O9-BUD-956

REINVENTING HUMAN SERVICES

MODERN APPLICATIONS OF SOCIAL WORK

An Aldine de Gruyter Series of Texts and Monographs

SERIES EDITOR

James K. Whittaker

Paul Adams and Kristine E. Nelson (eds.), **Reinventing Human Services: Community and Family Centered Practice**

Ralph E. Anderson and Irl Carter, **Human Behavior in the Social Environment: A Social Systems Approach** (fourth edition)

Richard P. Barth, Mark Courtney, Jill Duerr Berrick, and Vicky Albert, **From Child Abuse to Permanency Planning: Child Welfare Services Pathways and Placements**

Kathleen Ell and Helen Northen, **Families and Health Care: Psychosocial Practice**

Marian Fatout, **Models for Change in Social Group Work**

Mark W. Fraser, Peter J. Pecora, and David A. Haapala, **Families in Crisis: The Impact of Intensive Family Preservation Services**

James Garbarino, **Children and Families in the Social Environment** (second edition)

James Garbarino, and Associates, **Special Children—Special Risks: The Maltreatment of Children with Disabilities**

James Garbarino, and Associates, **Troubled Youth, Troubled Families: Understanding Families At-Risk for Adolescent Maltreatment**

Roberta R. Greene, **Social Work with the Aged and Their Families**

Roberta R. Greene, **Human Behavior Theory: A Diversity Framework**

Roberta R. Greene and Paul H. Ephross, **Human Behavior Theory and Social Work Practice**

André Ivanoff, Betty J. Blythe, and Tony Tripodi, **Involuntary Clients in Social Work Practice: A Research-Based Approach**

Paul K. H. Kim (ed.), **Serving the Elderly: Skills for Practice**

Jill Kinney, David A. Haapala, and Charlotte Booth, **Keeping Families Together: The Homebuilders Model**

Robert M. Moroney, **Social Policy and Social Work: Critical Essays on the Welfare State**

Peter J. Pecora, Mark W. Fraser, Kristine Nelson, Jacqueline McCroskey, and William Meezan, **Evaluating Family-Based Services**

Peter J. Pecora, James K. Whittaker, Anthony N. Maluccio, Richard P. Barth, and Robert D. Plotnick, **The Child Welfare Challenge: Policy, Practice, and Research**

John R. Schuerman, Tina L. Rzepnicki, and Julia H. Littell, **Putting Families First: An Experiment in Family Preservation**

Madeline R. Stoner, **The Civil Rights of Homeless People: Law, Social Policy, and Social Work Practice**

Albert E. Trieschman, James K. Whittaker, and Larry K. Brendtro, **The Other 23 Hours: Child-Care Work with Emotionally Disturbed Children in a Therapeutic Milieu**

Harry H. Vorrath and Larry K. Brendtro, **Positive Peer Culture (Second Edition)**

Betsy S. Vourlekis and Roberta R. Greene (eds). **Social Work Case Management**

James K. Whittaker, and Associates, **Reaching High-Risk Families: Intensive Family Preservation in Human Services**

REINVENTING HUMAN SERVICES

Community- and Family-Centered Practice

Paul Adams and Kristine Nelson
EDITORS

ALDINE DE GRUYTER
New York

About the Editors

Paul Adams is Professor, Graduate School of Social Work, Portland State University. He is the author of *Health of the State*, and has written numerous journal articles. Dr. Adams received his D.S.W. from the University of California, Berkeley.

Kristine Nelson is Professor, Graduate School of Social Work, Portland State University. She is the author of numerous journal articles, and is coauthor of *Alternative Models of Family Preservation*, and *Evaluating Family-Based Services* (Aldine). Dr. Nelson received her D.S.W. from the University of California, Berkeley.

ALDINE DE GRUYTER
A division of Walter de Gruyter, Inc.
200 Saw Mill River Road
Hawthorne, New York 10532

This publication is printed on acid free paper

Library of Congress Cataloging-in-Publication Data
Reinventing human services : community- and family-centered practice / Paul Adams and Kristine Nelson, editors.
p. cm. — (Modern applications of social work)
Includes bibliographical references (p.) and index.
ISBN 0-202-36097-0 (cloth : acid-free paper). — ISBN 0-202-36098-9 (pbk. : acid-free paper)
1. Human services—United States. 2. Social service—United States. 3. Community organization—United States. I. Adams, Paul, 1943- . II. Nelson, Kristine III. Series.
HV91.R445 1995
361.8'0973—dc20 95-8047
CIP

Manufactured in the United States of America

10 9 8 7 6 5 4 3 2 1

Contents

Foreword

SIMPLE FABLE FOR A COMPLEX PROBLEM

Once upon a time, in a better world, people knew their reality. A table was called a table, a house a house. Poverty was poverty, and lack of food, hunger. People, rich and poor, knew their reality because they heard everyone else using the same words.

As in all worlds, there were people who were poor and some who could not cope. Family, neighbors, and churches pitched in and tried to help. But with time, the number of the needy grew and exhausted the resources of their helpers. So some people studied to become helpers.

At first the helpers used the words that everyone used. But as they helped, they began to notice peculiarities among the poor, and they gave them names. The world of the helped was transformed. Some of the helped began to resemble their labels (such is the power of naming). And the helpers made more and more labels. As more words and signifiers appeared, organizations were developed to carry on the task of assigning the labels and writing formulas that explained the meaning of behaviors they had labeled. And as the behavior of the poor was categorized, and the meaning of their behavior, thinking, and feeling was elucidated, the helping professionals, in their zeal, proliferated and differentiated. Some specialized in working with children and others with adults. Some specialized in school problems and others in drug abuse. Some took children and put them in special places to heal, separating them from their parents, school, and neighborhood.

As more and more explanations appeared, specialists in one field stopped knowing what specialists in other fields knew. Agencies and governments, in their wish to help the poor, began to distribute money according to the needs of agencies working with certain categories of individuals. This became known as categorical funding. But as the helpers' knowledge increased in complexity, the poor found that, willy nilly, their world included the agencies that helped them. They were becoming more and more dependent on the rule makers, but they themselves no longer knew their reality. Besides being poor, they were ignorant of the ways in which their lives were conceptualized.

As history evolved, a number of the helpers began to notice that the poor did not always improve with help, and sometimes they got worse. Some helpers began to notice that the procedures implemented by the multiple agencies that work with the poor were contradictory. They began to write alternative explanations and suggest alternative ways of working.

To start, these new helpers accepted their own ignorance. This posture gave them the freedom to ask questions. Since the client populations were poor people, the wisely ignorant practitioners began to ask the poor people questions about ways of helping. From the start, these helpers had what previous helpers had not had—the capacity for curiosity.

These wisely ignorant helpers also knew the limits of their capacity. So they decided on programs of collaboration. A way of working evolved in which the helpers and the poor people together determined the goals of their joint tasks. Words like teamwork, co-construction, community, systems, neighborhood, ecology, family, and empowerment began to replace the tired old words like deficit, concern, problems. The new words were magical because they gave the new helpers new places to look. They found corners they had never seen before. For one thing, they looked at the fragmentation imposed by categorical funding and realized that, regardless of the clamoring of the individual, it is the family that is the indivisible smallest cell of the social system.

There was a major problem with this new thinking because, as in other fables, the family is at once the best and the worst we have. But the worst aspects of the family, and there are many, had been very well described. It was the strength of the family—the resources and possibilities—that had been left utterly unexplored.

Exploring family possibilities opened many new avenues to help. But how could a sense of possibilities be returned to poor families? The word empowerment had the sound of strength, but its implementation with the poor was uncharted territory. How can you empower from a position of power? The new helpers realized that they had to change their practice. For a poor family, empowerment can happen only in collaboration.

From this discovery, it followed as day follows night that other sources of help must be explored. Besides the professionals, they had to expand to include natural helping resources: extended family, neighbors, church, school—the old collection of dogooders that naturally connect the family to the community. Instead of a pyramid of power flowing from top to bottom, they had to create a mesa. Instead of a collection of agencies peddling their wares ("I deal with learning disorders!" "My specialty is child abuse!"), they had to map a family's needs with the family and match them with the services.

Once the helpers were able to listen, how did they match the helpers to the needs? That's what *Reinventing Human Services* is all about. Adams and Nelson et al. are championing a diversity of new approaches that are comprehensive, family centered, consumer directed, and focused on accessing the resources of the family in the community. But it is a difficult task, and most services to the poor are still managed by bureaucracies concerned with organizational survival, who keep traditional services functioning.

Like all fables, this one finishes with a moral. Different perspectives on poor families highlight different aspects, and MORAL: *some perspectives are better than others.*

Salvador Minuchin
New York, NY

Introduction

Dissatisfaction with a human services system that is unresponsive, stigmatizing, and ineffective has led to a ferment of experimentation in recent years. Practitioners in many fields, usually working in isolation from each other, have redesigned services and reshaped practice, transforming the relations between professionals and the families and communities they serve. The new approach to services is less reactive and more proactive and preventive, building on the strengths and resources of families and communities rather than focusing on individual or neighborhood deficits. In forming partnerships with family members, their social networks, schools, churches, and formal and informal organizations of many kinds, workers share responsibility rather than shouldering the burden of social problems alone. They interweave formal and informal care and control in the community. Both workers and managers use an empowerment strategy to effect change rather than simply follow procedures.

The need for a fundamental change in the practice and organization of the human services is clear. First, families and communities face urgent and growing problems. Working class and poor families are paying the social price of economic structures and policies that promote inequality and poverty. They pay in the form of attenuated social supports, formal and informal, and high rates of social problems like delinquency, drug abuse, and child maltreatment, which constitute the business of the human services. In many communities, as Fisher documents in Chapter 2, the situation is desperate.

Second, human services themselves are in a state of crisis, not only due to lack of resources. Public social services have responded to funding constraints and policy mandates by targeting services on the most critical "cases," and are increasingly contracting with private providers to furnish discrete packages of service. They have sought to protect themselves from scandal—a child suffering further abuse despite being known to the child welfare agency—by prescribing ever more exactly what procedures workers must follow. Attempts to substitute rules and procedures for the professional judgment of line workers have been reinforced by funding mechanisms that specify the kinds of diagnosis or other category the service user must fit before help can be provided. These efforts to ensure accountability push workers in both public and voluntary agencies to spend more time on paperwork and less in helping people. The resulting services are fragmented, unresponsive, and stigmatizing. They require people to wait until there is a crisis—a child is injured or seriously neglected, runs away or commits a seriously delinquent act—before they can get help.

What would it be like if services were designed to strengthen rather than substitute for the caring capacity of families and communities? What if services were shaped by and available to all citizens in their communities, so people could get a little help when they needed it, without always having to fit into a narrow category or be formally processed as "clients"? What if services were geared to recognizing and building on the strengths and resources of families and communities, rather than focusing on their deficits? What if workers were encouraged to use their professional judgment and creativity to get results and effect change rather than simply to follow the rules and get their paperwork done?

Fortunately, flexible, responsive, empowerment-oriented services already exist. Much of this work, however, takes the form of projects that flourish briefly on the fringes of the human services system. Schorr (1988) studied and publicized effective child welfare programs across the United States, but found a few years later (1993) that half of them had disappeared. There is much to learn from the experience of effective services. The challenge is to replicate and adapt what works so that good practice can survive and spread, with administrative infrastructures that support it.

REINVENTING GOVERNMENT

Our title, *Reinventing Human Services*, recognizes that the efforts to rethink and redesign human services are part of a larger push to "reinvent government" at local, state, and federal levels. Osborne and Gaebler (1992) drew wide attention to the phenomenon, celebrating and promoting "An American Perestroika" in their *Reinventing Government: How the Entrepreneurial Spirit Is Transforming the Public Sector*. Their book, written with infectious enthusiasm and full of telling case studies of successful government practices, had a powerful influence on the Clinton Administration. Under the leadership of Vice-President Gore (1993), the federal government embarked on an intensive 6-month National Performance Review and a sweeping effort to reinvent itself, called REGO.

The concerns that stimulated this movement—the fragmented, bureaucratic, rule-driven, ineffective way in which agencies conduct their affairs—are as characteristic of human services as of any other area of public responsibility. For example, Peters (1993, p. xviii) gives the example of a pregnant teenager who is also a juvenile offender on welfare and "must deal with at least six different government case workers, each regulated by a different set of rules—many at odds with one another." Osborne and Gaebler (1992, p. 21) quote Lou Winnick of the Ford Foundation as saying, "In government all of the incentive is in the direction of not making mistakes.... You can have 99 successes and nobody notices, and one mistake and you're dead." This fear of things going wrong, resulting in the micromanagement of line workers and managers by means of ever-more restrictive rules and regulations, is probably nowhere stronger than in the field of child welfare.

The problem, as President Clinton put it (Peters, 1993, p. xx) is that "We spend too much time in government...trying to keep bad things from happening [by issuing] rules and regulations that eventually prohibit sensible public employees from making good things happen." It is a system driven by fear and distrust, which only worsens what Gore (1993, p. xxx) calls the "performance deficit"—a government that not only wastes its resources, but that is ineffective. As Gore (1993, p. xxx) puts it:

> We spend $25 billion a year on welfare, $27 billion on food stamps, and $13 billion on public housing—yet more Americans fall into poverty every year.... We fund 150 different employment and training programs—yet the average American has no idea where to get job training, and the skills of our workforce fall further behind those of our competitors.

The main emphasis of the "reinventing government" literature, however, like that of this book, is not on the problems, which are well enough known. It is on successful practice to bring about change, to release and mobilize the creativity of those who are closest to the consumers of services. Osborne and Gaebler (1992, pp. 19–20) examined many examples of innovative, entrepreneurial government organizations. They looked for what those bodies had done "which, if other governments did the same, would make entrepreneurship the norm and bureaucracy the exception." They found several common threads:

> Most entrepreneurial governments promote *competition* between service providers. They *empower* citizens by pushing control out of the bureaucracy, into the community. They measure the performance of their agencies, fo-

> cusing not on inputs but on *outcomes*. They are driven by their goals—their *missions*—not by their rules and regulations. They redefine their clients as *customers* and offer them choices—between schools, between training programs, between housing options. They *prevent* problems before they emerge, rather than simply offering services afterward. They put their energies into *earning* money, not simply spending it. They *decentralize* authority, embracing participatory management. They prefer *market* mechanisms to bureaucratic mechanisms. And they focus not simply on providing public services, but on *catalyzing* all sectors—public, private, and voluntary—into action to solve their community's problems.

These are, with a couple of important exceptions, the elements of effective human services. The practices in various settings described and advocated in this book all involve empowering citizens by changing the relation between professionals and people who use their services. The shift to an empowerment-based practice, which builds partnerships with families and communities, involves some fundamental changes in the way human services are typically delivered. It requires a reinvention of the way we do business, in the sense advocated by Osborne and Gaebler, Clinton and Gore.

On two key issues, however, we part company with the advocates of reinventing government. The first of these is the relation between market and community. Enthusiasm for the market and market mechanisms is a pervasive theme of those who seek to reinvent government. In view of the unresponsive and ineffective character of government bureaucracies, it is easy to see why. Certainly, we seek no less than the official reinventors to promote an entrepreneurial spirit—in the sense of an enterprising, creative, innovativeness—in managers, workers, and service users (the last most literally in the program discussed by Raheim in Chapter 6).

However, the contradiction between the market and the community aspects of reinvention is nowhere sharper than in the human services. As Fisher shows in Chapter 2, the users of those services are very disproportionately the victims of a market economy that creates poverty and inequality among families and communities and of market-oriented social policies that work against efforts to improve matters. He argues that "market systems and market-based policies are in many respects anti-social, anti-community, and anti-family."

As for market mechanisms and promoting competition among providers, these have become, not a solution to the fragmentation, excessive paperwork, and stigmatizing of the human services, but a major part of the problem. As Chapter 4 by Adams and Krauth illustrates, public sector workers find themselves reduced to buying a given number of hours of therapy from a private provider who has an incentive to provide those hours of service whether all of them are needed or not. No one under this system has an incentive to be proactive, either in providing a little help to citizens when that would be enough to prevent their formal processing as cases, or in developing informal partnerships with other organizations such as schools, churches, or neighborhood groups. Rather than bringing an entrepreneurial spirit into the public sector, privatization and the purchase of services system have spread distrust, excessive paperwork, and fragmentation into the private and voluntary sectors that depend on government contracting for their income.

Our second disagreement is in the area of cuts. A major focus of the federal REGO exercise is cutting jobs—12% of the civilian, nonpostal workforce over 5 years, or 252,000 positions (Gore, 1993, p. xxv). In Britain, one of the most sweeping attempts to create a more responsive government at the local level, involving the reorganization of the entire social services department of East Sussex County Council into small, neighborhood-based teams, was accompanied by a secret mandate to cut spending by 8% (Hadley & Young, 1992).

There is certainly a need to make human services more effective and thereby get better value for money. But cutting spending on the human services, a trend of the last two decades, is not reinvention. It is more of the same. It reinforces a residual approach to policy that provides services only when there is a crisis and all else has failed. In that context, even the most creative, innovative, and empowering practice, like that associated with family preservation services, described in Chapter 5, then serves only a tiny minority of families whose situation has become desperate. The services and practices described here do not depend on large infusions of additional resources and are not add-ons to existing programs. They call for a redeployment of existing resources, a different way of doing business. At the same time, however, the scale of unmet need is enormous and its urgency great.

In this respect, paradoxically, the beginning of wisdom in reinventing human services may be a recognition of their marginality. Decentering human services, shifting them from the center of the picture of which they are a part, has two aspects. First, at a *policy* level, we need to recognize that human services depend for their maximum effectiveness on larger economic forces and policies. Efforts of professionals to build partnerships in communities that empower service users and other local people are essential. But they can achieve only a limited effectiveness in the face of economic structures and policies that foster poverty and inequality, unemployment, and homelessness. Even the best human services cannot substitute for decent jobs and adequate income supports.

Second, at the level of *practice*, community- and family-centered work starts from the recognition that professionals are not at the center of helping systems, that most of the caring and controlling in which social workers, nurses, teachers, probation officers, and even the police engage is done by others—families, kin, and neighborhood networks, informal groups, churches, schools, and other formal organizations. The effectiveness of human services depends on how well they interact with the whole complex of formal and informal elements to strengthen the community's capacity to care for its members and address shared needs and concerns.

This line of argument is all too easily misread as a case for cuts in public services, as shifting the burden of social care back to the shoulders of families and communities and—to the extent that they disproportionately carry the load as unpaid volunteers and family caregivers—to women. Further cuts, legitimated in this way, only worsen the plight of those, especially people of color with low incomes living in deteriorating inner-city neighborhoods, who already pay the highest social price for market policies and forces.

The point, however, is that the care of children or elderly people or those with disabilities is a shared responsibility (Moroney, 1986) involving families, local communities, and the state. Rather than intervening only when family caregivers and their networks are unable to cope, human services need to recognize and support, even give respite to, those who bear the main burden of care. We need a base of universal social policies that share the financial costs of such care—for example, maternity benefits and paid parental leaves, family allowances, and caregiver benefits. Neither having a child nor becoming old should precipitate poverty. Services, too, need to be broadened in their conception, so that they promote and enhance the development of families and communities, as well as respond to problems and deficits (Chapin Hall Center for Children, 1994). We are not advocating pushing more of the burden of care back on shoulders already suffering under the strain, any more than we advocate the impossible and undesirable aim of *substituting* paid, formal care for the efforts of families and their informal networks.

Although our focus is on services rather than income maintenance, we make no claim that even the best services can substitute for social policies that share the responsibility of caring for dependent family members through income supports. Nor do we offer a strategy for cutting the costs of services. We suggest instead ways in which services could be designed and delivered more effectively, in part by shifting from a residual, crisis-oriented approach to one that works with families and communities to meet shared concerns and promote healthy development. The dollars already allocated for human services are desperately needed, but they need to be spent differently. To borrow the image so tellingly developed by Smale in Chapter 3, some of the resources spent on paying specialized lifeguards to rescue drowning people who fall into the right category need to go toward sending workers upstream to work with local communities to prevent people from falling in the river and to teach them how to swim.

COMMUNITY

All the chapters in this book deal with the question of how to bring the community into the thinking and practice of the human services. They do not argue for reviving community organization as a specialized activity or abandoning work with individuals and families. The argument, rather, is to bring the community into all human services activities—including crisis-oriented work with individual cases.

Rather than rehearse the arguments of each of the chapters, we want to underline some points that distinguish our approach from much writing and practice dealing with communities and the human services. There is a growing realization of the need to involve local people in the planning and delivery of services to their communities. Such involvement takes a variety of forms, from participation of citizens and service users on agency and interagency boards to the involvement of parents in the development of service plans in child welfare and child mental health. In view of the difficulty of sustaining participation in boards and committees dominated by professionals, there is sometimes a tendency to define the task as one of encouraging the community to join the professionals in the carrying out of their tasks. This is often appropriate and may be a highly effective intervention with particular individuals. The danger, however, is that citizens may come to be seen as adjuncts or unpaid helpers who assist the professionals in their work. If we take the decentering of human services seriously, however, we see that it would be better to recognize that most of the caring and controlling in the community is normally done informally within families and neighborhoods. The task of the professionals, then, is to find ways to join the community and help it in carrying out *its* work of caring for its members.

A related problem is the professional tendency to see the community as a resource that the worker can use to supplement his or her repertoire of interventions, putting together a bag of resources from different places—a support group here, a helpful neighbor there—and presenting them to the consumer. Instead of that, we see changing the community itself as part of the task and the service user as a contributor to the process. Professionals do not, in this approach, use informal networks for their purposes, as a bag of resources to reach into, but seek to enable and support social networks to help them function more effectively. In this sense, the community both has resources for addressing its concerns and is the locus of problem-perpetuating patterns of interaction. Bringing resources to bear from a range of sources and intervening to change destructive patterns may be part of the same process, as when a family that has been defined by neighbors and professionals alike as a problem for the community is enabled to take on a new role in solving a neighborhood problem. (In the excellent example described by Holder & Wardle, 1981, not only were concrete needs met, but a whole pattern of relationships involving service users, other local people, and professionals was transformed.)

An important aspect of the decentering of the professional–consumer relationship is the recognition that it is part of a larger pattern of interactions that may involve other professionals, kin, neighbors, a school, a church, and a neighborhood association. The worker who is oblivious to this larger system may become part of the problem-perpetuating pattern (Imber-Black, 1988; Holder & Wardle, 1981).

One of the most transforming results of bringing community into professional thinking and practice is that it enables one to see "clients" more broadly than just users of services, consumers of resources, victims, or threats to the safety of the community or their children. It even enables one to go beyond recognition of the strengths, resources, and expertise that consumers can bring to bear on their own situations and on which the worker can build. Many of the following chapters—especially those by Smale; Adams and Krauth; Checkoway, Finn, and Pothukuchi; and Swenson—also point to the importance of recognizing the capacity of "clients" to *contribute* to the community.

In Smale's example, this perspective enables a worker to ask how a formally referred client, Joanne, may be helpful to the agency in its work in the neighborhood. Finding a way to involve her depends, however, on the prior work done by the human services team in proactively developing projects in the neighborhood they serve. This hypothetical example typifies the work done by the patch team described by Adams and Krauth, as well as by other locality-based, community-centered teams in the United States, Canada, and Britain. Checkoway, Finn, and Pothukuchi describe how a whole group of the population, youth in at-risk neighborhoods—typically seen as problems, victims, or perpetrators—may be engaged as contributors to the building of community. Swenson shows how a group of social workers who had a rich involvement with their own communities saw their clients' relation to community in more impoverished terms, most often as a relationship of consumers to resources.

Here, too, we depart from the "reinventing government" literature cited earlier, in emphasizing the users of services not as customers to be served but as fellow citizens and community members with whom human service professionals can *exchange* ideas, concerns, and resources. Thus, instead of conducting focus groups as a kind of consumer research to learn what services were wanted, the Iowa patch team followed the example of an earlier social services team in London. Invited to participate in exchange meetings, local people joined team members in discussing both common concerns and the resources that citizens and professionals alike could bring to bear in addressing them.

This kind of community or neighborhood orientation to professional practice is sometimes criticized, however, for assuming a degree of social homogeneity or a level of resources, including informal helping networks, extended families, churches, and social services, that no longer exists, especially in many distressed urban neighborhoods. It also may idealize the helpfulness of such networks and systems, even when they do exist. Indeed, some would argue, the racism, exploitation, and poverty embedded in our social structures make a mockery of the very notion of community in contemporary America.

However, in arguing that professionals should work with and within communities rather than try to substitute for them, we do not assume that communities are homogeneous or self-sufficient. Our position is not that communities do not need professional intervention to address their problems and should be left to pull themselves up by their own bootstraps. We assume that both the community and its resources are problematic. Indeed, as Smale argues in Chapter 3, the problems that bring individuals and families to the attention of human service professionals are best understood as the malfunctioning of a network of people. The task for community-centered practice is to understand problem-perpetuating patterns of interaction, involving perhaps multiple system levels (e.g., family, school, and social service systems) and intervene to change them. It assumes that there are strengths and resources to be mobilized within as well as outside the community, but that if you do not look for them, and for the capacity for change at all system levels, you will not find them.

Human service workers confront every day, in schools, hospitals, agencies, and neighborhoods, the impact of racism and poverty on the lives of families with whom they work. They see the conflicts of class and race within communities, the oppression that divides families and neighborhoods against themselves. It would be a mistake to assume that, because transforming this situation is a task beyond the sole responsibility or capacity of human service workers, the quality of services is of no consequence to the families who receive them or the workers who deliver them. Workers often have considerable power over the lives of citizens, and the way they do their jobs has the potential either to reinforce or to effect change in entrenched patterns of oppression.

REINVENTING PRACTICE

For reasons already given—the enthusiasm for the market and for cutting jobs in the "reinventing government" literature—we chose our title with some misgivings. But we wanted to focus on the positive aspects of the reinvention program as it applies to human services—the encouragement of a mission-driven, outcome-oriented, innovative practice that builds partnerships and empowers citizens, prevents problems, is proactive and entrepreneurial, decentralizes authority, and empowers workers to get results. We also had other reasons for wanting to talk about "reinventing" human services.

Reinvention implies rethinking the whole enterprise, not reforming it at the margins or dealing with a number of its problems, but fundamentally reshaping it. In the case of the human services, where large public service systems are entwined with complex rules, regulations, and categorical funding mechanisms arising from a crazy quilt of federal and state laws, this is a formidable undertaking. It is also necessary and achievable.

In another sense of the term, reinvention suggests an unnecessary activity, that of discovering again what is already known. There is no need, one presumes, to reinvent the wheel. Here it is important to recognize that the ideas and principles advanced in this book are not pure inventions of the authors. There is a long tradition of empowerment-oriented practice in American social work (Simon, 1994). The renewed interest in neighborhood-based services has important precedents in African-American communities, in the War on Poverty programs of the 1960s, and in the Progressive era in the early years of this century. The revived enthusiasm for community (see, for example, Etzioni, 1991; Bellah, Madsen, Sullivan, Swidler, & Tipton, 1985) has deep roots in the same American culture and history that also gave rise to an exceptionally strong individualism.

Indeed, the principles of community-centered practice, or of family-based services, once grasped, are so natural and compelling that they sometimes elicit the response, "But that is just good social work!" The task then is to figure out why good practice is so rare and how we can reengineer administrative, funding, and educational structures so as to foster rather than stifle it.

In talking of reinventing human services, we mean to draw on and learn from the experience of the past, and to recognize that if successful practices are to be adopted as innovations—for that is what they are for those to whom they are new—people will want and need to reinvent the wheel (Smale, 1992). The Not Invented Here syndrome is a powerful obstacle to adoption of effective practice, whether that practice was "invented" in the state legislature, the central office, or another country. Innovation in practice that involves building partnerships with service users and other local citizens and organizations has to be reinvented in the context of the choices of the participants. If higher authorities try to lay down a blueprint for local bodies to follow, they may well destroy the practices they want to promote. If effective services are to be widely replicated, local champions, drawing on the work of other times and places and supported by a network of like-minded innovators, will need to win support for a process of adapting key principles to their own situations. Thus they will have to "reinvent" already discovered solutions.

THE BOOK

This book is the product of an intensive interdisciplinary collaboration at the University of Iowa Center for Advanced Studies. Through the generous support of the Obermann Fund and The University of Iowa, a group of scholars and practitioners met at the Center during July 1993 examining, discussing, and debating family- and community-based approaches to social problems. The participants submitted their papers in advance and revised them substantially during and after the seminar. All but two of the chapters in this book are outcomes of this long critical and editorial process. (Despite their interest, Halpern and Checkoway were unable to attend the faculty research seminar, but have enriched the book by contributing chapters. Salvador Minuchin, who has written the book's foreword, participated in the seminar for a week.)

Reinventing Human Services examines the historical and economic context of current efforts to reinvent human services, showing the urgency and the difficulty of the task. It draws on successful practice in Britain and Canada as well as the United States to develop a new paradigm for social work practice, one that integrates individual, family, and community levels of practice and reconceptualizes professional–community relations. It shows how practitioners are developing community- and family-centered practice in a range of fields, including services to children, youth, and families; mental health; education; and employment services, and how they integrate services across systems. A chapter on community policing describes the parallel rethinking of relations between professionals and citizens that is underway in law enforcement. The interdisciplinary team of authors includes scholars, researchers, and practitioners from the disciplines of economics, urban planning, communications, criminal justice, psychology, marriage and family therapy, and education, as well as social work. The multidisciplinary and multisystemic nature of the book's authorship and development parallels that of the integrated practice it describes.

The book does more than describe promising innovations in the human services. It integrates different lines of development, in community social work, family-based services, services integration, community policing, and community and neighborhood development, in a fruitful interchange. For example, although family-based services have brought about profound changes in child welfare, the themes of this book differentiate it from most writing on family preservation. Here the topic is addressed in the context of a renewed focus on neighborhood-oriented approaches and the drive to reshape public services as a whole, to "reinvent government." This unique focus emphasizes the need to integrate family- and community-centered approaches to practice, and to move to a more proactive, preventive, and neighborhood-based services system. Such a system would respond to the needs of all families and children, and well before a crisis created an imminent risk of placement.

Reinventing Human Services is intended to further good practice. It draws on cutting edge experience to consider the theoretical and practical issues involved in reshaping human services and bringing community into the thinking and practice of social workers in all settings.

Part I provides an historical, economic, and theoretical context for community- and family-centered practice. Halpern locates the reemergence of neighborhood-based services—which now involve public child welfare and other agencies that deliver services often in worsening inner-city conditions—in a historical context of 75 years of public and private neighborhood-oriented initiatives. Fisher documents the persistent and growing poverty amidst plenty that results from the market economy in the United States and is perpetuated by social policies that weaken families and communities. Drawing on the best examples of community social work in Britain, Smale develops a paradigm for practice and practice theory that, as the Adams and Krauth chapter shows, is relevant to the task of reinventing human services in the United States.

Smale's emphasis on a community-centered, partnership-oriented, collaborative, and empowering approach to practice resonates in all the accounts of effective services and strategies in Part II. These chapters describe examples of the shift to community-centered practice in social services, education, and policing, considering both changes in front line practice and the management, administrative, and interorganizational structures needed to promote good practice. They show the importance of a family-centered approach that involves parents as partners and of going beyond a categorical, fragmented practice that is limited to individual families in crisis.

Part III of the book examines the shifts involved in including communities and families in practice. These chapters discuss how we understand and construct community, how we bring community to bear on work with individuals and families, and how professionals can work with families as full partners in the design and delivery of services.

The editors and authors owe a special debt of thanks to the funders of the seminar from which the book developed—C. Esco and Avalon L. Obermann and The University of Iowa—who made it possible for us to spend a month together discussing each other's work and developing our own chapters during and after the seminar. The Center for Advanced Studies at The University of Iowa sponsored our seminar and provided a congenial setting for our collaborative endeavor. The Center's director, Jay Semel, supported our work of directing the seminar and editing this book with persistence, a fine attention to detail, and humor. Lorna Olson, assistant to the director, assured the seminar's smooth running and the well-being of its participants. The National Resource Center for Family Centered Practice (formerly the National Resource Center on Family Based Services) at The University of Iowa cosponsored the seminar. Shad Jessen at Portland State University assisted in the production of the manuscript. All have our thanks, but responsibility for the quality of the final result is, of course, ours.

REFERENCES

Bellah, R.N., Madsen, R., Sullivan, W.M., Swidler, A., & Tipton, S.M. (1985). *Habits of the heart: Individualism and commitment in American life*. New York: Harper & Row.

Chapin Hall Center for Children. (1994). *Children, families, and communities: A new approach to social services*. Chicago: Chapin Hall Center for Children at the University of Chicago.

Etzioni, A. (1991). *A responsive society: Collected essays on guiding deliberate social change*. San Francisco: Jossey-Bass.

Gore, A. (1993). *Creating a government that works better and costs less*. The report of the National Performance Review. New York: Plume.

Hadley, R., & Young, K. (1990). *Creating a responsive public service*. New York: Harvester Wheatsheaf.

Holder, D., & Wardle, M. (1981). *Teamwork and the development of a unitary approach*. London: Routledge & Kegan Paul.

Imber-Black, E. (1988). *Families and larger systems: A family therapist's guide through the labyrinth*. New York: Guilford.

Moroney, R.M. (1986). *Shared responsibility: Families and social policy*. New York: Aldine.

Osborne, D., & Gaebler, T. (1992). *Reinventing government: How the entrepreneurial spirit is transforming the public sector*. Reading, MA: Addison-Wesley.

Peters, T. (1993). Foreword. In A. Gore, *Creating a government that works better and costs less* (pp. ix–xxii). The report of the National Performance Review. New York: Plume.

Schorr, L.D. (1993). Keynote address. In National Association of Social Workers, *Effective strategies for increasing social program replication/adaptation: A review of the literature and summary of a seminar* (pp. 7–18). Washington, DC: NASW.

Schorr, L.D., with Schorr, D. (1988). *Within our reach: Breaking the cycle of disadvantage*. New York: Anchor/Doubleday.

Simon, B.L. (1994). *The empowerment tradition in American social work: A history*. New York: Columbia University Press.

Smale, G.G. (1992). *Managing change through innovation: Toward a model for developing and reforming social work practice and social service delivery*. London: National Institute for Social Work.

I

THE CONTEXT OF COMMUNITY- AND FAMILY-CENTERED PRACTICE

The first part of this book explores the historical, economic, and theoretical context of community- and family-centered practice. Neighborhood-based services have a long and rich history in the United States and their reemergence must be understood in the context of 75 years of public and private neighborhood-oriented initiatives. Currently, however, these services are often called upon to address worsening inner-city conditions. Although this persistent and growing poverty amidst plenty stems from a market economy, it is perpetuated by social policies that weaken families and communities. In this context, the development of community-based services is both urgent and problematic. However, the best examples of community social work in Britain provide a model for addressing community needs and developing more effective and relevant human services in the United States.

In the first chapter, Robert Halpern traces the history of neighborhood-based services in low-income neighborhoods. Starting in the Progressive era with the Settlement House movement, neighborhood-based services have been an important vehicle for addressing urban poverty, delivering services, and advocating for social reform. Settlements and neighborhood centers have provided recreational and cultural programs, home visitors, and youth workers to assist successive generations of new residents adjust to urban life. Neighborhood needs and the services deemed necessary to address them were, however, determined by agency boards rather than community residents. Following the Progressive Era, increasing professionalization and bureaucratic organization in education, health care, and social services combined to diminish the role of neighborhood-based services and to encourage specialization and the development of categorical services.

Borrowing from the past and reinventing the concept of neighborhood-based services, the War on Poverty of the 1960s stimulated a variety of new programs. Community action agencies added paraprofessional workers from the neighborhood, a social action perspective, and the goal of reforming the public social service system, but also further fragmented service delivery.

Currently, with concern about worsening conditions in the inner-cities and widespread dissatisfaction with the social service system, neighborhood-based services have reemerged as an important aspect of social service practice and social reform. Halpern shows how the new community-centered approaches, building on the ideas and experiences of the settlements and community action agencies, incorporate empowerment-based practice models and include neighborhood residents as full partners in the process of identifying needs and defining appropriate services for increasingly diverse populations. Questions remain, however, as to how far neighborhood level services can succeed in communities geographically and socially isolated from the rest of the society.

Peter S. Fisher directs our attention in the next chapter to the economic context in which community-centered practice is situated. The widening gap between rich and poor since the 1980s creates both the need for the services advocated in these pages and, at the same time, a threat to their viability. Not only are children raised in poverty at higher risk for a variety of negative outcomes, but the communities in which they live have been drained of both economic and social resources. These hardships affect African-American and Latino children most, especially those in single-parent households.

These outcomes, however, are not an inevitable result of immigration, economic downturn, or international competition, but have been supported by market-based social policies. In addition to a lowering of wages for nonprofessional workers, the policy measures of the past two decades—privatization, user fees, deregulation, a redefinition of welfare, and reduction in federal aid to states and cities—have led to worsening conditions for poor families and communities, while directing a larger share of the nation's wealth to those at the top.

Consequently, the poor have become increasingly isolated in communities that lack the resources to provide the services they need. With high unemployment and a low tax base, communities with the most needs have the fewest resources to meet them. Effective economic and social reform has been blocked, however, because the rhetoric of the market has been widely accepted within the social services: economic efficiency is seen as more important than long-term results, reliance on welfare is denigrated as "dependence," while dependence on low-wage jobs or fragile marriages is deemed "self-sufficiency." In the market, those with the most purchasing power take the lion's share, while those with few economic resources are left out.

In the third chapter in this section, Gerald G. Smale seeks to redefine practice and integrate individual and community-centered practice to more effectively address current needs and situations of community residents. As they have developed over the past century, social services may well have become, for those in need of help, part of the problem rather than part of the solution. Categorical social programs "rescue" only those eligible for services, while ignoring others in need and directing attention away from prevention. Smale describes a model of community social work, as developed in England and Scotland, that provides an alternative approach—one that avoids "clientizing" those in need of temporary assistance and overcomes the false dichotomy between intervention at the individual and at the community level.

Community social work views professional services as marginal compared to the amount of help and care that is provided in informal social networks and avoids usurping natural helpers and creating disempowering reliance on formal services. Rather than "objects of concern," clients are seen as equal citizens with the same capacities and rights as professionals. In this new light, the professional's task is to promote partnership and collaboration by identifying strengths and mobilizing resources in the community, reframing situations, and modifying destructive patterns.

For community-centered practice to be successful, professionals must intervene indirectly with service agencies and communities as well as provide direct services to individuals and families, acting as change agents as well as delivering services. Since no one individual can possess all the necessary knowledge and skills, the smallest unit that can accomplish community-centered practice is a team. Only through teamwork can the strengths of all the partners, including "clients," their networks, and the broader community, be activated to resolve problems.

Although this type of systemic, ecological, and empowering practice has been advocated in social work for some time, practice theory to provide guidelines for social workers in the field has yet to be developed. Extensive observation, discussion, and analysis of innovative practice in England and Scotland provide the foundation for developing a new theory of social work practice that can resist the pull to individualize problems and provide a more respectful and effective approach to helping that integrates individual, family, and community practice.

1

Neighborhood-Based Services in Low-Income Neighborhoods: A Brief History

ROBERT HALPERN

This chapter provides an historical overview of neighborhood-based services, those services rooted institutionally and socially in low-income neighborhoods. These services start with the community's own traditions and relate to the community as a whole, rather than to a particular service field, professional discipline, or categorical domain. Neighborhood-based services are "friendly," accessible, responsive, and nonstigmatizing. They include assistance and advocacy in linking families to other resources. Not least, neighborhood-based services have a rich underlife; families can draw on programs informally for assistance and support in any area and at any time.

OVERVIEW

Since the emergence of the settlements over a century ago, neighborhood-based services have played an important role in poverty alleviation and social reform efforts in the United States. At the same time, within the framework of the human services, neighborhood-based services have played a steadily diminishing role. The early push for professionalization of social services, the growth of statutory and clinic-based service provision, and the attractions of bureaucratic organization, including centralized administration, pushed neighborhood-based services to the margins of the human services.

Neighborhood-based services never disappeared completely. At least until the late 1950s most poor neighborhoods sustained a diverse set of recreational and cultural programs for children and youth, public health nurses continued to visit young families, and vestiges of street-corner social work with gangs persisted. Nonetheless, declining public and private resources for the inner city, the flight of private social service agencies, and the growing financial restraints on remaining inner-city institutions such as churches, combined in the 1950s to undermine what was left of this infrastructure of supportive services.

Neighborhood-based services reemerged in the mid-1960s with the War on Poverty. Federal funding temporarily replaced much of the lost private and local public resources. Established neighborhood agencies such as settlement houses and youth-serving agencies were revitalized by the new funds and mission; and new programs emerged that reflected the assumptions and strategies of the era. Paradigmatic of these new strategies was the employment of nonprofessional community members as service providers, attempts to link social services to social action, and the deliberate use of neighborhood-based programs to try to change the culture of the larger human service system (Kahn, 1976).

During the 1970s and 1980s neighborhood-based services continued to grow, idiosyncratically, in thousands of local communities, usually as a local response to a community need. Borrowing from the past and reinventing, individuals and agencies developed parenting support programs, community schools, youth programs, school-based health clinics, and after-school programs. Many of these locally generated programs survived by responding to government or foundation requests to address prevailing social preoccupations and objectives, such as intervening with pregnant and parenting teens, diverting youth from the juvenile justice system, and preserving families in which parents had been abusive or neglectful. During this same period, neighborhood-based services became a vehicle for implementing broad human service reforms, such as decentralization and decategorization of services, and realigning the roles of professionals and clients. They also aspired to rebuild presumably deteriorated informal social support systems for families through family support programs.

The new and renewed roles for neighborhood-based services in the inner city highlighted a variety of longstanding issues. Neighborhood-based service programs have struggled continuously, if not always consciously, with issues of identity, role, and boundaries. Is their purpose to provide the best possible services to individual families or, on a larger scale, to bring new resources into the neighborhood, to reform the mainstream human service system, to seek or provide employment opportunities for community members, and to strengthen local democracy? What is their relationship to large public service systems such as child welfare? Should they try to assume traditional service functions or complement and extend them? What does it mean in practice to take the community as the reference point in setting priorities and designing services? How can families be both partners and clients at the same time? What roles should professionals play in neighborhood-based programs? What are appropriate roles and expectations of indigenous lay helpers? What kinds of knowledge—whose knowledge—should shape planning, advocacy, and direct services? To whom ought a program be accountable?

In a different vein, because they are so closely tied to and rooted in their neighborhoods—and so permeable to the environment surrounding them—neighborhood-based services have tended to incorporate the difficulties, stresses, and vulnerabilities of low-income neighborhoods, particularly in staff relations and sometimes in relationships with families as well. Poor working conditions for staff often compound the inherent stresses and strains of working with poor families in depleted neighborhoods. Because they are located in isolated communities, neighborhood-based programs themselves too often have remained isolated from the larger society and its institutions.

Today, as worsening social conditions in the inner city produce growing numbers of multiply vulnerable families with a host of complicated problems, neighborhood-based services often struggle alone to serve and help these families, sometimes by default, sometimes by choice and design. Yet neighborhood-based services remain the least adequately conceptualized, funded, and staffed elements of the human service system, unprepared in fundamental ways for this extraordinarily difficult job. Moreover, work with multiply vulnerable families tests many of the principles of neighborhood-based services, such as building on family strengths and asking families to take an active role in shaping, and even providing, services.

THE RISE AND DECLINE OF NEIGHBORHOOD-BASED SERVICES

Neighborhood-based services prevailed for only two brief periods in the history of the human services in the United States, for a decade or two at the turn of the century and again during the 1960s. The paradigmatic neighborhood-based service was the settlement. Settlements were the first institutional response to poverty that was shaped at least in part by the needs of poor people, rather than purely by the predispositions of reformers. Nonetheless, settlement leaders did not always or even usually trust neighborhood residents to determine their own needs and interests.

The primary attraction of settlements to neighborhood residents was the assistance provided in coping with the endless difficulties of everyday life, the specific skills taught, and the wide range of supportive services and recreational activities offered. Common elements included day nurseries, kindergartens, after school programs, sports, sewing, hobby and other kinds of clubs, and summer camps (in the countryside) for children; equivalent clubs, as well as day and evening classes of all sorts, for youth and adults; theatre, folk dancing, and art classes; and primary health care, help in finding jobs, legal assistance, counseling, emergency food, clothing, fuel, and bedding. Milk stations located themselves at settlements, as did visiting nurse associations and social workers charged with visiting families to determine eligibility for relief.

Settlement leaders and staff played an important role in a wide variety of neighborhood improvement campaigns, and used clubs, lectures, and community forums to mobilize community residents around specific issues (Bremner, 1972). A few settlement leaders, such as Robert Woods, had a more explicitly political vision for the settlements, viewing them as vehicles for community self-governance (Polsky, 1991). Nonetheless, the political potential of the settlement movement was constrained by most leaders' view of them as neutral organizations, integrators and conciliators in an increasingly segmented, conflict-ridden society. Most settlement leaders and staff felt uncomfortable with the whole idea that there were constituencies with different interests.

Local communities' sense of ownership also was undermined by patterns of settlement governance, financing, and staffing. Settlement boards usually were composed of people living outside, and often far from the neighborhood, and neighborhood residents had little say in how settlement funds were used. The settlements rarely hired neighborhood residents as staff, particularly in positions of authority (Philpott, 1978, p. 285). Settlement leaders and staff felt that it was more efficient and fair for them to make key decisions about use of resources; and they felt confident that they knew best what poor families needed.

The assumption that poor people, at the time mostly immigrants, did not have the ability to recognize, define, and formulate solutions to their own problems contributed an important (if inadvertent) rationale to the emerging human services with their accompanying professions (Kirschner, 1986). At the same time, the seeming necessity of justifying services by viewing poor people as lacking the knowledge and ability to meet their needs or define and address their situation created contradictions that haunt human services for poor people to this day.

From the outset, services for poor people embodied aims that were difficult to reconcile: to enable and at the same time to control recipients; to work from poor people's own understanding of their lives and to define and interpret their lives using external standards; to link poor people to mainstream norms, institutions, and opportunities, and, at the same time, to highlight their difference and deviance by diagnosing and sorting them into categories of dependency and dysfunction. The strong, if implicit, message of distrust of poor people underlying the emergence of formal helping complicated the already difficult task of forging trusting relationships across barriers of class and culture.

The settlements were far from the only neighborhood-based service model to emerge in the Progressive era. Schools had visiting teachers and developed social centers with a variety of activities for children and adults. Nurses had been expanding their role in communities since the last decades of the nineteenth century. For example, in Chicago the Visiting Nurses Association (founded in 1889) set up "baby tents" in poor neighborhoods, "portable, open-air clinics that brought comprehensive medical care for infants to the heart of immigrant neighborhoods" (Silberman, 1990, p. 11). In the first two decades of the twentieth century there was a rapid growth in the number of public health nurses, reaching 11,000 by 1924 (Melosh, 1984). Public health nurses used settlements, milk stations, infant welfare stations, and even schools as a base for a range of neighborhood activities including home visiting, surveillance of sanitary conditions, and public education campaigns.

In many neighborhoods, nurses, in concert with local public health departments, took their activities one step further, creating "neighborhood health centers" (the prototype for the community health centers of the 1960s). The basic idea was to create or use an existing neighborhood base for a concerted, comprehensive, local public health program: to provide an array of preventive, educational, and diagnostic (but not curative) health services, when necessary reaching out to "recalcitrant" or overwhelmed families; to gather systematic information on neighborhood health and social conditions; and occasionally to organize residents to press for social reforms (Stoeckle & Candib, 1969, p. 1385). Health centers organized within neighborhood boundaries, seeing all the families in a neighborhood as clients, at least implicitly. Some local centers actually set themselves the goal of conducting a home visit to every family that had given birth to a new baby within their catchment area. Wilbur Phillips, the Secretary of the New York Milk Committee's child health stations, pioneered the use of neighborhood residents as "aides" in neighborhood health centers to recruit patients, take household surveys, and even participate in center governance (Stoeckle & Candib, 1969, p. 1387).

Forces Undermining Neighborhood-Based Services

During those same years, between 1910 and 1930, a number of forces were already at work undermining neighborhood-based social and health services. In the health arena, growing knowledge of disease treatment was giving nurses new clinic-based roles in hospitals, making hospital-based practice more attractive. Equally important, physicians wanted to bring "independent" nurses into the clinic under their supervision and control. Physicians' explicit argument was that neighborhood-based work, especially home visiting, was inefficient, too expensive, and too time-consuming (Melosh, 1984). The real issue was physicians' desire to assure the emerging health care system so as to capture consumers and fees. The neighborhood health centers succumbed to the same forces.

Throughout the 1920s social services were also becoming professionalized and bureaucratized, the former in new schools of social work, the latter in growing urban systems of private, voluntary child and family service agencies and an emergent statutory social welfare sector. There were a number of forces shaping the emerging social work profession. One was a search for a new identity to replace that lost with the demise of progressive social reform. A second was the growth of the public social welfare sector, due to Mothers' Aid, child welfare, and related programs, which together were beginning to alter the axis of social services.

The private social welfare agencies were wary of the growing public sector role in social service delivery. At the same time social work as a profession wanted to demonstrate that its skills were critical to public, statutory work because that would solidify the place of the profession (see Polsky, 1991, Ch. 5). This required evidence that social work could be both efficient and effective. Bureaucratic organizational principles seemed to meet the need for greater efficiency and accountability, and social workers embraced these, if somewhat reluctantly. (Like nurses, social workers sensed in bureaucracy a threat to their autonomy.)

Helping itself could not be so easily rationalized and proceduralized. What was desired was an approach that was scientific, but not overly proceduralized and rationalistic. The emergence of clinical social work during the 1920s, with its strongly psychoanalytic orientation, met this need and at the same time was critical to the demise of neighborhood-based work with poor families. Psychoanalytic theory strengthened social work's claim to being a true profession with a scientific foundation (a claim first made by Mary Richmond in *Social Diagnosis* in 1917). It also accelerated the ongoing shift in social workers' attention from community to individual maladjustment.

Although psychoanalytic theory was not intended to explain poverty, it seemed to imply that poor peoples' difficulties were largely of their own making. The daily work of most social workers—"arranging foster care, adoption, and job referral; dealing with financial need...coping with children's difficulties in school; assisting with problems arising from desertion, separation or widowhood...aiding with housing problems"—would not change significantly until the 1950s (Kahn, 1976, p. 28). Nonetheless, the new clinical social worker, with an office-based therapeutic practice, was the model for the future of social work. Lubove (1965) notes that no other profession picked up the tasks that social work began to abandon in the 1930s and 1940s—helping families gain access to services or advocating for disenfranchised groups and communities. The vacuum left by social work helps to explain the strong resurgence of neighborhood-based services in the 1960s.

Settlements and other neighborhood-based agencies themselves began to experience the side effects of professionalization and centralization. For example, settlements increasingly were composed of numerous departments staffed by specialists defining their own sphere: casework, recreation, hygiene, and adult education. Large family welfare agencies such as the Children's Aid Society established district offices in numerous neighborhoods, each with several little departments that mimicked the main agency's administrative structure. As competition for scarce resources and clients grew, different neighborhood agencies that had once tried to be multifaceted community centers concentrated on specific services with inputs and outputs that could be quantified for funders.

When residents of poor neighborhoods walked into an agency to sign up for a program or seek help with a problem, they increasingly found themselves confronted with a maze of paperwork and procedures or were forced to go from office to office in search of the right starting point. As agencies centralized and became more clinically oriented, their staff spent less time in poor neighborhoods, causing both individual providers and whole agencies to lose their feel for the context of families' lives.

Even as human service agencies deliberately or inadvertently became "detached" from neighborhoods, they felt a need to reach out to reestablish bonds. By the 1920s a few social service leaders, for example Hyman Kaplan of Cincinnati, were concerned about the harmful effects of bureaucratic organization and specialization as a basis for social problem solving in poor communities. A few leaders were already arguing the need for "generalists" who could act as advocates and "buffer between client and technician" (Kirschner, 1986, p. 84). They pointed out that as professionals appropriated more and more social functions, from socialization of children to provision of social support and social control around childrearing, they inadvertently further undermined the very family and community capacities that they were trying to support and strengthen.

Such concerns spurred efforts during the 1920s, 1930s, and 1940s to return the human service system to its neighborhood-based roots and to recreate generalist helping roles. Hartford, Syracuse, and other cities experimented with neighborhood councils designed to assure citizen input into the planning and provision (though not the governance) of services (Dillick, 1953, p. 116). Settlements, innovators as always, promoted various approaches to addressing growing fragmentation of services including case management and centralized intake. For example, Mitchell House in Hartford tried to establish a single intake into the whole complex human service system in its neighborhood. Settlements also attempted to bring the services of separate institutions together. In the mid-1920s in Cleveland, the Hiram House settlement tried to link up with the schools in its neighborhood, offering to recreate the visiting teacher role: starting small clubs, home visiting, working with teachers to meet the needs of children having school and other problems, and street corner counseling (Dillick, 1953, pp. 103–104). By the mid-1930s community organizing, which had been suppressed both by the general spirit of the 1920s and the specific efforts of local philanthropic organizations in social welfare, reemerged in scattered places around the country, most notably in Saul Alinsky's efforts in Chicago and other cities.

Setting the Stage for the Neighborhood-Based Services of the Current Era

The 1940s and 1950s were characterized by discrete innovation and sporadic (but when taken as a whole, continuous) local reinvention of various neighborhood-based service approaches: a community school started in one neighborhood, an information and referral center or multiservice center in another, and a health outreach program in another. As was the case historically, efforts to reach out to vulnerable families with young children, to individual youths, and to youth gangs served to stimulate innovative programs, taking professionals out of their offices into the neighborhood. Kahn (1976, p. 29) points out that during this period the recognition of "multi-problem" families who drained public resources with their complex problems also stimulated a variety of innovative approaches. These included pioneering efforts to bring the whole array of agency services—assessment, casework, crisis management, and even long-term therapy—into families' homes. The idiosyncratic process of local invention and reinvention both fertilized the field and preserved ideas and approaches, kept them alive until the inevitable next wave of reform. It provided a kind of dictionary that reformers would be able to draw on, to name and define things, when the time came. It also helped hold together an increasingly fragile fabric of social support in inner-city neighborhoods.

During this same period, particularly through the 1950s, traditional neighborhood agencies such as settlements and youth-serving agencies struggled with changing inner-city populations, the growth of gangs, and geographic and physical change in their neighborhoods (see Trolander, 1987, Ch. 4). Neighborhood-based services continued their critical role of facilitating the adjustment of migrants to a new world, this time Puerto Rican, African-American, and Mexican. Settlements and other agencies tried to establish a presence and find a useful role in new public housing projects, sometimes as basic a role as building a sense of community (see Trolander, 1987, p. 83). Nonetheless, once a nursery school or after-school program or youth center was located in a project building, it became vulnerable to the dynamics of project life—for example, constraints imposed on children's mobility by gang turf—in ways that a strategically placed, free-standing facility would not have.

Many traditional neighborhood-based agencies—particularly those with religious or ethnic affiliations that no longer matched those of the local population—found the changes occurring around them extraordinarily disorienting and some abandoned neighborhoods that they had worked in for decades. In Chicago's Lawndale neighborhood, for example, the Young Men's Jewish Association simply ceded a local youth center facility to another youth-serving agency that was expanding its programs for African-American youth. Some agencies followed their traditional constituencies to the suburbs (Kahn, 1976, p. 28). Others, particularly settlements, a few nonsectarian youth serving agencies, and locally based churches with social programs, stayed on and struggled to reduce intergroup tensions created by rapid population change, notably in work with neighborhood gangs (see Hall, 1971, pp. 226–227). Agencies that remained in their old neighborhoods often found themselves questioning their role and relevance to new realities and populations. Their traditional enrichment activities, such as drama clubs or home economics classes, did not attract youth anymore. Even their efforts to create positive mirror-images of gangs, for example, providing space for self-organized youth "clubs," only reached a small group of children.

The 1950s also saw the intensification of three related trends within social work that would pull the few remaining social workers out of neighborhood-based work with poor families. One was a rapidly expanding state and federal social welfare system, which meant rapidly expanding bureaucracies. These in turn provided an engine for the continuing growth of statutory social work, particularly in public aid and child welfare. A second was the triumph of clinical social work over basic casework. The "prestige jobs, the well-paying jobs, and the socially respected assignments were in child guidance, Veteran's Administration, mental hygiene clinics, and family counseling agencies" (Kahn, 1976, p. 28). A third was a shift in the self-defined mandate of private voluntary agencies. While the state was assuming expanded responsibility for the welfare of dependent and vulnerable families, over the objections of the private "voluntary" social welfare agencies, these same agencies were rethinking—some observers said walking away from—their own responsibilities to this population (see Polier, 1989, p. 8).

The old line agencies argued that they had to restrict their services if they were to maintain quality; that is, to provide specialized therapeutic services using the best trained professionals. Underlying that argument was reluctance to serve a growing volume of poor African-American and Latino families (Bush, 1988, p. 32). This reluctance stemmed in part from financial concerns; traditional donors sometimes did not want their money used for these new populations of children and families. It stemmed also from a belief that African-Americans and Latinos would not benefit from what they had to offer. As inner-city neighborhoods changed in ethnic composition, the private agencies exchanged the traditional "particularism of serving one's own kind for the particularism of serving those people who might benefit from the specialized skills of trained social workers" (Bush, 1988, p. 35). From there it was only a short step to an inference that such clients did not reside in the inner city (see Lerner, 1972).

No single loss to the traditional human services in inner-city neighborhoods was critical in and of itself. It was the accumulation of losses—youth serving programs, the old line child and family service agencies, and settlements—that eventually would prove so devastating, especially in combination with losses in other domains such as employment, public housing, and resources for schools. The damaging effects of professional and institutional abandonment were masked for almost two decades by the remains of a new service network created by the War on Poverty. In retrospect it was clear that this new network did not replace the old. The staffing and posture that were "optimal for mobilization and protest did not prove to be the best prescription for ongoing service delivery" (Kahn, 1976, p. 36). Nor did this new network have much influence on the overall quality and quantity of remaining traditional services in inner-city communities; both continued to decline throughout the 1970s and 1980s.

NEIGHBORHOOD-BASED SERVICES IN THE 1960s

The renewal of neighborhood-based services during the 1960s was stimulated and shaped by a number of factors, some complementary and some that led to tensions in purpose and strategy. The major demonstration projects of the era, such as Gray Areas and Mobilization for Youth, provided both a rationale and prototypes for many of the specific federally funded neighborhood-based programs that emerged during that period. These demonstrations, particularly the Ford Foundation's Gray Areas, were the first to note the increasing dysfunctionality of the mainstream human service system, particularly with respect to inner-city children and families. They were the first to articulate the idea that new intervention models were needed to prepare poor children, youth, and adults to take advantage of new economic realities and demands.

As in the Progressive era, neighborhood-based services in the 1960s were conceived by those living outside of inner-city neighborhoods—this time the federal government and its professional consultants—as a response to the unique problems of those neighborhoods. As earlier, the idea was to make the neighborhood the referent and locus for organizing services and supports to poor families. The overriding focus was on things that could be accomplished within the boundaries of the local community with an emphasis on assimilation and acculturation of African-American migrants and Latino immigrants, and an orientation toward self-help. Many of the objectives of the new neighborhood-based services were also reminiscent: improving women's and children's health, altering poor children's life chances and developmental trajectories, rebuilding the social fabric of the neighborhood, increasing civic participation, helping "immigrants" to the city adjust to the demands of urban life.

At the same time, the social, political, and institutional context for neighborhood-based services in the 1960s differed from that of the Progressive era in ways that made the traditional tasks of neighborhood-based services harder to achieve and suggested new tasks. For one thing, well-established, rigid public bureaucracies had tremendous control over most aspects of poor families' lives. For another, many helping professionals—teachers, social workers, physicians—felt threatened by a potential loss of status and monopoly on services. However, at least a few wanted to reform their professions and/or foster social change.

The inner-city neighborhoods of the 1960s were more depleted economically and institutionally than immigrant neighborhoods had been 50 years earlier (Halpern, 1995). Residents and service providers had fewer resources to work with—to build on, mobilize, draw together—and fewer realistic objectives. As a group newly urbanized African-Americans brought with them a history of exclusion, discrimination, and denigration, not in some far country but in their own society. A growing number of families could no longer see their way out of the ghetto; not so much because they were trapped by a self-perpetuating culture of poverty as because paths into the labor market were narrowing and receding.

Other forces shaping neighborhood-based services in the 1960s included the Civil Rights movement, grass-roots protest groups that focused on issues ranging from welfare rights to community control of schools, and the efforts of African-American and Latino leaders to create pride in ethnic identity. The Civil Rights movement encouraged attention to the rights of minorities and poor families above and beyond their needs and obligations. It enabled public interest lawyers and community organizers to question the right of large public bureaucracies to define, label, and categorize poor people. In the context of growing ethnic pride and identity, because "caseworkers came from outside the neighborhood, from what was indeed an alien culture, they were seen as unable to grasp their clients' experience and aspirations" (Polsky, 1991, p. 176). This perception profoundly affected relations between professional helpers and their clients in America's inner cities. The general abandonment of inner city neighborhoods by traditional human service agencies was exacerbated by repeated attacks during the 1960s on the relevance and usefulness of those few that remained.

Rebuilding the Infrastructure of Neighborhood-Based Services

Specific programs created as part of the federal government's War on Poverty provided the infrastructure and defined the priorities of efforts to renew neighborhood-based services in the 1960s. These included Head Start, neighborhood health centers (which would later be renamed community health centers), neighborhood service centers (later called multiservice centers), the Neighborhood Youth Corps, and community mental health centers. Specific programs emerged from task forces or working groups composed primarily of social scientists, consulted and in some cases recruited into government service by the Kennedy and Johnson administrations. Most were administered under the umbrella of the community action program.

While each had distinct purposes and provided different services, all the programs shared certain generic features: a focus on serving the community rather than diagnosed or labeled individuals; a specific target population with an orientation toward the whole family and the whole community; employment of community residents in direct service and auxiliary roles; involvement of community residents as partners or advisors in policy setting; outreach to isolated, overwhelmed, or distrustful families to bring them into community life; a preventive orientation; a self-defined role as mediator or, when necessary, as advocate between families and the large public bureaucracies; provision of an array of services within the same program; and, not least, a desire to embed the program physically, socially, and even temporally in neighborhood life.

Each program was seen loosely as a piece of a larger puzzle that the Office of Economic Opportunity (OEO) and its local community action agencies were trying to piece together. The puzzle was simultaneously conceptual and geographic. In conceptual terms, the pieces comprised the array of supports poor children and families needed to escape poverty; which of these should OEO address and which should be left to other federal and local, public and private agencies; what should be part of each program; and how should different programs (including old and new services) work together to create a whole? Driving these questions was a growing appreciation of the large number and interrelatedness of inner-city families' problems and support needs.

The neighborhood created both frame and canvas and provided at least some of the ingredients for addressing the conceptual questions. For the first of many times in succeeding years these questions were asked: What should the array of services—the "service system"—look like in each poor neighborhood? How should these services work together? What should be the responsibilities of public service systems in creating a more supportive service system for poor families? At the same time, the neighborhood focus constrained thinking and planning. No one at the time (and to some extent few even today) asked how services or cultural and recreational resources within inner-city neighborhoods should be tied to those outside; or whether and how services and resources outside the neighborhood—schools, social services, museums, arts programs for children—should be made available to inner-city children and their families. By the 1960s many inner-city children had little contact with the world outside their neighborhood.

In reaction to a half century of fragmentation of people and their problems everything was now viewed as connected: youth were embedded in families that were embedded in support networks, institutions, the neighborhood. Nonetheless a tension quickly emerged with respect to where and at what level the effort to make things whole again, to create a coherent service experience for families, would be located. Ideally comprehensiveness and coherence were objectives for the local service system as a whole. But as specific programs began working with families and their staff began to experience directly the complexity of family support needs and the loss of human service infrastructure in the community, they felt compelled to respond through their particular program.

Most programs tried to become more internally comprehensive, adding services and helping functions, in effect nudging aside the more abstract idea of locating comprehensiveness at the neighborhood level. For example, the model that emerged in Head Start included not just preschool education but health screening, meals, service brokerage for the whole family, and, in some centers, mental health counseling. Neighborhood health centers not only tried to provide all kinds of health and mental health services, but started day care programs and became involved in advocacy for educational and welfare reform. The historic settlement idea of bringing an array of services together under one roof was revived in the neighborhood service or multiservice center (March, 1968), as well as in specific categorical programs.

There were other forces impelling programs to become internally comprehensive. One was a rejection of the historic response of specialized agencies to clients or client needs that did not fit what they had to offer, that is, referral to another program. A second was a desire always to have secondary functions as insurance against loss of funds or shifts in priorities. Thus when Head Start's effectiveness as a child development program was questioned in the late 1960s, its advocates argued successfully that Head Start was not just a child development program, but a child health and nutrition program, a parent support program, and an employment program for community residents (Skerry, 1983, p. 19). A third force was the idea that neighborhood-based programs were inherently better at many functions than specialized agencies. Neighborhood health center staff were convinced that they could provide not only better primary health care than hospitals, but treatment for many diseases as well. They understood patient beliefs about health and were more inclined to explain, follow-up, be patient, and so forth.

Beyond the common problem of programs being distracted from their core mission when they tried to do too much, tensions emerged in many neighborhoods around the issue of comprehensiveness. Existing providers wanted the new federal programs to focus on services they did not provide and populations that they did not serve. Each program tended to see the issues with which it was concerned—child development, health care, youth employment—as the best basis for mobilizing neighborhood residents and then organize them to address the full range of neighborhood concerns.

Participation as a Major Theme

Many of the contradictory pressures shaping neighborhood-based services in the 1960s intersected around the issue of participation. The historic rationale for the human services—helping clients adjust to the realities of their lives, that is to hardship, exclusion, and insecurity—was coming to be viewed as a form of oppression. At the same time, children and families with difficulties requiring highly skilled help—such as substance abuse, inattentive or erratic parenting, parent–child conflict, learning problems in school, and behavioral problems outside of school—were not getting help. If services were still to be a part of social problem solving, new paradigms were needed. Democratic helping was the alternative to authoritarian helping that reformers saw at the time, which quickly came to mean community resident participation in service design, management, and provision.

As in the community action program, generally, there were ongoing struggles in many programs about appropriate roles for community residents, particularly in the arena of policy setting. In Head Start, for example, two very different visions of parent involvement (beyond their roles as volunteers and staff) clashed during the early years of the programs. At one extreme was the vision of parents primarily as clients needing guidance in childrearing, home management, and related domains. At the other was the vision of parents actually running the program: planning, hiring, supervising staff, and managing budgets (Valentine & Stark, 1979, pp. 297–298). The opposing visions of participation in Head Start, as in other programs, reflected very different analyses of both the capacities of poor people and the core problem in inner-city communities.

An interesting exception to the ever more circumscribed parental and community authority in Head Start and other neighborhood-based programs is the "neighborhood" health center sponsored by Tufts University in Mississippi (Geiger, 1969, p. 138). A strong commitment to genuine participation led to the formation of 10 local health associations and a broad definition of health that allowed each association to set its own priorities (e.g., drinkable water, child care, home care for the elderly). Each of the 10 associations also had a voice on an overall health council, which defined an overarching priority, in this case the need for more food. The professional staff of the health center, taking its cue from the council, focused its energy and program resources on organizing a farm co-op. Also making participation work in this case was a clear, multistep process, with rules, parameters, and objectives jointly set by community members and professionals and a trust in that process among all the stakeholders.

Paraprofessionals as Service Providers

In most programs of the era, however, participation came to mean primarily use of community residents in volunteer and paid staff roles, the latter a departure from usual practice, if not unprecedented. Community residents cooked meals and worked as classroom aides in Head Start programs and in schools; did outreach to search for pregnant women, to instruct new mothers in infant care, and to check that people were taking their medications for neighborhood health centers; counseled youth in mental health centers; worked as "job developers" (i.e., job-finders) in employment agencies; and led youth in public works crews for the Neighborhood Youth Corps. Community residents provided transportation, served as translators, provided help with homework in after-school programs, visited new parents to provide guidance and social support, and even worked as case managers (for example, in the Lower East Side Family Union; see Weissman, 1978). In some programs paraprofessionals' roles were clearly defined and delimited. In others they recreated the generalist helping role of the settlement workers and the early social workers.

A diverse coalition of proponents brought very different rationales to the movement to employ community residents with different, sometimes conflicting, purposes. To some the paraprofessional movement was a vehicle for both creating jobs and bringing community residents into the labor force while raising aspirations and self-esteem. To others the paraprofessionals saved professionals from having to spend so much time on routine, nonskilled, or unpleasant tasks (Grosser, 1969, pp. 117–118).

To still others the paraprofessional movement was a vehicle for altering the culture and enhancing the sensitivity of the human service system; and perhaps for improving its image among the poor. As helpers, paraprofessionals had the advantage of shared life experience—presumed by some to be more powerful than theoretical knowledge or professional experience—in understanding and communicating with clients. As members of "recipient" communities, they could help the human service system learn more about client culture and, perhaps, alter sterotypes about clients. As agency employees, paraprofessionals could present a friendlier face to the public. To a few, the indigenous paraprofessional movement was seen as an attack on professionalism and on the traditional human service system as a whole.

Paraprofessionals were rarely viewed as partners with professionals in programs with a full complement of professional staff. In a few programs, including many Head Start programs that were not sponsored by school systems, pay scales were such that paraprofessionals constituted most of the staff. However, in terms of training, preparation, and competence it was unclear whether paraprofessionals were supposed to learn professional skills, to rely on "natural skills, acquired not through education but through life experience" (Reiff, 1969, p. 62), or to combine both.

Eventually the principle of participation would be partially inverted in many programs with professionals turning community residents back into clients. This process was evident not just in Head Start, with its growing emphasis by the late 1960s on parent education, but in the neighborhood health centers, community health centers, and job training programs. It proved extraordinarily difficult to "bracket" status differences and relate to each other "as if they were social equals" (Fine, 1993, p. 683). But the confusion, disorder, and doubtful decisions that followed upon thrusting poor people into complex new roles in ill-defined new programs with little training or support also bounded participation. By the late 1960s the discussion of poverty was returning to its historic narrow track focused on the poor themselves (Katz, 1989, p. 3).

Neighborhood-Based Services and Broader Service Reform

Among other things, the new neighborhood-based programs of the 1960s were expected to serve as catalysts for systemic change within the human services—in social services, health care, and education. This meant both altering the values of mainstream services and helping to create a more rational, coherent overall system. Throughout the 1960s the human service landscape in inner-city neighborhoods was steadily repopulated. In addition to the various federally funded programs, scores of small programs emerged, seeded by community action or foundation funds and located in storefronts, church basements, or anywhere space could be found (Kahn, 1976, p. 30). As the decade wore on, the large human service bureaucracies and old line agency networks reluctantly responded to a variety of pressures from below, both by adopting participatory rhetoric and by reentering the neighborhood-based services arena themselves through the mechanism of decentralization. Decentralization seemed to address the criticism of irrelevance and the demand for community control, while further buffering downtown headquarters from responsibility for difficult local problems (Yin & Yates, 1975).

One by-product was an even more complex, fragmented, and incoherent local service system for poor children and families. There were more entry points, service sites, categorical programs, and specialized roles than a decade earlier. Different types of programs provided almost identical services. Multiple programs served the same family at cross-purposes, and no one provider had overall responsibility for a particular child or family. When a child or family slipped through the cracks of the system, there were no mechanisms to examine that failure, let alone figure out who might be responsible. Many programs were committed to improving community well-being, but dozens of uncoordinated efforts failed to do so.

Strategies had already been incorporated into OEO programs to address fragmentation at the individual client level (e.g., case management) and at the program level (e.g., co-location of services and interagency agreements). Programs such as the neighborhood centers and Model Cities were initiated specifically to "knit together" the dozens of categorical programs in inner-city neighborhoods. However, there was no vision of what a more coherent local human service system would look and act like from an individual client's perspective, nor how it might be governed and funded. Further, as was the case with community action agencies, new human service agencies or programs did not have the credibility or leverage needed to alter prevailing patterns of collaboration or to influence negative provider attitudes toward poor families. Their staff did not have funds to purchase client services, nor did they have control over a flexible grant-funding stream. Established service providers tended to collaborate only to the point at which their autonomy in funding, problem definition, eligibility determination, recordkeeping, and helping approach was threatened.

For all their difficulties, local efforts at service coordination during the 1960s yielded important lessons. One was that differences in objectives or perceptions among providers could not be swept under the rug or ignored. They had to be recognized by all parties as legitimate and reconciled within that framework. In addition, it was not always easy to get representatives of client groups and clients themselves to articulate what good services would be like, other than being community controlled (in the arena of schools) and geographically accessible with a minimum of "red tape" and respectful staff (Perlman, 1975, Ch. 1).

Another lesson of the era was that in poor neighborhoods the combination of service system fragmentation, families with many and complex support needs, and an overall context of scarcity and disorganization interacted in ways that dramatically heightened the difficulties of service provision. Providers often had little control over the services poor families said they needed, whether they were direct services such as a preschool program or health care or other resources such as jobs or housing. However, people with pressing problems wanted the program to address whatever concerns they brought with them, regardless of program mission, not to be referred from agency to agency. The pull to provide comprehensive services to poor families was strong, but the services most needed were usually the most difficult to provide.

CONCLUSION

Neighborhood-based services have always embodied multiple purposes—to assist poor people in coping with the hardships of poverty and economic insecurity; to guide and monitor them in their roles as parents; to teach them middle-class ways and link them to mainstream opportunities; to provide basic health care; and to counsel, encourage, organize, and advocate for them. At the same time, the primary role of neighborhood-based services has been different in each historical era, reflecting the situation and composition of low-income neighborhoods themselves. In the early decades of the century, neighborhood-based services were conceived as a means of bringing mainstream society into poor neighborhoods and later as a means of compensating for the effects of bureaucracy within the expanding service system. In the 1960s they became a vehicle for the poor themselves to use, to organize, and to control public resources, and to create their own society within the larger one.

The federally funded neighborhood-based services of the 1960s helped buffer the effects of a deteriorating social and institutional fabric in inner-city neighborhoods. Those who designed, managed, and provided these services also struggled with, but could not resolve, the problem of recreating good quality human services in the inner city. To some extent their efforts were constrained by competing purposes, forced upon and embraced by them, conceptual confusion, specific strategic errors, and lack of support from the helping professions and traditional human service institutions. The efforts of neighborhood-based services also were constrained by worsening social conditions in inner-city neighborhoods. The tasks of neighborhood-based services seemed to become more ambiguous, even dissonant, as the situation of inner-city communities changed fundamentally from port of entry to isolated and excluded enclave. Many programs found it impossible to ignore community organizing, advocacy, and related tasks, even though these often distracted from their primary mission. Providers of neighborhood-based services increasingly felt compelled to address the causes and consequences of social problems that they were ill-equipped to address.

To some extent there were also inherent obstacles to creating conceptually clear, internally healthy and helpful services for devalued populations in devalued communities. Neighborhood-based services draw their identity, resources, and sustenance primarily from the neighborhood in which they operate. This can be problematic in isolated, depleted, and disorganized neighborhoods. Neighborhood-based services in low-income neighborhoods have helped both to sustain and inadvertently to maintain those neighborhoods. They are now one of the few remaining sources of structure and institutional support in many inner-city neighborhoods. Yet too often they seem as isolated and stressed as the neighborhoods in which they are embedded.

Historically, neighborhood-based services have appeared to be a creative response to the difficulties of inner-city life. One can argue that, along with the community development corporations, they have constituted a series of natural experiments concerning the means of rebuilding community in the ghetto. Nonetheless, friendly, responsive services can only do so much to help devalued, excluded people feel valued and included. The notion of rebuilding a sense of community through networks of neighborhood-based services can only be taken so far when the majority of poor children and families are geographically and socially isolated from the rest of society.

REFERENCES

Bremner, R. (1972). *From the depths: The discovery of poverty in the United States.* New York: New York University Press.

Bush, M. (1988). *Families in distress.* Berkeley, CA: University of California Press.

Dillick, S. (1953). *Community organization for neighborhood development: Past and present.* New York: William Morrow.

Fine, M. (1993). [A]parent involvement: Reflections of parents, power, and urban public schools. *Teachers College Record, 94,* 682–709.

Geiger, J. (1969, November). Community control—or community conflict. *American Lung Association Bulletin,* 4–10.

Grosser, C. (1969). Manpower development programs. In C. Grosser, W.E. Henry, & J.G. Kelly (Eds.), *Nonprofessionals in the human services* (pp. 116–148). San Francisco: Jossey Bass.

Hall, H. (1971). *Unfinished business.* New York: Macmillan.

Halpern, R. (1995). *Rebuilding the inner city.* New York: Columbia University Press.

Kahn, A. (1976). Service delivery at the neighborhood level: Experience, theory and fads. *Social Service Review, 50,* 23–55.

Katz, M. B. (1989). *The undeserving poor: From the war on poverty to the war on welfare.* New York: Pantheon.

Kirschner, D. (1986). *The paradox of professionalism.* New York: Greenwood Press.

Lerner, B. (1972). *Therapy in the ghetto.* Baltimore, MD: Johns Hopkins University Press.

Lubove, R. (1965). *The professional altruist.* Cambridge, MA: Harvard University Press.

March, M. (1968). The neighborhood center concept. *Public Welfare, 10,* 97–111.

Melosh, B. (1984). More than the physician's hand: Skill and authority in twentieth century nursing. In J. Leavitt (Ed.), *Women and health in America* (pp. 482–496). Madison, WI: University of Wisconsin Press.

Perlman, R. (1975). *Consumers and social services*. New York: Wiley.

Philpott, T. (1978). *The slum and the ghetto*. New York: Oxford University Press.

Polier, J. (1989). *Juvenile justice in double jeopardy*. Hillsdale, NJ: Lawrence Earlbaum.

Polsky, A. (1991). *The rise of the therapeutic state*. Princeton, NJ: Princeton University Press.

Reiff, R. (1969). Dilemmas of professionalism. In C. Grosser, W. Henry, & J. Kelly (Eds.), *Nonprofessionals in the human services* (pp. 57–65). San Francisco: Jossey Bass.

Silberman, D. (1990). *Chicago and its children: A brief history of social services for children in Chicago*. Chicago: Chapin Hall Center for Children.

Skerry, P. (1983). The charmed life of Head Start. *Public Interest*, *73*, 18–39.

Stoeckle, J., & Candib, L. (1969). The neighborhood health center: Reform ideas of yesterday and today. *New England Journal of Medicine*, *280*, 1385–1391.

Trolander, J. (1987). *Professionalism and social change*. New York: Columbia University Press.

Valentine, J., & Stark, E. (1979). The social context of parent involvement in Head Start. In E. Zigler & J. Valentine (Eds.), *Project Head Start: A legacy of the War on Poverty* (pp. 291–314). New York: Free Press.

Weissman, H. (1978). *Integrating services for troubled children*. San Francisco: Jossey Bass.

Yin, R., & Yates, D. (1975). *Street level governments*. Lexington, MA: Heath.

2

The Economic Context of Community-Centered Practice: Markets, Communities, and Social Policy

PETER S. FISHER

Social service providers find themselves working, to a large extent, with families in poverty. This is not because the poor have a monopoly on drug abuse, violence, or child neglect since they are found, as well, among the upper and middle classes. However, poverty *is* associated with *higher rates* of child abuse and neglect, homicide, substance abuse, physical and mental health problems, and crime. In addition, children in poor families are much more likely to be poor as adults, or, worse, to die before they reach adulthood.

The purpose of this chapter is to show how the market economy in the United States creates inequality and poverty among families, how unequal resources among communities help to maintain poverty, how inequality has increased over the past 15 years, and how a market-based public philosophy works against efforts to reduce inequality and improve social conditions. I will argue that market systems and market-based policies are in many respects antisocial, anticommunity, and antifamily. To produce a lasting improvement in people's lives, social policy, as well as attempts to bring about more fundamental structural change, must strengthen families and informal social relationships and restore a deeper sense of community and of collective responsibility at all levels. Rather than adopting the "official" language and modifying policies to conform to the rhetoric of the market or appealing to market efficiency, advocates should attack the ideological basis of public policy and expose market rationales as legitimizing the current unequal distribution of wealth and power.

THE CONSEQUENCES OF POVERTY

Poverty affects the physical and mental well-being of children and families in a number of ways. Being poor can lead to inadequate nutrition, affecting the health of adults and children and the birth weight and viability of newborns (Garbarino, 1992; Najman, 1993; Wilkinson, 1989). Substandard housing conditions increase lead-poisoning (through the ingestion of paint or the use of old lead plumbing), rat bites, and disease generally. The psychological stress of living at a subsistence level can lead to depression (Belle, 1990) and increase violent responses to frustration—including child abuse, spouse abuse, murder, and suicide (Garbarino, 1992; Gelles, 1992).

Poor families tend to live in poor neighborhoods, which compounds their problems. Poor neighborhoods may have less access to health services because of lack of transportation, and poorer quality health care, public services, and schools. Poorer education and social isolation, in turn, can affect employability and access to jobs that would raise a family out of poverty (Anderson, 1991; Crane, 1991; Mayer, 1991). Finally, growing up in a poor family in a poor neighborhood increases the likelihood that one will be poor as an adult and, therefore, raise another generation in poverty.

Much of the literature focuses on the extent to which these problems are the direct result of growing up in or living in a poor family and the extent to which they are the result of growing up in or living in a poor neighborhood or going to a school with a high concentration of children from poor families. Part of the "neighborhood effect" is clearly due to resource and structural problems associated with poor neighborhoods, but part may also be due to socialization effects. It is difficult to deny that community norms, role models, and peer pressure influence attitudes and behavior, for to do so would be to deny the importance of social processes in general and to subscribe to an extreme form of individualism. Nonetheless, some have carried the idea of the importance of neighborhood socialization to the point of hypothesizing a "culture of poverty," a highly controversial notion that, at least as used by some, seems to beg the question of why these local norms and role models develop in the first place and how they relate to broader societal values and norms and that, somewhat paradoxically, places the blame for being poor on the behavior of the poor themselves rather than on the structure of economic opportunity and the social conditions under which they live.

MARKETS, POVERTY, AND INEQUALITY

Poverty Amidst Plenty

It is common to talk about "the paradox of poverty"—how poverty, and the problems it creates, can persist in a country as wealthy as the United States. Why hasn't economic growth and the rising standard of living in the twentieth century eliminated poverty or at least enabled public policy to do so?

I would argue that the coexistence of poverty and wealth in the United States is not a paradox, but a product of the economic system in which we live. Although there is not the space here to elaborate on this argument, I will make two points. First, poverty is best understood not as an affliction, but as part of a relationship of inequality among family members, between families and communities, among communities, and between social classes. Second, the history of the twentieth century shows that the persistence of inequality and poverty is a fact that must be accounted for.

Recent Trends in Poverty and Inequality

Something began happening to the distribution of income in the United States in the 1970s. Since the end of World War II, two decades of expansion (interrupted only briefly by recessions) and an unprecedented rise in the general standard of living sharply decreased inequality of family incomes. This trend toward greater equality peaked in the late 1960s, followed by an upturn in inequality that at first appeared to be merely a cyclical response to recession and stagnant growth. Sometime in the 1970s, the distribution of income, measured in a variety of ways, shifted toward greater inequality,[1] a trend that has continued through the 1980s. Why has this happened? The answer lies partly in changes in the structure of the U.S. and world economies and partly in changes in public policies.

Until recently, long-term economic growth was like a rising tide that lifted all boats; now we have been forced to recognize shifting tides that lift some boats more than others, or that cause some to fall. These recent trends are depicted in Figure 2.1, which shows the adjusted family income[2] for all individuals from 1967 to 1989 at five points: the 10th, 25th, 50th, 75th, and 90th percentiles. That is, it shows how the income level that divided the bottom 10% of individuals from the top 90%, for example, changed over that 22-year period. Income is adjusted both for inflation and for the poverty level.

In 1973 the 10th percentile cutoff was exactly 1.00; the poorest tenth of the population that year was below the poverty level for that year; the other 90% were above the poverty level. By 1987 the cutoff had declined to 0.90. The poorest tenth were worse off in absolute terms, all having incomes below 90% of the poverty level. But we can see that the poor also suffered relatively; the absolute cutoffs for the 75th and 90th percentiles actually rose during this 10-year period, so that the absolute spread between the 10th and the 90th percentiles widened. The former

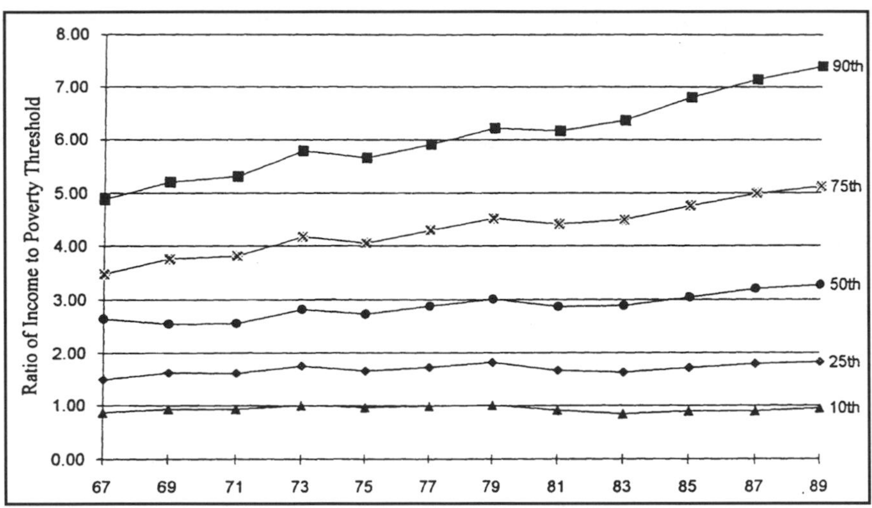

Figure 2.1. Changes in the absolute and relative distribution of income, 1967 to 1989 (by percentile). Constructed from data in Karoly (1993, pp. 86–87).

is absolute impoverishment; the latter is relative impoverishment, or increasing inequality.

Different population subgroups have been affected differently by this rising inequality. Most importantly for our discussions in this book, families with children experienced a greater increase in inequality from 1973 to 1987 than did all families. For families with children, the income of the poorest tenth declined by 22% over that period, while that of the richest tenth rose 23% (Karoly, 1993, p. 43). In terms of both absolute and relative well-being, the poorest families with children were much worse off, and this decline in welfare was more pronounced than for all families or for all individuals. This is another way of saying that the proportion of the nation's children living in poverty has risen; the poverty rate among black children remained high between 1968 and 1986 (about 42%), while the poverty rate among white children increased from 9.9 to 14.7% over this period (Gottschalk & Danziger, 1993, p. 176).

The sharper rise in inequality and poverty among families with children is closely related to the increase in the proportion of families that are female-headed, single-parent families. Though there was an increase in the incidence of poverty among such families between 1968 and 1986, the more significant trend was that such families, which have always been disproportionately poor, have come to constitute a much larger share of all families. In 1968, 32.3% of black children and 7.1% of white children lived in female-headed families; by 1986 these proportions had increased to 57.2 and 18.3%, respectively (Gottschalk & Danziger, 1993).[3]

This, of course, is the phenomenon known as the feminization of poverty, which is in large part a result of the increase in divorce rates and births outside marriage, which usually leave the mother without adequate support from the father, and the structure of opportunity for women—educational channeling, occupational segregation, and wage discrimination. Among white families, although inequality increased, everyone was better off. Among black and Hispanic families, the poorest 25% of families became poorer, but the richest 25% became richer (Karoly, 1993, p. 43).

The rise in inequality of incomes is due in substantial measure to rising inequality in wages, whether measured hourly, weekly, or annually (that is, taking into account changes in annual hours worked). The increasing inequality of wages can be traced to changes in the structure of the economy over the past 20 years, particularly the decline of better-paying blue-collar jobs, a higher premium for college education (i.e., the difference between the average wage for those with a college education compared to those without) (Murphy & Welch, 1993), and an increase in the share of income that came from property (rent, interest, dividends, capital gains, royalties) (U.S. House of Representatives, 1992, p. 1544). In addition, with the decline in the proportion of the labor force that is unionized and the decline in the strength of unions, bargaining power shifted toward management, enabling capital to protect its income from the effects of heightened international competition by shifting the location of production without effective opposition from unions.

PUBLIC POLICY AND INEQUALITY

Just as inequality has increased over the past two decades, so a public philosophy based on market theories has limited the effectiveness of government in reducing that inequality. Orthodox economic theory has in the last 20 years become the dominant paradigm in the public policy arena, producing a whole range of policies and programs. It is worthwhile to examine this ideology and to identify some of these policies and their effects on inequality and poverty.

Market-Based Public Policies

A market is a pattern of regularized exchange between buyers and sellers. It is one way of determining how goods, services, labor, income, and wealth are to be allocated among the members of a society. But markets have no soul, there is no place for fairness or justice. The outcome of a market exchange is simply the result of the bargaining power that parties bring to the market, and bargaining power is largely a function of the choices one has. The more alternatives you have—other workers waiting in line, other communities eager for your factory, other sources of income—the easier it is to walk away from any particular exchange, and that threat is what brings bargaining power. If your choices are all poor ones—a worse job, no job at all, a humiliating welfare system—you have little to bargain with. In this way, markets reproduce the inequality of resources that buyers and sellers, workers and owners, bring with them to the bargaining table. When we as a society decide to leave certain kinds of decisions to the market, we are deciding to let the outcomes be determined by those with market power; we are deciding to perpetuate the status quo distribution of wealth. Following are some of the policies that have resulted from this market-based public philosophy and their specific effects:

- *Privatization of public services.* Lower wages, increased use of part-time workers, and reduced employment opportunities for people of color have generally followed privatization.
- *Shift to user charges rather than taxes to finance public services.* User fees are alleged by market theory to improve efficiency in the use of services; their substitution for taxes usually results in a greater burden being placed on lower income households.
- *Replacement of universal service with willingness-to-pay as the guiding criterion in regulated industries.* In transportation and communications, universal service implied a basic right of citizens or communities to have access to the transportation network or the telephone system. Deregulation has meant the end of requirements to serve low-volume places or to price basic phone service low enough to ensure near-universal service; instead, the market principle—the service is sold to those who can afford to pay for it—is given greater weight.
- *Governmental competition.* According to the market-based philosophy, competition among governments is healthy, because it forces them to compete away excessive tax burdens on business. Competition among school districts is healthy because it keeps teachers and administrators on their toes, like owners of competing pizza franchises, striving to improve the quality of their service to attract customers (students).
- *Capital mobility.* Policies aimed at restricting the mobility of capital, such as plant closing legislation that mandates early notification and worker compensation, represent inefficient interference in the market, according to conventional economics. For the same reason,

government policy should not attempt to prop up declining communities and regions; if the market has dictated that they are inefficient locations for production, so be it. People will just have to move to where the jobs are.

- *Welfare reform.* By and large, conservatives have succeeded in defining the welfare problem in the 1980s and have provided the language in which public debate on the issues of work and welfare is carried on by liberals as well as free market ideologues. Conservatives have been able to shift the terms of the debate away from benefit levels (and have thus avoided addressing their adequacy) and instead have focused on "welfare dependency," "self-sufficiency," and direct ties to the labor market, quite clearly shifting attention away from the economic system and its failure to provide decent jobs at wage levels that can support a single-parent family. Whereas the receipt of welfare is described as dependency, the receipt of wages is defined as independence or self-sufficiency. State welfare reform programs are usually described as efforts to promote independence and self-sufficiency, which is defined as supporting oneself entirely by performing wage labor. In the new world of welfare reform, one is never dependent on work or on a husband's work, nor is one self-sufficient on welfare.
- *The new federalism.* State and local governments, in the market philosophy, have become irresponsible, just like citizens dependent on welfare. Taking cities off the federal dole forces them to adopt some "market discipline" and straighten out their finances, which often means laying off employees and cutting services to the poor in order to keep taxes down and avoid driving away the "best customers" (upper income taxpayers).

These public policies have some striking commonalities. They are based on a utilitarian individualism that denies the existence of community and defines the social good as simply the sum of individual desires. The individual, in turn, is a consumer and a factor of production, but not a citizen; citizens have rights, consumers only have demands. And the only kind of demand that counts is effective demand—which is to say, willingness and ability to pay. Needs or wants not backed up by the income to purchase their satisfaction do not count. Communities have no standing as social institutions; they are only places where consumers happen to live and, perhaps, own assets such as houses. Efficiency is the overriding goal of public policy; it requires that everything possible be marketed rather than distributed outside of markets. Where markets do not exist, government should establish property rights so that they can exist. Inequalities that persist despite the workings of markets to eliminate them must be the fault of the individual.

The Effects of Market-Based Public Policies

How have government taxing and spending policies, developed in the context of the market philosophy in the past 10 or 15 years, altered the pattern of inequality? So far we have discussed trends in inequality measured by money income before taxes. The material well-being of families and individuals, however, is substantially affected by a variety of public policies: federal, state, and local taxes reduce disposable income, while in-kind government benefits such as subsidized housing or food stamps increase a family's resources, but are not reflected in money income. Fortunately, we do have some data on the income distribution of households according to more comprehensive definitions of income. These measures allow us to assess the effect of tax and spending policies on income inequality.

Income inequality. A convenient summary measure of income inequality is the gini coefficient. Perfect inequality (100% of the income earned by the richest individual) would yield a gini of 1.00; perfect equality would yield a ratio of 0. Table 2.1 presents the gini coefficients for the distribution of income among households in 1979 and 1990, using four different definitions of income. "Market income" is wages and salaries, income from ownership of property, alimony and child support, and employer contributions to health insurance, all before taxes and before any government transfers. "After tax income" is market income less federal and state income taxes and federal payroll taxes, plus the earned income tax credit. "After social insurance" is after-tax income plus social insurance entitlements (non-means-tested transfers): social security, railroad retirement, unemployment benefits, workers' compensation, and Medicare. The final definition of income adds the means-tested cash and in-kind transfer payments: AFDC, Medicaid, food stamps, SSI, and subsidized housing.

As can be seen, the gini coefficient increased between 1979 and 1990 for all four measures of income. Inequality of market incomes, as measured by the gini, increased almost 6% during those 11 years.[4] Inequality increased even more (7.5%) for after-tax income, indicating that the

Table 2.1. Gini Coefficients for Household Income Distribution

	1979	*1990*	*Percent Change, 1979–1990*
Market income	0.460	0.487	5.9
After tax income	0.429	0.461	7.5
Percent reduction in inequality	6.7%	5.3%	
After social insurance	0.375	0.400	6.7
After means-tested transfers	0.359	0.382	6.4

Source: U.S. Bureau of the Census (1992).

tax system was becoming less progressive. Looking at it another way, the tax system reduced inequality by 6.7% in 1979, but only by 5.3% in 1990. It is noteworthy that the social insurance entitlements do far more to reduce inequality than the means-tested transfer programs. This pattern has also been found by Gramlich, Kasten, and Sammartino (1993).

Poverty rates. When we look at the effect of government on poverty rates rather than overall inequality, a similar picture emerges. In both 1979 and 1990, the effect of taxes was to increase the percent of persons in poverty, but the effect was larger in 1990. Transfers were less effective in reducing poverty in 1990 than in 1979. The poverty rate in 1979 was reduced from 24.1% based on after-tax income to 11.0% after all transfers, a 54% reduction in poverty incidence. In 1990, the poverty rate was reduced from 26.8% (based on after-tax income) to 15.1% by transfer programs, a 44% reduction in the poverty rate (U.S. Bureau of the Census, 1992, Table 2).

The diminished importance of taxes in reducing income inequality is attributable to two principal factors. First, the progressivity of the federal income tax was substantially eroded by the tax cuts of 1981 and 1982 and this progressivity was restored only slightly by the Tax Reform Act of 1986 (Wallace, Wasylenko, & Weiner 1991). Second, there have been significant changes in the mix of federal and state taxes over the past 20 years (see U.S. Advisory Commission on Intergovernmental Relations, 1991, pp. 120, 126). Greater reliance has been placed on payroll taxes at the federal and state level; these taxes are less progressive than income taxes and in fact are regressive at the high end of the income distribution. In addition, a greater share of government revenue comes from state income taxes, as revenue-raising responsibilities have been shifted down to state and local governments. State income taxes are considerably less progressive than federal taxes. States have also increased their reliance on gambling revenues and user charges, both of which are regressive forms of finance. Finally, there has been a reduction in the importance of taxes on property and the income from property (corporate income taxes); the net effect again is a reduction in progressivity, at least among higher income groups.[5]

POOR COMMUNITIES

The Geographic Concentration of Poverty

These changes in government policy have had an enormous impact on poor families and poor communities. Poor communities could simply be places where the poor tend to live, but they also tend to be places where public resources are scarce. The concentration of poor families in certain geographic areas is important for at least two reasons: (1) it may increase the isolation of the poor from labor markets, reduce the likelihood that children raised in poor families will escape poverty as adults, and exacerbate the various problems associated with poverty; and (2) high-poverty cities have higher public service costs and fewer resources available to redress the social problems attendant to poverty. In a sense, the private poverty of the cities' households is compounded by public sector poverty. The residents of affluent suburban jurisdictions, on the other hand, are able to use city boundaries to protect their private wealth from the claims of the poor and to add to that wealth with lower-cost public services.

This suggests three questions: (1) To what extent are poor families concentrated in high-poverty neighborhoods and has this concentration been increasing? (2) To what extent are the poor concentrated in cities in poor fiscal condition and has this been changing? (3) To what extent are rich cities getting richer and poor cities poorer, mirroring the changes in the distribution of income among individuals and families since the 1970s?

Census data indicate that poverty rates (the percent of families who are poor) in all areas increased between 1979 and 1992: in central cities, and in metropolitan areas outside central cities, as shown in Figure 2.2. But poverty has risen most rapidly in central cities, from 12.7% in 1979 to 17.5% in 1992, and least rapidly in nonmetropolitan areas, where it actually declined between 1987 and 1992.

For the United States as a whole, the picture in 1987 was little changed from 1979: about 41% of poor families resided in poverty areas. But the total population of these areas was declining; whereas nearly

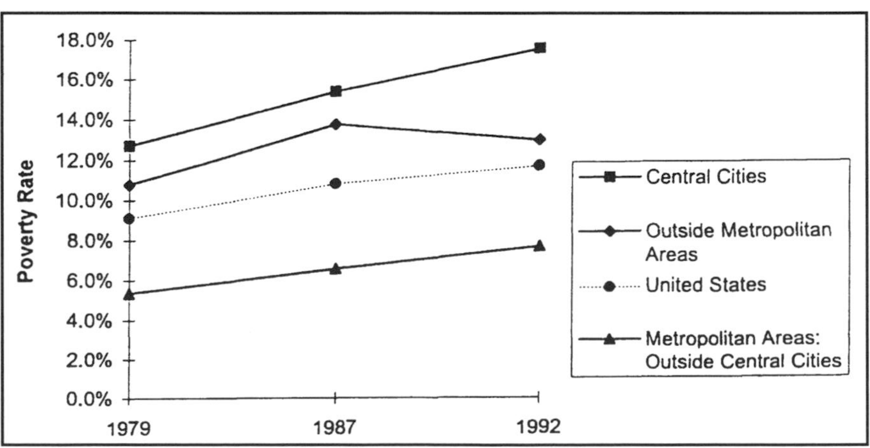

Figure 2.2. Percent of families below poverty, by place of residence. From U.S. Bureau of the Census (1981, p. 85; 1989, pp. 72–73; 1993, p. 137).

18% of all families resided in poverty areas in 1979, only 14.5% did so just 8 years later (U.S. Bureau of the Census, 1981, 1989). It appears that the nonpoor are exiting poverty areas while the poor on balance are not, leaving these areas with a substantially higher poverty rate (30.4% in 1987 as opposed to 20.6% in 1979).

It is also clear that a larger share of poor families resided in poverty areas of central cities in 1987, compared to 1979; and a smaller share resided outside poverty areas, as shown in Figure 2.3. Finally, the data show an increasing share of the poor living in metropolitan areas outside central cities, and a decreasing share living in nonmetropolitan areas. However, there is tremendous variation among cities in metropolitan areas and the central city–outside central city dichotomy conceals much.

Few studies have examined actual patterns of exit and entrance of households from and to poor neighborhoods. That is, the poor population may remain relatively constant, but composition data alone do not tell us whether this was because the same poor persons that resided there in 1980 are entrapped and are still there in 1990, or whether there has been a large out-migration offset by a large in-migration. One study that examined a panel of families between 1979 and 1985 found some rather

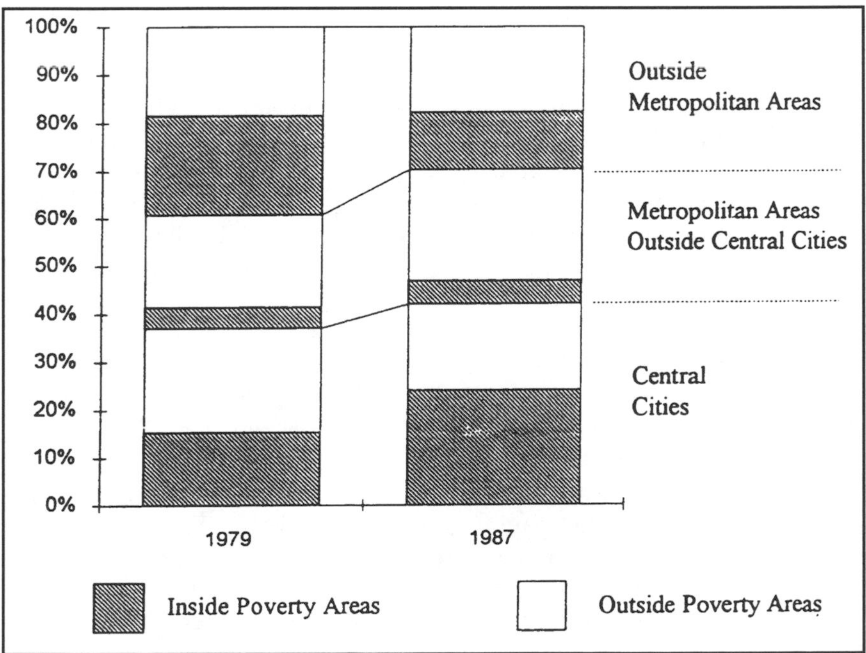

Figure 2.3. Poverty concentration: Percent of all families in poverty. From U.S. Bureau of the Census (1981, p. 85; 1989, pp. 72–73).

surprising results (Gramlich, Laren, & Sealand, 1992). Fully 27% of poor white families with children residing in a poor census tract (defined as one with a poverty rate of 40% or more) in one year were residing in a nonpoor tract one year later. For black families, the rate was much lower, 10%, but this still implies high turnover over a period of years.

When the authors traced through all of the implications of the exit and entrance rates for various population groups, however, they found that migration tended to produce the following pattern: "most white adults are clearing out of poor urban areas, the one exception being poor whites in families without children. Most black adults in families without children are also clearing out, but all groups of black adults in families with children, even those with high incomes, are entering on balance" (Gramlich, Laren, & Sealand, 1992, pp. 282–283). The result is a rising poverty rate in poor urban areas, an increase in the share of "persistently poor" in such areas, a rising share of black children who grow up in poor urban areas, but a declining share of white children who grow up in such areas.

Fiscal Disparities Among Cities

The second and third questions raised earlier related to the concentration of poor households in fiscally poor cities and the extent of resource inequality among cities. Probably the most comprehensive study of city fiscal condition to date was conducted by Ladd and Yinger (1991). Instead of looking only at resident incomes or the property tax base as measures of fiscal capacity, they attempted to construct an index of fiscal health that incorporates estimates of six factors.[6] They found that, on average, for 71 of the largest central cities, fiscal health declined between 1972 and 1982, but improved somewhat between 1982 and 1988, a period of economic recovery. They also found that population size, per capita income, and the poverty rate together explained 68% of the variation in fiscal health among the 71 cities in their study. The addition of two other variables, percentage of housing built before 1940 and the share of metropolitan population, raised this figure to 77%.

These predictive factors are closely related to three of the six determinants of city fiscal health: the public service needs of the population, service costs, and the tax-paying ability of residents. They do not take into account differences among states in the allocation of service responsibilities to cities or differences in the kinds of taxes permitted (the major determinant of a city's ability to export the tax burden through sales taxes or taxes on the income of commuters).[7]

Ladd and Yinger's index of fiscal health indicates the relative cost (in terms of the tax burden on residents as a percent of resident income) of providing a standard package of public services. A city with a high index can provide average service levels at relatively low taxpayer burden (or, looking at it another way, can provide high quality services with only an average tax burden), due to some combination of low population need, low cost of production, high resident resources, or high ability to shift the burden to nonresidents. A city with a low index must tax its residents heavily to provide an average level of services or can provide only a low level of services with an average tax burden, due to some combination of factors such as a population with high demands for social services, a high cost of producing services, low taxable income of residents, or low ability to export tax burdens.

Using an approximation of Ladd and Yinger's index of fiscal health, I examined disparities among cities in four metropolitan areas in 1980 and 1990. The metro areas were Los Angeles–Long Beach, San Francisco–Oakland, Boston, and Atlanta. In all four more than two-thirds of the metro area poor resided in the 6 to 11 cities in the lowest fiscal health category in both 1980 and 1990. These poorest cities generally consisted of the large central city and a handful of older industrial suburbs. In three of the four metro areas (the exception being Atlanta), there were modest improvements in the fiscal health of the poorest cities, but much larger gains in fiscal health for the richest cities. Relative disparities in fiscal health within these metropolitan areas increased in the 1980s.

Fiscal health has thus far been discussed in terms of a city's own resources. To the extent that state and federal aid to cities is targeted at poorer cities, actual disparities in service levels or tax burdens will be reduced. Ladd and Yinger (1991) found that, among the 71 largest cities, fiscal health (considering own resources) declined between 1972 and 1982, but state and federal aid increased, just about offsetting the decline in potential own-source revenues. During the 1980s, however, federal revenue sharing was eliminated and a whole range of other local government aid programs was cut substantially—urban development action grants, housing subsidies, job training programs, community development block grants, and grants for wastewater treatment and transportation. Federal aid to cities represented 10.8% of own-source revenues in 1972; this figure had increased to 18.4% by 1982, but only 6 years later had declined to 7.5% (Ladd & Yinger, 1991, p. 323). The cutback in federal funds has not been offset by the states. State aid to cities, as a percent of own-source revenues, peaked in 1975, declined until about 1984, and has changed little since (Ladd & Yinger, 1991, pp. 324–325).

Economists have long argued that income redistribution cannot effectively be carried out at the local or even at the state level because of the mobility of households. Efforts, particularly by cities, to finance benefits or services to low-income households through taxes on their own middle-class tax base will in the long run be self-defeating. The rich and the middle class will move to more homogeneous higher income communities, where they need not be taxed to support services to the poor. There is no lack of evidence to support this thesis. Nonetheless, recent history has not seen a shift in responsibility for redistributive programs to the federal government. Nor is the problem limited to clearly redistributive programs such as AFDC or public housing. Even if all health, welfare, housing, and social service programs were federally financed, poor populations would still place higher demands on city budgets, as long as they are more dependent on public transit, as long as poverty areas generate higher rates of crime, as long as the poor live in substandard housing with higher incidence of fires, etc.

The fiscal problems of cities have been worsening. State budgets, which once produced a sizable net surplus of revenues over expenditures, have become extremely tight during the 1980s with many states continually on the verge of deficit financing (Gramlich, 1991). Any new initiatives in the form of family- or community-centered practice must be undertaken in a climate of fiscal austerity at the state and local level and with the understanding that the same conditions that are aggravating the problems—namely, the increasing concentration of the poor at least in northern and Midwestern central cities and poverty areas—are also weakening the ability of local governments, cities and counties, to deal with the problems, as fiscal disparities widen.

CONCLUSION

The heightened international competition of the past 20 years has induced corporations to drive harder bargains and to seek the assistance of governmental authority in imposing market discipline on labor and on the beneficiaries of government programs. Public policy has contributed to the intensification of competition in U.S. labor markets and the extension of markets into new areas of life. The results have been an increasing inequality of income, in the form of a declining share of labor income and an increasing share of capital income, and a greater inequality of wages within industries and within virtually every population subgroup. Inequality manifests itself in poverty. Poverty among families with children, an increasing share of them female-headed, has grown significantly in the last 15 years. A larger share of the nation's children are growing up in conditions that we know put them at greater risk of dying in infancy, of being neglected or abused, of failing to finish high school, of committing a crime, and of being the victim of violence. Poverty destroys families and imperils children.

It is now well established that the greatest share of the gains in income during the Reagan recovery of the 1980s accrued to a small number of the wealthiest households in the United States. It appears that these gains have been used to increase the degree of economic segregation in some metropolitan areas, as the rich have continued to balkanize metropolitan areas to protect their suburbanized wealth from the claims of the poor. The poor have increasingly become concentrated in the central cities of the northeast and midwest, and in some of the older suburbs, where tax bases have been declining and service costs rising. The inequalities of market income are replicated in the inequality of resources among or within cities.

When we rely on markets rather than democratic political processes or informal relations to do things, we are disenfranchising all interests that have no standing in markets. Communities, in particular, cannot represent themselves in a process of exchange. In fact, the market works to undermine community in many ways; places have no significance in markets except for their ability to support production, so capital and labor in a market system move from place to place according to the cold calculus of profit or wage maximization or simply out of the necessity of finding a job. Communities need permanence, families with roots, jobs that have stability, and businesses with a commitment to a place. These interests get left out of the market calculus, and communities and the networks of social relationships that enrich lives and support families in trouble are weakened in the process. The market reproduces poverty and at the same time undermines the ability of families and communities to respond to the crises in the lives of families that poverty produces.

It is difficult to design or argue for policies to reduce inequality if one has to defend them in the terms of the dominant market philosophy. To some extent, the success of alternative kinds of social policies depends on the ability of advocates to recapture the rhetoric of public policy from the market ideology that now predominates. To create alternatives to the inequalities reproduced and intensified by markets, public discussion of social problems and policies must be carried on with a nonmarket rhetoric. Notions of family and community have not yet lost their non-market meanings; we should see that they do not.

What would a community-friendly rhetoric sound like? We would talk more about citizens and the rights or entitlements of citizenship and less about individuals only in their capacity as factors of production or consumers of products. We would talk less about individuals being responsible for themselves, sink or swim fashion, instead of dependent on government, as if those are the only two alternatives, and talk more about collective and shared responsibility. We would reframe the notion of self-sufficiency, returning to an earlier concept of individual and collective competence—an ability to do things ourselves, outside of markets, with the help of informal ties of family and friendship and community—instead of letting the market ideologues equate self-sufficiency with dependence on wage labor for income and dependence on the cash economy for the satisfaction of all our needs. In the process, it can be hoped that the efforts we make to reduce the human toll of poverty will not inadvertently reproduce the old relations of dependence, control, and inequality.

NOTES

1. The income distribution can be measured among households, families, or individuals as the unit of analysis. The distribution of family income presents only part of the picture because it ignores unrelated individuals. Both family and household income trends can be deceptive because they are driven partly by changes in family size. For example, during the 1980s average family and household size declined, so that the same income was supporting fewer individuals at the end of the 1980s. As a result, per capita income increased.

2. Adjusted family income divided by the poverty threshold appropriate for that family size and composition. By using poverty thresholds, we take into account the economies of scale in supporting larger families. Thus we end up with a distribution of ratios of income to the poverty level.

3. The effects of these trends on the rate of poverty among children would have been larger but for the decline in the average number of children per family and the increase in women's earnings over this period (Gottschalk & Danziger, 1993).

4. The gini coefficient should be viewed as an index, not a percent. A change in the gini can be presented in absolute terms (the 1990 gini minus the 1979 gini) or in percentage terms, as is done in Table 2.1: the absolute increase in the gini divided by the 1979 gini.

5. It is difficult to determine who actually bears the burden of taxes on corporate income or on business property. If tax burdens are assumed to fall on income from capital, these taxes are quite progressive. To the extent that part of the burden is actually shifted to consumers, the tax incidence becomes regressive among lower income groups. The changes in corporate income taxes, property taxes, sales taxes, and the user charges were not incorporated into the above analyses of income inequality because of the difficulties in attributing tax burdens to households. If they had, the increase inequality between the late 1960s and the late 1980s would have been greater. It should be noted that the most recent attempt to allocate the burden of all taxes to households, based on the tax system as of 1985, found that the overall tax system reduced income inequality by only 1 to 2.5%, depending on the assumptions made (Pechman, 1985). This supports the contention here that the 5 to 6% reduction in the gini coefficient as a result of income and payroll taxes and the EITC (Table 2.1) greatly overstates the role of the tax system in reducing inequality because it omits the more regressive or proportional taxes.

6. These are (1) the characteristics of the population of the city and the kinds of demands they place upon city services; (2) the city's topography, climate, wage structure, land cost, and other factors that determine the cost of providing services; (3) the allocation of service responsibilities among different levels of government (state, county, school district, township, city); (4) the financial resources of the resident population that can be tapped to finance services; (5) the ability of the city to export part of the burden of financing to nonresidents, such as commuters, absentee owners of property, consumers of goods produced in the city, or state or Federal taxpayers through intergovernmental grants; and (6) the kinds of taxes permitted under state law and state-imposed limitations on tax rates.

7. Ladd and Yinger examined all cities with a 1970 population above 300,000 plus central cities in the 50 largest metropolitan areas, which included several cities in the 50,000 to 300,000 range. The estimated index should give a reasonable picture of the relative fiscal position of cities within a particular metropolitan area in a particular state, since the same service responsibilities and tax restrictions will be faced by all cities. While it could be argued that the exact parameters of the regression equation are strictly valid only for 1982 and only for cities in the size range employed in the regression analysis, the predicted fiscal health can be interpreted simply as an index number, a composite of several factors known to be closely related to overall fiscal health. As such, it is arguably a better indicator of fiscal health than other measures of fiscal capacity that have been used in the past, such as per capita income alone, or a weighted tax base index that fails to account for differences in costs or service needs at all.

REFERENCES

Anderson, E. (1991). Neighborhood effects on teenage pregnancy. In C. Jencks & P. Peterson (Eds.), *The urban underclass* (pp. 375–398). Washington, DC: The Brookings Institution.

Belle, D. (1990). Poverty and women's mental health. *American Psychologist, 45,* 385–389.

Crane, J. (1991). Effects of neighborhoods on dropping out of school and teenage childbearing. In C. Jencks & P. Peterson (Eds.), *The urban underclass* (pp. 299–300). Washington, DC: The Brookings Institution.

Garbarino, J. (1992). The meaning of poverty in the world of children. *American Behavioral Scientist, 35,* 220–237.

Gelles, R. J. (1992). Poverty and violence toward children. *The American Behavioral Scientist, 35,* 258–274.

Gottschalk, P., & Danziger, S. (1993). Family structure, family size, and family income: Accounting for changes in the economic well-being of children, 1968–1986. In S. Danziger & P. Gottschalk (Eds.), *Uneven tides* (pp. 167–193). New York: Russell Sage Foundation.

Gramlich, E. M. (1991). The 1991 state and local fiscal crisis. (With discussion). *Brookings Papers on Economic Activity, 2,* 249–287.

Gramlich, E. M., Kasten, R., & Sammartino, F. (1993). Growing inequality in the 1980s: The role of federal taxes and cash transfers. In S. Danziger & P. Gottschalk (Eds.), *Uneven tides* (pp. 225–250). New York: Russell Sage Foundation.

Gramlich, E., Laren, D., & Sealand, N. (1992). Moving into and out of poor urban areas. *Journal of Policy Analysis and Management*, *11*, 273–287.

Karoly, L.A. (1993). The trend in inequality among families, individuals, and workers in the United States: A twenty-five year perspective. In S. Danziger & P. Gottschalk (Eds.), *Uneven tides* (pp. 19–98). New York: Russell Sage Foundation.

Ladd, H. F., & Yinger, J. (1991). *America's ailing cities: Fiscal health and the design of urban policy. Updated edition*. Baltimore, MD: Johns Hopkins University Press.

Mayer, S. E. (1991). How much does a high school's racial and socioeconomic mix affect graduation and teenage fertility rates? In C. Jencks & P. Peterson (Eds.), *The urban underclass* (pp. 321–341). Washington, DC: The Brookings Institution.

Murphy, K. M., & Welch, F. (1993). Industrial change and the rising importance of skill. In S. Danziger & P. Gottschalk (Eds.), *Uneven tides* (pp. 101–132). New York: Russell Sage Foundation.

Najman, J. M. (1993). Health and poverty: Past, present and prospects for the future. *Social Science & Medicine*, *36*, 157–166.

Pechman, J. A. (1985). *Who paid the taxes, 1966–85?* Washington, DC: The Brookings Institution.

U.S. Advisory Commission on Intergovernmental Relations. (1991). *Significant features of fiscal federalism, 1991: Vol. 2. Report M-176-II*. Washington, DC: Author.

U.S. Bureau of the Census. (1981). *Characteristics of the population below the poverty level: 1979*. Current Population Reports, Series P-60, No. 130. Washington, DC: U.S. Government Printing Office.

U.S. Bureau of the Census. (1989). *Poverty in the United States 1987*. Current Population Reports, Series P-60, No. 163. Washington, DC: U.S. Government Printing Office.

U.S. Bureau of the Census. (1992). *Measuring the effect of benefits and taxes on income and poverty: 1979 to 1991*. Current Population Reports, Series P-60, No. 182-RD. Washington, DC: U.S. Government Printing Office.

U.S. Bureau of the Census. (1993). *Poverty in the United States 1992*. Current Population Reports, Series P-60, No. 185. Washington, DC: U.S. Government Printing Office.

U.S. House of Representatives, Committee on Ways and Means. (1992). *1992 green book: Background material and data on programs within the jurisdiction of the Committee on Ways and Means*. Washington, DC: U.S. Government Printing Office.

Wallace, S., Wasylenko, M., & Weiner, D. (1991). The distributional implications of the 1986 Tax Reform Act. *National Tax Journal*, *44*, 181–198.

Wilkinson, R. G. (1989). Class mortality differentials, income distribution and trends in poverty 1921–1981. *Journal of Social Policy*, *18*, 307–335.

3

Integrating Community and Individual Practice: A New Paradigm for Practice

GERALD G. SMALE

"If only they had been there to give me a little bit of help when I really needed it things might not have got so bad."

In the helping professions there is a long-standing belief in the necessity of engaging in preventive activity where possible, in addition to helping people in crisis. Preventive action is sometimes referred to as "upstream work" from the metaphor of rescuing drowning people (Egan & Cowan, 1979).

The life guards jump into the river to rescue first one person, then another, and then another. When the fourth appears they realize that somebody has to go upstream to try to stop these people getting into the water or to find a way for them to get out before they are exhausted.

In the United States the categorization of funding for different client groups and for specific problems, often based on different services or methods of help, leads to a picture of a row of life guards lined up on the river bank, each with a different color hat. Each is able to enter the water only if the drowning person wears a matching color. People without clothing that matches a colored hat go on down the river. Because they get paid only when they enter the water, none of the life guards goes upstream.

Categorical funding influences the nature of social work and the people served. Linking funding to particular activities values specific work and excludes other activities. Upstream work becomes truly heroic in such circumstances. First, it will probably be impossible to prove that you saved any lives; second, you will not get paid; and third, you will lose the friendship of your colleagues downstream, deprived not only of some or all of their income, but also of their more obvious heroism.

This is of course only metaphor and theory. Luckily for the helping professions, in real life there is no end to the number of ways that people fall, get pushed, or jump into the river, and fail to get out. With good teamwork it is also possible to work both up- and downstream. Currently there is growing concern and action to overcome these problems, including, in the United States, moves to decategorize funding of social services, to promote collaboration between agencies, and to develop community-centered services, all of which may initiate upstream work without sacrificing those already in the water.

In the United Kingdom there is also a growing acknowledgment that most people are kept afloat, or helped out, by others in their social network. Although crucial to some, social services are peripheral to most care in the community, just as the justice system is to most social control. It is recognized that service users and the caregivers of dependent people need to have far more say in how services work and that professionals[1] work in partnership with all of these people, rather than take on the problems themselves. Inventive practitioners are reformulating the role of the professional, despite pressures to adopt models similar to those developed in the United States: managed care in an increasingly pluralistic welfare market with highly specialized therapeutic practice focused on specific diagnoses. In contrast are efforts that developed throughout the 1980s to sustain innovative community-centered practice based on partnerships with others.

This chapter draws on the experience of practitioners and managers who have been at the forefront of developing the "patch," or community social work, approach in British social services and presents a framework for practice based on this work. This approach recognizes that social services and social work are normally marginal to the management or resolution of people's problems and that partnerships between people and professionals and collaboration among agencies are essential. This approach also integrates individual, family, and community practice and views citizens as partners and not just objects of concern or study. Finally, the experience of the National Institute for Social Work's Practice and Development Exchange suggests how new practice theory can be developed.

THE NEED TO DEVELOP PRACTICE THEORY

Innovations in practice are running well ahead of practice theory and research. Theoretical developments relevant to integrating practice with individuals, families, and communities (Swenson, this volume; Pincus & Minahan, 1973; Goldstein, 1973) have yet to be translated into theories of how to act: practice theory. This is particularly so when intervention includes a wide range of people who cannot be identified as in any way pathological, but who are essential parts of the social system within which a problem is locked. Practice theory is even more important when intervention is based on partnerships with all of these people and recognizes their equal rights as citizens.

Questions such a practice theory must address include the following:

- How to develop partnerships between citizens who engage in community care through family or similar ties, professionals, and people who feel no immediate responsibility, but whose families, jobs, or social life bring them into contact with those "in need"?
- How to communicate across class and cultural boundaries; how to tackle the inequalities that persist in social services delivery and in most forms of organized social control?
- How to approach citizens as partners to carry out social control functions on behalf of other citizens?
- How to integrate social work with other services such as education, health, or juvenile justice and alternative interventions such as community development?
- How, as citizens with different responsibilities and roles, to engage with service users and each other in the planning of social work and other professional services to get optimum value and to maximize the efforts of all who contribute to care in any community?
- How to integrate theories of individual pathology with structural approaches to understanding social problems?
- How to use quantitative and qualitative research to understand the different dimensions of social problems? Do theory and research have to be revised when decision making includes empowered citizens?

Developing Practice Theory

When a person, or a family, is referred to the authorities for physically abusing their child, an investigation takes place to test the validity of the allegation. Unless the allegation is demonstrably without foundation, all too often this leads to a chain of events that makes the situation worse long before it gets better. Many children avoid enormous suffering and many families are helped in such situations. Although these interventions are often essential, they are not without unintended consequences. Typically parents and children acquire a variety of labels, as much to release resources as to provide useful information for intervention or treatment.

An essential assumption is that an episode of abuse is an indication of family breakdown that requires either remedial intervention to put things right or the placement of children in alternative homes. Either way, the social service or mental health system becomes central, at least in the eyes of the professionals, to the resolution of children's and family problems.

The least harm done is the stigma involved in picking up a label. Professional intervention becomes part of the family's problems, at least an unfortunate symbol of their other problems. If the children are removed, there is the cost of further emotional trauma to all members of the family, as well as the expense of alternative treatments. Without extensive work to rectify the unintended consequences of this help, these traumas will become part of the problems that are experienced by those coming into contact with the family, either in further efforts to help them or as victims of their behavior.

Alternative Starting Points

Community social work differs from traditional practice at the point of access and the starting points of intervention. The following example illustrates these differences:

> Joanne is referred to the Department of Human Services (DHS) on the suspicion that she has been abusing her child, Jason, perhaps causing injury by physically chastising him. DHS refers the "case" to the patch team working in the neighborhood. Joanne is approached by a social worker working in the patch team. The nature of the referral is explained to Joanne, as is the mandatory obligation this places on the social worker to act on behalf of DHS and to continue contact with her. Some time is spent sharing information. (An "exchange model" for developing partnerships with people in such situations, in contrast to "questioning" or "procedural" models of intervention, is described in Smale, Tuson, Biehal, & Marsh, 1993.)
>
> Joanne is understandably anxious, suspicious, and possibly hostile as she guardedly explains her situation; she is particularly vague about her parenting of Jason. This relationship is observed by the worker as Jason interrupts, periodically tears through the conversation, or demands something from his mother. He is a very active little boy, like most children of his age a bundle of loud energy, curiosity, and mischief, constantly demanding interaction. Depending on how you feel, he is an annoying, stimulating, bor-

ing, exasperating, interesting, amusing, or irritating little boy: a typically exhausting child.

Joanne describes herself as not knowing anybody in the area, uncertain of her neighbors. Like many people in the city she thinks of the neighborhood as a "rough" one and has been apprehensive about talking to people in the street since she moved into the area some months ago. She reveals that she was evicted from her previous home for rent arrears following separation from her partner and the worker guesses that Joanne is by no means sure that she will herself be acceptable to her new neighbors.

The eldest child from a big family, Joanne moved a long way from them with her ex-partner. The worker recognizes that she has plenty of experience looking after little children, even if she now has little confidence that she is being a "good mother" to Jason. As the exchange develops, Joanne is given information about various resources available in the neighborhood including projects related to the team's work. She is invited to bring Jason to a play group, to see if she would like to be a volunteer helper. The trade off will be that if Jason likes the group, she will be able to leave him some mornings after he has settled. She will also meet other mothers in the neighborhood who help at the playgroup and meet for coffee when they bring their children.

Without denying the seriousness of the situation or the authority and responsibilities social workers have, the patch worker reframed the problem. She moved away from the labeling inevitably involved in such a referral to helping Joanne identify and use resources without confirming or reinforcing her feelings of failure. This reframing is not just a linguistic ploy. To provide an authentic alternative response the worker explores different questions, such as "how can this woman help us with the work that we are doing in this neighborhood?" This is as important a question as identifying family needs and resources, or how problematic behavior may be changed. Reframing is part of the worker's acting in a different way.

To make such responses to Joanne, the social worker and her colleagues on the team had first to have engaged in a variety of other community social work tasks. They will have looked at the neighborhood's needs and resources: the incidence of different social problems; the ways that these are currently being managed and responded to; and the agencies, self-help groups, and other institutions in the area. Understanding the community involves identifying how people in the neighborhood relate to each other and to local institutions; what relationships are part of the area's social problems and need to change; what people and groups are part of the normal solutions to problems in the neighborhood; and how more people and organizations can be mobilized to be part of new solutions.

The Debate: Work with Individuals and Families or the Community?

This is not the common approach to practice. Typically the individual client and/or the immediate family is the focus of most, if not all intervention. Even where it is recognized that a systemic or ecological perspective is required, there is a tendency in stressful circumstances to individualize social problems when action needs to be taken (Egan & Cowan, 1979; Smale, Tuson, Biehal, & Marsh, 1993; Smale et al., 1994). For some decades, psychotherapy and, more recently, family therapy have become the predominant methods in social work and have been criticized by those taking a community development approach. Engaging in this debate Specht and Courtney (1994) recently argued that psychotherapy has diverted social work from its original vision, a vision of "the perfectibility of society," the building of the "city beautiful," the "new society," and the "new frontier."

For Specht and Courtney, the solution to the "psychotherapy takeover of social work" lies in restating the "original vision" of social work and turning away from intensive approaches to individual change, so that the unfulfilled mission of social work might be resuscitated. This mission, to deal with the enormous social problems under which society staggers, is a problem for all of society, or at least all of those directly or indirectly involved, not just social work. Allocating the task of solving these problems to social work, however defined, and focusing attention just on its traditional clientele is a recipe for ensuring that many people will carry on with their current behavior and so perpetuate these problems.

Some people do have personal relationships and inner resources that help them come to terms with the problems that incapacitate others. Many are able to develop their ability to change some important dimensions of their lives. Individual and family interventions can increase some people's capacities to make such changes. But many individuals are part of communities and neighborhoods caught up in environments that contribute to the maintenance and perpetuation of their problems, even if they do not cause them. These problems are beyond the personal power of individuals involved. This is true whether they are a "client" or a community development social worker.

It is reasonable to assume that social workers have turned their back on some of these problems because their scale and scope are enough to induce hopelessness in all but the most optimistic. The social work task may appear to be a "mission impossible." This problem is compounded if the practice theory of community action is based solely on sociological insights into large scale social forces. Helping individuals with traditional psychotherapy can seem to be a much more manageable task than changing their environments, even though "social problems" cannot be confronted by focusing on the individual alone.

DEFINING "SOCIAL PROBLEMS" AND PRACTICE THEORY

Novice Buddhist monks are set the impossible task of imagining the sound of one hand clapping. It seems as if the Western mind has no difficulty with such a problem. Many interactional events are seen as if only one partner is involved. Sporting defeats are discussed in terms of the mistakes of the team being analyzed, as if the opposition did not play their part in winning the game. In many discussions of social problems, attention focuses on the identified "clients" of the helping professions and the justice system.

People have many different problems, the causes being located in many different aspects of their own attributes, in their environment, or in the interaction between the two. These "causes" are not often known in a strictly scientific sense. Individual problems become a social problem when they are not resolved by the individual or when needs cannot be met by people in the immediate social circumstances of the person or people who "have the problem." Thus a frail, elderly woman having difficulty in feeding herself, fearful of being alone, and without somebody with whom she can share her depression about her physical condition clearly has "problems." Some may say these problems are an inevitable "fact of life," a feature of aging.

To refer such a situation to a social service, social work, or voluntary agency or to identify it as a "social problem" is more a comment on how needs are, or are not, being met by others, than on the condition itself. To focus on an individual's needs alone is not only to ignore potential sources of support, in fact the normal resources called on in these circumstances, it is to misunderstand the very nature of the social problems presented by this situation. When they do this, social workers and other professionals stand little chance of producing positive change in the networks they have been called upon to help. They will depend on negotiating for public or other external resources to help such people, and essentially take responsibility for these problems on to themselves as representatives of their agency. This is a valid option and one that is vital for many. But it is far from the only option, and when used routinely it compounds the tendency to "clientize" all who ask or are referred for help.

From this perspective social problems are the malfunctioning of a network of people. Networks are typically composed of family, friends, or neighbors and other members of the wider community. The "problem" may be that there are no, or too few, significant people in the system. I want to emphasize the fact that the vast majority of people's needs are met by caregivers in the community without professional intervention. People's needs only become a "social problem" when they are not met. Being old is not a serious problem any more than is being a baby. Only without appropriate relationships with others is either a "social problem."

The "unitary approach" to social work practice attempted to link and integrate different approaches within a framework of systems theory (Pincus & Minahan, 1973; Goldstein, 1973; Specht & Vickery, 1977). But the contrast between individuals, families, and "the community" persisted. These theories did not go far enough in recognizing that professionalized interventions with individuals and families are the way in which many people in the community typically delegate to others significant aspects of social problems. The distinction remained intact between those labeled "the problem" and those labeled "healthy" within the many interactions perceived as social problems.

These processes enable some parties to abdicate responsibility at the expense of stigmatizing those held primarily responsible. In effect the majority, or those with the power to define the situation, say "we do not have to be involved in the resolution of these problems, beyond employing social workers to deal with the problem people." Providing professionals to work with individual family pathology is a community response. Thus, there is no real choice between working with families and individuals and taking action in the community. It is a mistake to think that you can work effectively with those excluded from society without affecting society itself. These dichotomies are "illusions of alternatives" (Watzlawick, Weakland, & Fisch, 1974). Perpetuating these illusions may maintain as many people in social problems as it relieves from their misery.

Community or Individual and Family: Steps Taken to Resolve the Illusion

Throughout the last few years, staff at the National Institute for Social Work have been working throughout England and Scotland with practitioners who have been combining these "alternatives" into a coherent practice approach called community social work (Barclay, 1982). The aims were to describe and conceptualize their innovative practices (Smale & Bennett, 1989; Darvill & Smale, 1990), to analyze the steps they went through to change from orthodox practice to community social work (Smale, Tuson, Cooper, Wardle, & Crosbie, 1988; Smale, 1993), to develop training exercises (Hearn & Thompson, 1987), to evaluate our development strategy (Crosbie, Smale, & Waterson, 1989), and to identify the skills used in practice (Smale & Tuson, 1988).

The alternatives of community or individual and family melted away when we discussed practice with these workers and managers. Had we asked them if they worked with the community to "build meaning, a purpose, and a sense of obligation for the community," or with individuals and their families one by one, they might have been tempted to answer simply, "yes."

Teams practicing community social work deliberately engaged in a whole spectrum of activities. Subsequently it became clear that this was also true of most social workers and to some extent all social services agencies. A crucial difference was the degree to which different levels of work were seen as legitimate professional practice and so given appropriate thought, planning, and workload weighting by management.

The spectrum of work includes the following:

1. Direct Intervention: Work carried out through partnerships with individuals, their families, and their immediate network to tackle problems that directly affect them.

2. Indirect Intervention: Work with wider community groups, other professionals and agencies, relevant organizations, and institutions to tackle problems that affect a range or class of people. This includes the individuals and families involved in direct intervention, those concerned about them, or victims of their behavior.

3. Service Delivery: Providing resources to people to meet needs that are not met, or cannot be met, by others in their immediate social network to maintain the current social situation and avoid further distress or institutionalization. Resources may also be provided to community groups or other organizations so that they can meet the needs of identified families and individuals.

4. Change Agent Activities: Intervention aimed at changing the pattern of relationships within a social situation or system. This includes changing the ways people relate to each other in response to individual problems; intervening in the interactions that precipitate or perpetuate social problems at family, group, neighborhood, or wider community levels; and working with those who have resources so that they can be released to meet needs.

These dimensions of the social work task are not alternatives. Somebody has to be doing something about all of them. They may be left to chance in the hope that resources will be available, or collaboration possible when resources are needed, but only if the aim is to rescue a few of the casualties within some particular categories rather than to confront social problems.

The whole social work task can be represented by a map based on this framework (Figure 3.1). This is a framework to be filled in with the different activities that have to be undertaken to tackle the problems that exist within a specific community or area. It is only a map, a guide to the territory, not a picture of reality, still less reality itself (Bateson, 1979). It should make clear that there are at least two ways in which practice can be differentiated.

Change agent and service delivery activities vary according to who takes what degree of responsibility for the problem. To deliver a service, that is, to add a resource to the family, is to take some responsibility for the problem and give something toward its management or solution. Change agents do not take responsibility for the resolution of a problem from the participants. The problem can be resolved only if the participants change and they are responsible for their own behavior.

Direct intervention focuses on people identified as having or being a problem. The focus moves outward as more and more relevant people and organizations are involved. It is rarely sufficient to work just with an individual or a nuclear family; typically such practice involves others in

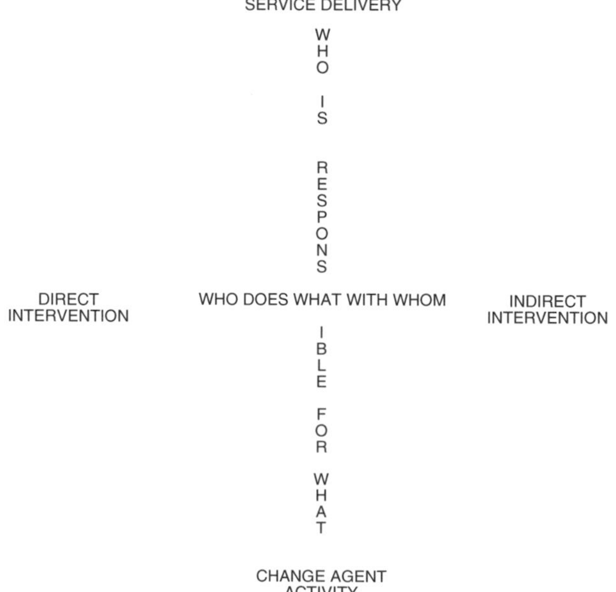

Figure 3.1. A framework for community- and family-centered practice.

the immediate social situation. Indirect interventions start at the other end of the spectrum, focusing on relationships between agencies, institutions, and classes of people. Building interagency collaboration is typical of such interventions. Change agents will work to change the relationships between people and between systems that precipitate social problems or perpetuate our failure to introduce desired change.

In most situations professional interventions will include some combination of service delivery and change agent activities. All social problems will require direct intervention of some kind with people identified as having a problem and with others they relate to. Recognizing that all these dimensions are essential enables time and resources to be deliberately allocated to all necessary activity. For each dimension to be given appropriate thought and action, properly planned and reviewed, requires the deliberate integration of these different efforts.

Most innovative work is composed of different elements that fall outside the traditional arenas of social work practice. Workers developing community social work draw on different theories, yet it is a misconception to dub the approach eclectic. They have a clear feel for where they are going and an awareness of mission that sets them apart from many of their colleagues (Harrison, 1989). They do not feel demoralized or powerless in the face of increasing demands and limited resources. Yet the stage of theory development is such that they find it easier to say what they are against rather than articulate a coherent theory of practice (Sainsbury, 1990). Based on what they do, and their explicit and implicit values and perceptions of social problems, the map presented above is a framework for the necessary dimensions of practice.

More Alternative Starting Points

The example of Joanne illustrated an alternative way of responding to an individual referral. The work described can be plotted on the map. Awareness of the many problems in the neighborhood is another reason for action. The work of the Canklow team in Rotherham's Social Services Department in Yorkshire, England, illustrates a different starting point (Eastham, 1990). Staff recognized that a very high number of referrals came from a large public housing project. The project produced a high percentage of children in placement, while housing a relatively small percentage of the children in the local authority area. Indirect change agent interventions began by setting out to improve the department's relationships with residents and other agencies and by identifying how they could form partnerships to make the social services' responses to the high level of referrals more effective. Direct change agent interventions and service delivery activity continued to be offered by the department through family and individual counseling, advice and advocacy, and linking identified families to specific agency services such as homemakers and day care.

In providing resources to community groups and other agencies in the patch area for support facilities and alternatives to high-risk activities, the team engaged in indirect service delivery. In other indirect change agent interventions, they established relationships with extended families and wider networks, encouraging people to help those who might otherwise have been referred for services.

Change Through Teamwork

The map highlights the crucial role of teamwork in developing community social work. The scope and range of activities involved require workers with different skills and aptitudes. We found that the smallest unit of staff that can engage in community social work is a team of workers. Individuals cannot be community social workers on their own, since the variety and breadth of the tasks go well beyond the capacity of any one person. On the other hand, it has been demonstrated that teams of workers can adopt a community social work approach even if, and often despite the fact that the rest of their department works in a different way. Indeed it follows from our assumptions that the aims and objectives of social work and social services should be negotiated and planned in partnership with a variety of citizens and other professionals and that teams working in different environments will adopt different approaches to community social work (Smale, Tuson, Cooper, Wardle, & Crosbie, 1988).

Team members do their work through a wide range of partnerships with others. In some rural situations and specialist agency settings, field workers will operate as the single representative of their agencies. They will then need to engage in teamwork with other professionals and people in the community.

Team, as used here, is not synonymous with currently organized agency teams. A team is a group of people who depend on each other to some extent to accomplish a task. Teams may be located in or across field, day care, or residential settings and may cross agency or professional boundaries. To be effective many teams will include all partners in a combined effort to tackle problems and issues, including members of the public who are normally seen only as clients, caregivers, or previously uninvolved members of significant social networks. A "package of care" "managed" by a "case manager" may be more appropriately seen as a team of people, partly convened by the family or neighbors and partly by the professional worker (Smale, Tuson, Biehal, & Marsh, 1993; Smale et al., 1994). This worker cannot be responsible for "managing" the team, only for managing the agency's contribution to the situation.

To put into practice a future vision of social work not only requires social workers to turn from exclusively working either with individuals or on community development, but to turn from working *as* individuals toward *teamwork*. The problem does not just lie in the individualization of social problems with overemphasis on the individual client. Nor does the problem lie in working with communities to the exclusion of individual pathology. More significant is the continuing reliance on the social worker as heroic individual—whether therapist or activist—rather than a person dependent upon teamwork with others to influence change.

WORKING IN PARTNERSHIP AND PRACTICE THEORY

I have stressed that community social work is based on a recognition that the bulk of care, supervision, and control in the community is undertaken by members of the community—parents, neighbors, relatives, informal caregivers, and other people operating through their normal social relationships or networks. This act of recognition in itself affirms the strengths that people have in the community and the peripheral nature of social work intervention, often overlooked by both practitioners and policymakers alike (Barclay, 1982; Smale et al., 1994). Based on this awareness, it is an underlying assumption of community social work that social workers should get together with local people, agency managers, politicians, and others to work out the approach that meets the unique circumstances of that particular situation (Smale, Tuson, Cooper, Wardle, & Crosbie, 1988). Recent national policy statements in Britain have endorsed these basic assumptions, asserting the crucial significance of the partnerships that professionals can forge with other citizens, be they people who use social services, their caregivers, parents of children at risk, those who help on a voluntary basis, or other professionals (Department of Health, 1989, 1990). Work is underway with user groups to increase their participation and to develop user-led services (Beresford & Croft, 1993; Beresford & Harding, 1993; Croft & Beresford, 1993).

But what does it mean to "work in partnership with people"? The implementation of community care reforms and new legislation on child protection in Britain is making many people reconsider their attitudes toward the public they serve. This is highlighting the lack of a theory to support the changes in practice required to work in partnership with people.

Much social work theory assumes that the citizen is a "client," "service user," "carer," "patient," or "customer." In any of these roles the person is defined through their relationship with "the professional" or "service provider." The implication is that the person has less knowledge, information, expertise, or resources than the professional. The "citizen" is not an equal person, but the object of concern and so of professional attention. These perceptions of social workers and their "clients" are now obsolete.

To move to a new type of practice requires a change in attitude that recognizes that the "clients," "carers," "service users," or "customers" of social work and social services are all citizens and the same sort of beings as professional workers and other members of the community. Systemic approaches stress the need to intervene in the relationships that precipitate or perpetuate social problems. Thus a family systems approach has stressed the need to shift the focus from the individual "patient" to the relationships within which the problem behavior is often enmeshed (Minuchin & Fishman, 1981; Haley, 1976). This meant involving other people in interventions who were not originally, or conventionally, seen as part of the problem. Changing the pattern of such relationships means changing the reciprocal behavior of all of these people, those labeled as "having" or being "a problem" and the others with whom they relate. As a social systemic or ecological approach widens the networks of people involved, the change agent is working more and more with people who have not been identified as having problems.

The individualization of social problems has enabled professionals to see the identified individual, or family, as less able than those who do not have the problem. If, as systems theory suggests, the problem lies in the relationships among many people, are we to assume that all participants are deficient? Shifting the emphasis from the individual to the family has pathologized many families instead of a child or a parent. Applying the same analysis to wider social situations makes it more difficult to pathologize individuals or individual families, though the idea of the bad neighborhood is common enough. But once it becomes apparent that whole systems perpetuate social problems, even the experts whose job it is to change identified clients, pathologizing becomes clearly untenable (Elizur & Minuchin, 1991).

It may seem obvious that when change agents intervene in these systems, different people will bring different things to the partnership, with different authority, power, and expertise, and in control of different parts of a social situation, but at root they are all, or should be, equal citizens. In theory and practice, however, "professional" intervention and service provision are based on assumptions that differentiate between "professionals" and "clients," often in quite radical ways. Consider, for example, the assumption that the professional worker can pick up new methods of work from a few days training, that is, new ways of thinking and acting in complex social situations, such as child abuse in all its various forms. However, the same professionals, their trainers, and educators typically assume that their "clients" will need extended "treatment," "behavior modification," "task centered casework," "family therapy," "support through a package of care," or some other kind of "intervention" to "reduce risks to children" or whatever the identified problem is, if, of course, they have any faith in the capacity of identified clients to change their behavior at all. Where they lack this faith, or where the system encourages them to take immediate action, they will always "rescue" the child.

Much applied social science looks for factors that influence the circumstances or behavior of those who are, or experience, "social problems." It examines the relation between their personal or social characteristics and the problems. Outcome research on the effectiveness of professional intervention and services is typically designed to see if workers, their methods, or services have a significant impact on the "clients," their problems, or their "needs." The underlying assumption is that they should be able to influence the person or their situation in such a way that the pathological factors in their past or current lives are overcome and the "problem" solved or managed in such a way that it does not perpetuate undesired "symptoms" or arrangements. The people under study *are not equal people, but the objects of study.*

It is typically assumed that policymakers, professionals, and academics have the freedom to choose between different models of practice or between different ways of tackling social problems. There would be little point in this volume unless we all assumed that this were so. But it often seems that we assume that actions of "clients" to resolve their problems are determined by intrapsychic and/or social forces and that they cannot make the same choices or exercise the same freedom. The professionally centered view of social change and social problem solving is based on this disparity of ability and knowledge. It is not confined to those wedded to individual therapies. It is also evident, for example, in Specht's critique of psychotherapy in social work. His final sentence reads: "That is how we make healthy people" (Specht, 1990, p. 356).

Practice is not based on theory alone nor can it just be based on research evidence. What the social worker actually does is the product of the dynamic interplay among values, skill, and knowledge applied to understanding the behavior of all the people involved in the patterns of relationships that precipitate or perpetuate social problems. These factors will inform and limit the judgments and decisions that social workers make and remake, and the actions they take as circumstances change over time. What the social worker does is as dependent upon the behavior of others as their behavior is on the social workers. This is not to suggest that there is equality or parity of influence, authority, or power, but to acknowledge that all parties to an interaction are just that and have some control and power over different aspects of the relationship and subsequent outcomes.

If professionals can make choices and act on their judgment in these relationships, then so can other people. A practice theory should recognize that people's behavior is not only determined by influences and "causes," including the interventions of social workers and others. Behavior is essentially guided by the decisions they make based on their judgments of the situation, which are presumably made in the same way by lay people and professionals alike. What people do, whether they are the traditional "clients" of social workers or those with the power to change their circumstances, will be limited by their behavioral repertoire and guided by the judgments that they make over time.

Practice theory should, therefore, be directed at explaining how all the people involved in a social situation make their decisions and sustain or change their behavior. This involves understanding at least five areas:

1. Insight into the recurring patterns of relationships among people, groups, and organizations that precipitate and perpetuate social problems and the enhancement of their ability to identify who should do what, with whom, to bring about positive change;
2. Understanding of the way different people construe their worlds and, specifically, what kinds of behavior or unmet needs they see as social problems;
3. Ability to reconcile the inevitable conflicts that arise between different perceptions of social situations and social problems and to manage different vested interests;
4. Ability to negotiate with people about who can do what to resolve social problems and to manage the coordination of the resources required;
5. Ability to work with people to increase the choice and control they have over their lives; to expand their behavioral repertoire, so they can put new solutions into practice if they choose.

At present social workers, and other change agents from the personal social services do not have a contract to work with all of these people to bring about change. The pervasive individualism and the division of labor in all areas of life have contributed to the professionalization of social problem solving. These processes have led to targeting the individual and family level. Just as family therapists often have to renegotiate the problem if they are to work with the whole family and not just the individual patients, so social change agents will have to enter into constant renegotiations with the many significant actors involved in social problems.

The major issue is not simply that many people in social work are basing their work on the popular psychotherapies, family systems, or ecological or community development alternatives, or that many are guided mainly by the procedures of their employing bureaucracy. The difficulty is the enormous pull toward the individualization of people's problems. Even when there is an intellectual acknowledgment of "community" or structural dimensions to people's problems, many agencies and their workers continue to intervene exclusively at an individual level. Individualized philosophies of practice support the status quo within our social work institutions, within a mixed economy of welfare. The prevailing ideology of individualism (Bellah, Madsen, Sullivan, Swindler, & Tipton, 1985; Specht & Courtney, 1994) seems to be a more powerful influence on practice than concern over our obvious failure to resolve many social problems.

Further Implications for the Role of the Professional Worker

People are, and always will be, the experts in themselves, their situation, their relationships, and what they want and need (Bricker-Jenkins, 1990, Smale, Tuson, Biehal, & Marsh, 1993; Smale et al., 1994). They always bring their expertise about themselves to the assessment and subsequent management or resolution of their, or other people's, problems. They will also have a certain degree of control over their own behavior that professionals will never have over them and so are able to influence the present and future relationships that underpin any new solution to a problem.

Professional change agents will need to have expertise in the process of participating with others to effect change in social systems. This includes the skills listed in Table 3.1.

To resist becoming central to the management of social problems, the professional change agent needs to be *marginal to these relationships* and to contribute the valuable "third party" perspective common in many forms of conciliation and negotiation. Marginality can be defined as the worker's ability to operate effectively as a participant and as an observer in social situations; to avoid becoming a part of problem-perpetuating

Table 3.1. Skills Needed by Professional Change Agents

1. The ability to negotiate and conciliate between individuals, families, and groups of people who have different perceptions, values, attitudes, expectations, wants, and needs that formed over many years or that are part of the structure of the community. This will require knowledge and skills associated with family therapy, community development, and other approaches yet to be identified.
2. Expertise in facilitating people's attempts to articulate, and so clarify, their own needs and what they want and what they can do to get them met.
3. Sensitivity to language, cultural, racial, and gender differences and how cultural differences relate to the way that social problems persist, how their resolution is normally approached, and how new resolutions can be formulated.
4. The ability to help people through major transitions involving loss. Interventions will often take place at times of great stress, including loss of a family member or some physical capacity, public recognition of behavior perceived as delinquent or pathological, or some other change that has precipitated referral.
5. The capacity to identify patterns in the relationships between people: how participants' behavior supports current relationships, and how this may be changed so that the problem can be managed differently or resolved.

interactions, a permanent part of "the solution," or a permanent outsider in the networks of people with whom they are involved.

All people have expertise in these areas, some more than others. It is essential that professionals recognize that they do not start with a monopoly of this knowledge. An essential part of their responsibility is to add to, but keep out of the way of, others' exercising their own social problem-solving skills.

Citizens are expert in themselves and their relationships as they see them from inside their situation. But as the anthropologist, Gregory Bateson (1973) pointed out, "you cannot hear the music if you are one of the notes." The marginal broker can participate without becoming enmeshed in the situation and contribute by listening to the music. Change agents should not become deluded into thinking that they can conduct the music. Normal life is much more like an improvising jazz band than a symphony orchestra. The essence of working in partnership is to work with the people involved, to find out what key they are playing in, and to contribute. This does not have to involve taking responsibility from the other players or attempting to control their behavior. It requires that the professional work with all the significant people involved, linking those with unmet needs to those with appropriate resources, to build on and add to what people do and the choices they have in how care and control in the community work for them.

HOW PRACTICE THEORY CAN BE DEVELOPED

The National Institute for Social Work's Practice and Development Exchange (PADE) emphasized learning from the practice wisdom of social workers and managers and identifying the practice implications of research (Smale & Statham, 1989; Crosbie, Smale, & Waterson, 1989; Smale, 1992). PADE enabled participants to "escape" from the assumptions and constraints of their own agencies. Their belief in the possibilities of change was enhanced by sharing experience with people who worked in different agencies, where different assumptions about practice, management, and culture apply. This enabled them to recognize that many barriers to change were problems to be overcome within their organizations and not permanent features of "reality." To work in partnership with all those involved in social problems requires a fundamental paradigm shift, going beyond the assumptions of the "helping professions" altogether.

Although practice exchanges have developed practice theory more relevant to practitioners, we have not yet gone far enough to ensure their relevance to all those directly involved in social problems. Theory-building exchanges need to continue to reflect on practice wisdom and research and include the experiences of those receiving services and those who are the subject of interventions. Thus they need to involve all those citizens who are to be partners in the process of bringing about change: the people directly caught up in social problems, other significant members of the wider community, and other professionals and services providers. Paradigm shifts come about when new information is introduced that cannot be accommodated in the conventional wisdom (Kuhn, 1970). This information will come from the voices of service users, "clients," caregivers, and other significant participants in problematic social situations that will transform the way that we think about practice.

CONCLUSION

Throughout this chapter I have suggested that we need to move beyond the illusion of alternatives in approaching social problems on an individual, family, or community level. Another way of looking at these different perceptions is to use the metaphor of camera lenses. The telephoto lens is the one adopted by those who focus on the individual: by caseworkers, case managers, psychotherapists, and counselors. The wide angle lens is used by those who concentrate on the wider community, the context within which individuals with social problems live. These workers may be neighborhood community developers, those involved in community action at different levels, or those participating in the formulation of social policy. Systems thinkers and change agents have gone beyond the polarization that has often been a consequence of using just a wide angle or telephoto lens. It could be said that they have adopted zoom lenses to enable them to switch from focusing on the individual to the family, and so to see the relationship between the two. Community social work and other ecological approaches have extended the range of these lenses to give us a better picture of relationships among people in wider social systems.

The trick now is to recognize that these relationships are not in front of us, they are all around, and include us. To develop a practice theory to act on this perception means giving up a reliance on photography. We need to increase our, and other people's, understanding of how to bring about change in the processes that perpetuate problems. The nature of the relationships among a whole range of significant people in these situations needs to be understood and changed, reunderstood and changed again. We, the professionals, will need to constantly reinvent our practice through forming and reforming partnerships, as we all struggle to address the increasingly complex world we live in.

NOTE

1. Throughout we refer to "the professional." The term is used here in the sense that some athletes are "professional," meaning that they are paid, that their training and skill make them fitter and more consistent than amateurs who can and do play the same games. This, of course, is not always true. By this definition, a parent aide is as much a "professional" as an MSW. Professionals are also expected to conduct themselves in certain ways to meet ethical standards to protect those they serve, so as not to "bring the game into disrepute" (Smale & Tuson, 1988).

REFERENCES

Barclay Report. (1982). *Social workers: Their roles and tasks.* London: Bedford Square Press.

Bateson, G. (1973). *Steps to an ecology of mind*. St Albans, UK: Paladin.

Bateson, G. (1979). *Mind and nature: A necessary unity*. London: Wildwood House .

Bellah, R.N., Madsen, R., Sullivan, W.N., Swidler A., & Tipton, S.M. (1985). *Habits of the heart: Individualism and commitment in American life*. New York: Harper & Row.

Beresford, P., & Croft, S. (1993). *Citizen involvement: A practical guide for change*. London: Macmillan.

Beresford, P., & Harding, T. (Eds.). (1993). *A challenge to change: Practical experiences of building user led services*. London: National Institute for Social Work.

Bricker-Jenkins, M. (1990). Another approach to practice and training: Clients must be considered the primary experts. *Public Welfare, 48*, 11–16.

Croft, S., & Beresford, P. (1993). *Getting involved: A practical manual*. York, UK: Joseph Rowntree.

Crosbie, D., Smale, G., & Waterson, J. (1989). *Disseminating community social work in Scotland: An initial appraisal*. London: National Institute for Social Work.

Darvill, G., & Smale, G.G. (Eds.). (1990). *Partners in empowerment: Networks of innovation in social work. Pictures of practice* (Vol. II). London: National Institute for Social Work.

Department of Health. (1989). *An introduction to the Children Act: A new framework for the care and upbringing of children*. London: Her Majesty's Stationery Office.

Department of Health. (1990). *Caring for people: Community care in the next decade and beyond*. London: Her Majesty's Stationery Office.

Eastham, D. (1990). Plan it or suck it and see? A personal view of the Canklow Community Project. In G. Darvill & G.G. Smale (Eds.), *Partners in empowerment: Networks of innovation in social work. Pictures of practice* (Vol. II, pp. 57–75). London: National Institute for Social Work.

Egan, G., & Cowan, M. (1979). *People in systems: A model for development in the human services professions and education*. Pacific Grove, CA: Brooks/Cole.

Elizur, J., & Minuchin, S. (1991). *Institutionalising madness: Families, therapy, and society*. New York: Basic Books.

Goldstein, H. (1973). *Social work practice: A unitary approach*. Columbia, SC: University of South Carolina Press.

Haley, J. (1976). *Problem solving therapy: New strategies for effective family therapy*. San Francisco: Jossey-Bass.

Harrison, W.D. (1989). Social work and the search for postindustrial community. *Social Work, 34*, 73–75.

Hearn, B., & Thompson, B. (1987). *Developing community social work in teams: A manual for practice*. London: National Institute for Social Work.

Kuhn, T.S. (1970). *Structure of scientific revolutions* (2nd ed.). Oxford, UK: Pergamon.

Minuchin, S., & Fishman, C.H. (1981). *Family therapy techniques*. Cambridge, MA: Harvard University Press.

Pincus, A., & Minahan, A. (1973). *Social work practice: Model and method*. Itasca, IL: Peacock Publishers.

Sainsbury, E. (1990). *The work of the community social work exchange*. (Available from the Practice and Development Exchange, National Institute for Social Work, London, UK.)

Smale, G.G. (1992). *Managing change through innovation: Towards a model for developing and reforming social work practice and social service delivery.* (Report to the Department of Health, Social Services Inspectorate.) London: National Institute for Social Work.

Smale, G.G. (1993). The nature of innovation and community based practice. In E. Martinez-Brawley (Ed.), *Transferring technology in the personal social services* (pp. 14–26). Washington, DC: NASW Press.

Smale, G.G., & Bennett, W. (Eds.). (1989). *Pictures of practice, Volume I: Community social work in Scotland.* London: National Institute for Social Work.

Smale, G.G., & Statham, D. (1989). Research into practice: Using research in practice and policy making. In M. Stein (Ed.), *Research into practice: Proceedings of the Fourth Annual JUC:BASW Conference.* Birmingham, UK: British Association of Social Workers.

Smale, G.G., & Tuson, G. (1988). *Learning for change: Developing staff and practice in social work teams.* London: National Institute for Social Work.

Smale, G.G., Tuson, G., Cooper, M., Wardle, M., & Crosbie, D. (1988). *Community social work: A paradigm for change.* London: National Institute for Social Work.

Smale, G.G., & Tuson, G. with Biehal, N., & Marsh, P. (1993). *Empowerment, assessment, care management and the skilled worker.* London: Her Majesty's Stationery Office.

Smale, G.G., Tuson G., Ahmad, B., Domoney, L., Darvill, G., & Sainsbury, E. (1994). *Negotiating care in the community: The implications of research findings on community based practice for the implementation of the Community Care and Children Acts.* London: Her Majesty's Stationery Office.

Specht, H. (1990). Social work and the popular psychotherapies. *Social Service Review, 64,* 345–357.

Specht, H., & Courtney, M. (1994). *Unfaithful angels: How social work has abandoned its mission.* New York: Free Press.

Specht, H., & Vickery, A. (Eds.). (1977). *Integrating social work methods.* London: George Allen and Unwin.

Watzlawick, P., Weakland, J., & Fisch, R. (1974). *Change: Principles of problem formation and problem resolution.* New York: W.W. Norton.

II

CREATING COMMUNITY- AND FAMILY-CENTERED PRACTICE: EXAMPLES FROM THE SOCIAL SERVICES, EDUCATION, AND POLICING

The chapters in Part II of this book describe effective services and strategies that involve community-centered, partnership-oriented, collaborative, and empowering approaches to practice. These accounts of community-centered practice in social services, education, and policing consider both changes in front line practice and the management, administrative, and interorganizational structures needed to promote good practice. They show the importance of a family-centered approach that involves parents as partners and of going beyond categorical, fragmented programs limited to individual families in crisis.

Chapter 4, the first in this section, expands on the British model of community social work described by Smale in Chapter 3. Paul Adams and Karin Krauth describe the "patch" approach to providing human services that was developed in Britain during the 1970s and 1980s in reaction to a bureaucratic and overly specialized service system. In the patch approach, workers from different disciplines with different skills are deployed in neighborhood-based teams to address local needs. They work with natural helping networks, interweaving the efforts of formal and informal sources of support including kin, neighbors, voluntary agencies, churches, schools, and neighborhood organizations. Patch allows social services to be delivered in an entirely different way--to be proactive rather than reactive, flexible rather than bureaucratic, informal rather than formal, and focused on strengths rather than on problems.

The patch approach fits well with reform efforts in the United States, including those directed at services integration, decategorization, family preservation, and neighborhood family support. Adams and Krauth trace the development of the patch approach in a demonstration project in Iowa, focusing particularly on changes in workers' attitudes and practice as they went from working outside the community to working in partnership with the people in the community, respecting their strengths, and learning about their culture. Teamwork enabled the workers to share their knowledge and skills, while building a common vision and strategy for their work.

Despite its successes, Adams and Krauth remind us that "going patch" also carries several dangers. One is that the expectation of work in the community is simply added on to already staggering workloads without the necessary support for a new approach to practice. A second is that agencies fail to devolve to line workers the authority to implement decisions made in partnership with families. To avoid these dangers, agencies need to reform their whole approach to service delivery, rather than simply add a patch program to existing services.

Family preservation services, the subject of Chapter 5 by Kristine Nelson and Marcia Allen, have followed this path as they developed from small programs within the continuum of existing child welfare services to providing the basis for system-wide reform. Family preservation services are innovative in focusing on the family as a whole and in providing comprehensive, integrated services planned in conjunction with the family. They seek to empower families by building on family strengths in collaborative relationships and by recognizing that families are the experts on their own situation. The professional's contribution is seen as increasing families' options and removing barriers to change.

Nelson and Allen furnish examples from a number of states, among them Maryland, Oregon, and Idaho, to indicate how family-centered services have expanded from their beginnings as add-on programs intended to prevent costly placements to a larger role in early intervention and system reform. In Idaho, a bottom-up effort applied the empowerment principles of family-centered services to staff in a system-wide reform that integrated child protective, juvenile justice, child mental health, employment, adoption, and substance abuse programs both at state and local levels.

In Chapter 6, Salome Raheim expands on one of these areas, the development of family- and community-centered services in job training and employment, addressing issues raised by the policy debate on welfare reform. Outlining the various dimensions of empowerment practice, Raheim analyzes how self-employment development strategies help to empower families in a realm that is usually considered outside the reach of human services. Through building partnerships, increasing choice, recognizing strengths, and encouraging critical thinking, self-employment programs provide participants with new skills and knowledge in the context of a supportive group. Although the programs help to mobilize and advocate for necessary resources, participants make their own plans and decisions, seek financing on their own, and develop a sense of efficacy and control over their lives.

The development and implementation of a self-employment plan are complemented by the support provided to participants--usually families at high risk of relying on public assistance for some time--through family development services. Based on the principles of family-centered services, family development provides intensive case management that helps families identify their strengths, set goals, remove obstacles, and develop new competencies. Working in partnership, families build a new vision for themselves and the means to achieve it.

In Chapters 7 and 8, scholar–practitioners discuss the role of schools in community and family-centered practice. Chapter 7, by Jo M. Hendrickson and Donna Omer, describes the concept of the comprehensive service school (CSS) that attends to the service needs as well as the educational needs of children and their families. Responding to the failure of traditional educational strategies to meet the needs of changing and increasingly diverse communities, the CSS establishes integrated, interdisciplinary services delivered within the school setting through the collaborative efforts of many community agencies.

The CSS approach recognizes that for children to be successful in school, the multiple needs of families in poverty require an integrated response involving agencies outside the educational system. In one example, Florida has established a statewide collaborative network that supports the development of CSSs in local areas. Through a process of collaboration among families, service providers, and communities, Florida was able to avoid adding on new programs and build links, increase communication, and reduce duplication among existing services including health care, education, parenting, employment, mental health, child care, and early intervention programs.

Unlike the United States, many countries have comprehensive health and welfare benefits that reduce the risks accompanying poverty; however, they also confront problems in meeting the educational needs of low-income, ethnic minority, and immigrant groups. In response, they have developed programs that link schools to community services through collaborative networks. In Chapter 8, Mary R. Lewis explores efforts in western Canada to improve educational outcomes for underachieving children, many of whom are at risk of dropping out of school. Finding that add-on programs serving individual children do not work as well as programs that integrate family, school, and community in collaborative efforts, interdisciplinary teams have created successful partnerships to serve families in at-risk neighborhoods.

An example from Calgary, Canada, shows how an interdisciplinary team comprising a public health nurse, a police officer, a mental health worker, a resource teacher, a child welfare worker, and family aides developed new roles and protocols to increase flexibility and preventive work. Working as a team, in many cases they have been able to avert the need for more formal and intrusive services. Achieving such integrated services at the line level, however, requires parallel structures and support at the supervisory and management levels to ensure that policies and goals mesh and barriers to effective service are overcome.

Addressing related concerns, Quint C. Thurman argues in Chapter 9 that a new model of policing rather than more police is what is needed in dealing with alienated and disenfranchised youth. This new model of community policing has much in common with innovative approaches to practice in the human services. Recognizing that social order arises first from the beliefs, values, and sanctions of the community and only secondarily from law enforcement, the goal of community policing is to return to the community responsibility that has been delegated to professionals and to involve local citizens in "co-creating" order.

Many of the same concepts apply as in human services. Community policing develops local knowledge, works in partnership with citizens in the community, and moves toward earlier and more informal intervention. It locates officers in schools and on foot in the neighborhood to develop informal relationships and intervene in matters of concern to the residents. Their work may include advocating with other governmental units for such things as better street lighting, enforcement of housing codes, and provision of better and more services to the community. Two examples from community policing efforts in at-risk neighborhoods in Spokane, Washington, illustrate the innovative aspects of community policing and their similarity to reforms underway in the social services.

In the final chapter of Part II, Barry Checkoway, Janet Finn, and Kameshwari Pothukuchi address the problems of youth from a strengths and empowerment perspective. They argue that rather than limiting youth to passivity or resignation, social workers should recruit them as active participants in assessing needs and resolving community problems. Drawing on examples from around the country, Checkoway and his colleagues describe projects that involve youth in social action, community planning, public advocacy, and service development. In addition to benefiting the community with, for example, rehabilitated housing or a cleaner environment, the youth develop positive peer support, greater responsibility, enhanced competencies, and higher self-esteem. They learn new skills and critical thinking, which in turn increase their motivation and academic achievement. In addition, they develop political and organizational skills that connect them positively to the community.

These examples of community- and family-centered practice in diverse fields provide guidelines and techniques to improve the responsiveness and effectiveness of human services. They point to the kind of collaboration, teamwork, and broad participation that are required to support this new model of practice and that can be adapted by many different kinds of agencies and programs to enhance service delivery and create change.

4

Working with Families and Communities: The Patch Approach

PAUL ADAMS and KARIN KRAUTH

Patch-based community social work as an approach to practice in the human services has developed in Britain over the past 20 years. Experience in Iowa and Pennsylvania has shown the potential of the patch approach to make an important contribution to reorienting human services in the United States. The patch system is a community-centered model of service delivery. The term *patch* refers to a limited geographical area that is served by a locally based team of human service workers. It is also used to refer to the approach.

The patch system localizes workers with different levels and types of skill in neighborhood offices. This enables patch teams to offer accessible, flexible, and holistic services based on their knowledge of the local cultural and physical environment and on the formal and informal partnerships they develop in their neighborhood or patch. The team is a central element of the patch approach that enables the sharing of knowledge and expertise. Although a team may include several specialists, it is still able to provide a generalist, holistic service.

Patch brings public services into neighborhoods and into more collaborative relationships with private providers. Patch teams based in public agencies find creative ways of meeting statutory responsibilities in individual cases while working proactively in the neighborhood. By picking up signs of trouble early, they are able to intervene sooner and more informally. Families receive a little help when they need it, instead of having to wait for a crisis. There is no need to be categorized, diagnosed, or "clientized" to get help. When implemented effectively, this approach results in an increase in referrals but a decrease, sometimes dramatic, in the formal processing of families through the system (Hadley & McGrath, 1984). The same principles can be applied to the care of elderly people, but here the focus is on families with children.

In this chapter, we describe the emergence of patch and community social work in Britain and discuss their relevance for human services in the United States. We then describe the initial experience of an attempt in Linn County, Iowa to adapt this approach to an urban setting, showing how this approach to interagency collaboration and integration of services changed the practice of line workers. Finally, we discuss some issues and challenges involved in "going patch" as an approach to reinventing human services.

PATCH AND COMMUNITY SOCIAL WORK

Patch and community social work developed in the United Kingdom, beginning in the 1970s and gaining broad support in the 1980s, as a response to widespread dissatisfaction with the social services and social work practice. Following the Seebohm Report's (1968) criticisms of the fragmented and overspecialized service delivery system, in 1971 a large-scale reorganization of local public social services combined child welfare, mental health, and services to the elderly and people with developmental disabilities (and in Scotland the probation service) into integrated departments. The new integrated departments improved the situation in many respects—they attracted substantially increased resources—but exacerbated some of the problems to which Seebohm had drawn attention.

The unified departments were supposed to enable social services workers to work more generically and flexibly instead of remaining within narrow fields of specialization to which the complex and multiple needs of families and communities often did not correspond. In practice, however, the implementation of the Seebohm recommendations, in the context of the 1974 local government reorganization, produced big, centralized, bureaucratic departments that were often relatively inaccessible and unresponsive to the people they served.

Several factors converged in the late 1970s and early 1980s to stimulate local experiments with a more decentralized, less hierarchical, less clinical, and more community-centered approach to social services. One of these was the dissatisfaction of practitioners with the continuing fragmentation and specialization within the new departments. Several studies of social workers and social services departments in the 1970s and early 1980s painted a consistent picture, summarized by Bayley, Seyd, and Tennant (1989, p. 8): "That picture is one of the dominance of one-to-one casework, little teamwork, poor relationships between workers and managers, poor and sporadic contacts with workers from other disciplines and domiciliary workers [homemakers], little contact with the wider social networks of clients, few contacts with or adaptation to the localities in which work was being carried out, a narrow departmentally limited approach, and a management system and professional orientation which reinforced this."

The shift to locally based, community-oriented services began with the entrepreneurial activities of line workers and managers who sought to change practice at the local level, even when the rest of their departments continued to work in traditional ways. Local politicians became interested in these new approaches, as Hadley (1993, pp. 36–37) puts it, "to offset cuts in expenditure by improved methods of working and to defend local services by making them more relevant and answerable to the citizen."

The Barclay Report (Barclay, 1982) on the roles and tasks of social workers gave strong impetus to this development. Emphasizing the forgotten elements of Seebohm, which had already urged social workers to learn from and build on the strengths of the neighborhoods in which their clients lived, the Barclay Report advocated "community social work" in place of a narrowly psychotherapeutic and individual-focused casework. It provided a vision of social work as upholding and supporting the networks that were essential to clients' welfare. The report both reflected and stimulated the move to "going local," which characterized both Conservative- and Labour-dominated local authorities in the early 1980s.

A central feature of this localization was the redeployment of workers in small, neighborhood-based offices. These offices typically combined workers of different levels of skill and professionalization, such as professional social workers, case aides, and other ancillary workers. In many cases they also combined workers from different departments, such as social services and housing (as in the London Borough of Islington) or social services and health (as in Dinnington). The workers in these offices became responsible for addressing the needs of a limited geographical area or "patch." Cases were allocated to teams on the basis of residence within the patch, a neighborhood ideally of between five and ten thousand people, but often somewhat larger.

Patch provided the opportunity for workers to be more accessible to consumers and to develop a knowledge of the neighborhood context of their lives. It facilitated a more flexible, responsive style of work, with blurring of roles between different kinds of workers and a lowering of barriers between human service professionals and those they served. It fostered the "interweaving of formal and informal care" (Bayley, Seyd, & Tennant, 1989). The patch team supported and built on the resources of informal networks of kin and neighbors and combined the efforts of voluntary and statutory agencies, churches, schools, and neighborhood organizations, to solve both individual and community problems.

If "patch" referred to the localization and integration of services, and the deployment of workers in neighborhood teams, "community social work" referred to a different kind of community-centered practice. This practice did not emerge or survive automatically by virtue of geographical relocation. In some neighborhood offices, especially in areas where local authority social service departments "went patch" from the top down, the practice of the workers on the front lines changed little, while their level of resentment increased. For example, although Islington placed its social workers in custom-built neighborhood offices with housing officers, and even merged housing and social services departments into a unified Neighborhood Services Department, the social workers in a neighborhood office studied by one of the authors in 1992 were only on the most formal of terms with the housing staff and worked in a traditional way independently of them.

On the other hand, workers who adopted a community orientation and a unitary or integrated approach to practice have been able to achieve significant changes in practice even without deployment into the neighborhood or other changes in organization (Sinclair, Crosbie, O'Connor, Stanforth, & Vickery, 1984; Bayley, Seyd, & Tennant, 1989, pp. 14–15). Realizing the full potential of this approach, however, requires changes in attitudes and organization, practice and structure (Bayley, Seyd, & Tennant, 1989).

In Britain, realizing this potential has not been easy. The struggle to implement a community-centered approach continues in the face of persisting traditional practices at line and management levels; of antithetical conceptions of professionalism among many social workers and social work educators; of a central government approach to decentralization that aims to undermine local government and substitute competition and market mechanisms for local cooperation, planning, and public service (Hadley, 1993); and even of recent separate pieces of legislation concerning children and elderly people that, in principle, support community social work. In reorganizing to implement this legislation, however, many social services departments have separated their children's and elderly services and broken up successful patch teams in the process of trying to implement a patch-like approach more widely.

PATCH AND HUMAN SERVICES IN THE UNITED STATES

How replicable is the patch approach, which arose in the specific political, economic, and social service environment of Britain, in the policy context of the United States?

Britain has a unitary and more centralized state system than the United States, with local authorities deriving their limited powers to tax and deliver services from the central government. Services are less categorical and more universal than in the United States: it is generally not necessary to fit into a specific category or to be poor to receive help. The voluntary or private sector plays a much smaller role in Britain and the purchase of service relationship between public funders and private providers is much less developed than in the United States, though this is changing. The post-Seebohm reorganization of local authority social services provided a structural framework for integrated service delivery and social work practice, but this too is beginning to change. Recent legislation for child welfare and services to elderly people has strengthened tendencies to renewed fragmentation and specialization.

However, patch offers a body of principles and experience the more usable in the United States because it

1. addresses the same concerns and goals as those who want to reinvent governmental services here;
2. draws on American as well as British intellectual roots and influences; and
3. is congruent with recent developments in the United States, such as the renewed push for services integration, the growth of family-based services and family support, and the revived interest in neighborhoods and their importance for children, youth, and elderly people.

Where patch has been successful in Britain, it has put into practice many of the principles espoused by reformers in the United States. Meeting the same criteria as successful programs in the United States, it is geographically accessible, comprehensive, and integrated. It provides for flexibility and front-line worker discretion. It is family-centered and family-supportive, mission-driven, responsive to neighborhood and community, and based on partnerships between service users and professionals (Schorr, 1988). Such services already exist in many settings and locations in the United States, although they tend to subsist only briefly on the margins of the human services system (Schorr, 1993).

Patch itself did not arise independently of developments in thinking about human services in the United States. American influences included the work on informal helping networks and ways to work with them of Collins and Pancoast (1976) and others at Portland State University. Indeed, a strong link developed between those at Sheffield University working on the Dinnington Project (a university-led and researched project in a Yorkshire mining village) and those at Portland State working on informal helping networks (Bayley, Seyd, & Tennant, 1989).

The work of Pincus and Minahan (1973) on a unitary approach to social work practice and systems thinking in general also had an important impact. Before it took a more narrowly therapeutic turn in Britain, the family systems movement provided a way of thinking both about individuals in relation to the family system in which they were embedded, and also about the relationship between the family and larger systems. It enabled such advocates of community social work as Smale and his collaborators (1988) to understand that communities are not simply resources for workers to utilize. Relationships within the community could be seen as precipitating or perpetuating the problems they were called upon to resolve. Professional intervention then required both forming partnerships with the people involved, and understanding and intervening to change patterns of interaction, between home and school, for example, or family and police, as well as among family members.

Of great importance for the development of new management attitudes and the adoption of a more entrepreneurial, less bureaucratic, and more consumer-oriented approach to the administration of public social services was the literature on excellence in management. Especially influential among managers, such as those at East Sussex Social Services Department which radically reorganized itself into patch teams, was the Peters and Waterman (1982) book, *In Search of Excellence: Lessons from America's Best-Run Companies*.

The American literature on informal helping networks, on systems thinking and integrated practice, and on entrepreneurial management, is an expression of dissatisfactions in the United States similar to those that produced a movement to reinvent human services in Britain. The impetus for reform in the United States, for a shift to a more empowering, accessible, responsive, and integrated approach to meeting needs is apparent in several developments. These include the revived interest in services integration, including efforts to decategorize child welfare funding and involve local communities in a comprehensive planning process, the development of family-based services, and the renewed interest in neighborhood-based initiatives (U.S. Advisory Board on Child Abuse and Neglect, 1993), all discussed elsewhere in this volume. Together they provide a friendly environment for the development of patch initiatives.

At the same time, the American human service system presents particular challenges, some of which are also beginning to confront the British system. There is a strong tendency in American human service systems for innovations such as family-based services to take the form of discrete packages of service produced for sale on the human services market. Innovative approaches to practice tend to become reduced to specific programs. Although there are attempts to reform whole systems toward family-based practice (see Chapter 5 by Nelson and Allen), the stronger tendency is for such work to be isolated in specialist units while the rest of the system continues largely unchanged.

The purchase of service system that has developed over the past 25 years in the United States appears to offer workers and agencies the flexibility and scope for entrepreneurial initiative for which British reformers strive. Yet the result is, paradoxically, fragmentation, rigidity, and resistance to change. Private providers depend upon the purchase of their services by public agencies, which are cutting funds and increasing accountability requirements. Put differently, their scope for proactive or preventive work is limited. They depend on people being "clientized"—formally processed and fit into a funding category—a process that typically requires a crisis. A parent must hurt a child or the child must commit a seriously delinquent act before help is forthcoming. In addition, an adversarial relationship tends to develop in this situation between the public agencies that control (within narrow limits) the purse strings and the providers who depend on them, as well as among the providers themselves.

The public social services worker who buys a service seems to have great flexibility in putting together an appropriate package of care. Yet the development of the purchase of service system in the context of staffing cuts and rising caseloads has produced "case managers" with little time for assessment, let alone creative interventions. Workers then think of their jobs in terms of lining up their clients with discrete packages of service from private providers and filling out the paperwork required to justify the expenditures they wish to incur.

This form of "case management" is different from the kind of one-to-one casework that British writers see as characterizing the traditional model of practice and to which they counterpose community social work. Public agency workers do work case by case, reacting to crises in narrowly prescribed patterns, just like their "traditional" British counterparts. But they do not work in isolation on their cases. Rather, they develop a professional network with workers in other agencies from whom they purchase services. They develop confidence in some agencies and some workers and not in others. It is a pattern toward which British services may be moving, as purchase of services becomes a more common practice.

PATCH IN IOWA

Both in Pennsylvania and Iowa, variants of the patch approach are being adapted to local circumstances. A grant from the Administration for Children and Families, U.S. Department of Health and Human Services to the University of Iowa provided the possibility of combining a patch approach to service delivery with the Iowa Decategorization Project, which merges some child welfare funding streams and involves the community in service planning.

The social services system in Linn County, Iowa, has all the characteristics we have described. On the one hand, there are many private providers competing for shrinking public dollars and a public human services system whose case managers (social workers and juvenile probation officers) buy services from them. There is also, on the other hand, a concerted attempt, expressed in the Linn County Decategorization Project, to reshape the service system to make it more integrated, comprehensive, responsive, and driven by client needs rather than funding categories or other bureaucratic imperatives. Because patch was introduced from the outside, with little knowledge on anyone's part of what going patch would entail in this setting, all the actors had to learn and adapt as they went along.

After a year of planning and development work, a patch team was established in Linn County, consisting initially of four social workers from the state Department of Human Services involved in child protection casework, a city housing inspector, a juvenile probation officer, a supervisor of a county protective homemakers program, a county health officer, a project coordinator, and a volunteer from the community who was later employed part-time in the patch office. The composition of the team changed over time and later included a worker from an African-American led community center, a line worker from the county homemaker program, and an assistant coordinator.

Several social work students have joined the patch team for periods ranging from a few months to an academic year, and some have also been employed as research assistants. Here we draw on the research of one of the students, Karin Krauth, co-author of this paper, who studied the team as a participant observer. The quotations that follow are from semistructured interviews with those workers from state, county, and city agencies who had well-defined jobs and legal responsibilities prior to their joining the patch team and who were faced with the task of carrying out those tasks in a new way as part of an interagency, neighborhood-based team. All had a dual responsibility, to their own employing agency and to the team and its coordinator.

The Patch Project was from the first an initiative of the Linn County Decategorization Project and, by the end of the federal grant period, was adopted as a local funding responsibility. The director of the Linn County Department of Human Resources Management also chairs the Linn County Decategorization executive committee, the Patch advisory committee, and a workgroup consisting of managers from agencies with workers on the team, the team coordinator, and a representative from the University of Iowa. During its first 2 years of operation, until October 1994, the team was housed in a church basement shared with a Headstart program.

Instead of trying to tell the whole story of the Patch Project's development, we will focus on one aspect of the story, how going patch changed practice, even in the first year of the team's operation.

Bayley, Seyd, and Tennant (1989) distinguish three stages in the transition to community-based practice. Stage One, working "outside the community," is the norm in offices where there is little or no community orientation and where "demand is filtered through a referral system that processes requests for help via receptionists, duty officers, intake teams, and so on" (p. 52). Stage Two, working "alongside the community," involves some shift in attitude and may require some organizational change. Organization is small-scale and workers begin to develop a sense of identity as an interagency locality team. They focus more on the client's network and may utilize a wide array of formal resources. They link up with other workers and may bring in an occasional volunteer. Workers think now about preventive work in the community, but see this as an add-on to their normal statutory work with clients (Bayley, Seyd, & Tennant, p. 54).

In describing Stage Three, Bayley, Seyd, and Tennant (1989, p. 54) express well the ideal of patch or community-based practice. In this stage, working "within the community," workers display the characteristics of the matrix team (Payne, 1982). Team members have a dual responsibility, to their own agency and to the team. They have incorporated a community orientation into their everyday work. It is no longer an add-on, done after their required work is complete, if there is time. Their knowledge of the area enables them to be proactive, to respond early, and to mobilize resources so as to prevent or lessen the severity of problems in the future. "Thus, working 'within the community' means that workers do not just focus on clients and their networks, but also on particular groups or streets within their area. They now call upon a range of community-based resources, from workers in other agencies, to self-help groups, individual volunteers and voluntary groups" (Bayley, Seyd, & Tennant, 1989, p. 54).

The workers' comments at various stages of the first year of the team's operation illustrate the shift that going patch entails. British experience had shown that prevention, accessibility, integration with other formal and informal services, and the inclusion of informal networks were all important to the development of community-oriented services (Barclay, 1982; Hadley, Cooper, Dale, & Stacy, 1987; Martinez-Brawley & Brawley, 1992).

At the beginning, team members tended to see prevention in limited terms, as avoidance of new abuse charges or new delinquent acts by people already formally involved with the system. Accessibility was taken to mean the ease with which these existing clients could reach their caseworkers. In contrast to traditional practice in the United Kingdom, however, workers spent considerable time communicating with workers from other human services agencies. These communications were connected with referrals to private providers rather than with collaboration. They resulted in fragmented rather than integrated services.

One worker commented on a change in her work role as a DHS social worker over the previous 10 years. "It used to be that when you were assigned a case you went out and talked to people to see their needs, determine whether there was something you could do or someone else could do. There was a lot more contact; you didn't wait to hear." Now workers spend more time "sitting at their desks talking to providers, not to their clients." She described the current role of a DHS worker: "As a case manager you go into court and sit down and the providers all talk to the court about what's going on. You're a nonentity. You just have the money strings. I think a lot of times we're just plugging in providers and not effecting a change, and we're paying beaucoup bucks."

At the beginning, all the state workers described themselves as working closely with providers but as having little contact with local organizations such as schools, churches, or volunteer groups. Few of the workers tried to involve or consult family or neighborhood networks. One worker explained this in terms of the "time it would take to train families and friends to work with clients and the issue of confidentiality."

Practice at this point, before the team became operational, clearly reflected conventional approaches to service delivery that can be characterized as "working outside the community" (Bayley, Seyd, & Tennant, 1989). Services were provided by centralized, hierarchical agencies on a categorical basis. Requests for service were channeled through receptionists, intake workers, and supervisors. Most services were provided only when problems were in advanced stages, that is, they were reactive rather than preventive. There was little involvement of informal helping networks. Worker roles were narrow and inflexible (Hadley, Cooper, Dale, & Stacy, 1987; Bayley, Seyd, & Tennant, 1989).

HOW PRACTICE CHANGED

Marginality and Partnership

Fundamental to patch practice is the realization that formal human services "represent no more than a single strand in the complex web of relationships and services, formal and informal, statutory and non-statutory, which together provide care and control in the community. The overall effectiveness of provision depends not on one part of this network alone but on how well the whole is woven together" (Hadley, Cooper, Dale, & Stacy, 1987, p. 95).

As the Patch team in Linn County absorbed this perspective, its own approach to practice shifted. It came to displace the human service worker from the center of the helping system, seeing the worker–consumer relation instead as one part of a system that includes family members, neighbors, informal groups, churches, voluntary organizations, schools, and other health and human services providers.

Whether working with individual formal cases on projects, or with groups, team members came to see families as embedded in networks, which might be attenuated or problematic, but were also sources of support. They saw their own relation to family and neighborhood networks as one of marginality (Smale, Tuson, Cooper, Wardle, & Crosbie, 1988; Smale & Tuson, 1988). That is, they tried to avoid either becoming enmeshed in the problem-perpetuating patterns in the network or standing outside the network, marginalized and helpless.

This shift of perspective, decentering the professional–client relation, looking at other lines of support, and seeing service users in their natural settings, had profound implications for everyday practice. Workers began to see their task in terms of building partnerships, not only with other agencies, but with consumers, family members, and other local people, as well as with neighborhood organizations, churches, and groups.

Strengths and Diversity

For the team a key to changing practice was the shift from a deficit to a strengths perspective on families. When presenting cases, workers began to ask each other to name a family's strengths and to look for ways to help people build on their positive qualities. This change in workers' attitudes was evident in how they began to view their own roles. As they looked to people's strengths they started to see themselves less in the role of saviors who told families what to do and more in the role of partners developing plans with families.

As workers' respect for families and their capacities to cope in the face of difficult circumstances increased, they learned from families about their cultures and the oppression they confronted in their daily lives. Issues of racism, sexism, and poverty emerged during team meetings, and the workers became more critical of ways in which social services at times perpetuated these problems. In one situation, a team member mediated between a Nigerian family and a worker from a private agency with respect to conflicts between legal and cultural expectations of parental discipline and became an advocate for the family as it navigated the welfare system and dealt with a teenage daughter's pregnancy.

Workers attempted to extend their professional roles so as to relate on a more personal level to patch residents and to bring their full humanity and array of skills and interests to bear on their work. As the following quote suggests, patch was a way of working that touched workers' feelings about being human. "Patch is not an institution. Patch is a way of thinking. People have to be people to make patch work. A skill is being sensitive to how other people are feeling. You can't see your neighbor hurting and not do something about it—it's not right. So patch is a frame of mind that says, 'I'm no different than my neighbor.'"

Teamwork

A shift from individual work to a team approach is essential for community-centered practice. It enables workers to exchange information, share ideas, and coordinate activities. Teamwork is indispensable to "going patch" for workers (1) to develop a detailed and comprehensive knowledge of the locality they serve; (2) to bring a wide range of skills to bear on the tasks they need to undertake at family, neighborhood, and service system levels; and (3) to develop a common vision and strategy. Workers saw the team approach as one of the most positive aspects of the project and as leading to more comprehensive, flexible, and responsive services.

The concept of "team" extended beyond the core patch team. Workers began to see themselves as members of an extended team of other human service workers, community leaders, and consumers. They developed a shared vision for the neighborhood and also a shared responsibility for meeting these goals. One worker expressed this expanded sense of the possible: "I'm seeing more and more that we as patch team members can help facilitate change in the neighborhood."

The team's efforts to develop a shared vision with others and to promote collaborative teamwork were evident in the range of visitors who attended team meetings to discuss their programs and ideas. During one such meeting, the team drafted a list of ways they thought patch could support initiatives in the community. These included "Support concept of starting someplace now; help to generate interest and push for new ideas; start with the patch concept of building on the strengths of the family/community; attend community meetings; bring people/agencies together to work on these ideas together; set up, back off, and move on to the next idea; work to enhance existing programs." These approaches indicate that the patch team members were moving away from seeing themselves only as individuals intervening on the individual case level to recognizing the power of teamwork within and beyond the core team. A year later, in March 1994, the team drafted an excellent document about the requirements of team membership and practice, which appears in the appendix to this chapter.

The patch team worked hard to build partnerships with local schools, churches, agencies, and groups such as the two neighborhood associations. Because of their focus on a limited geographical area, the workers developed considerable local knowledge and came to know neighborhood residents better. The housing inspector who lived in the neighborhood became an active member of the neighborhood association and, as a result, became the local contact for residents with housing concerns. She was also invited to give presentations to the association about home safety and the prevention of accidents.

Another patch worker noted that her relationship with the schools had improved dramatically since she joined the patch team. "Before patch, I didn't make as much effort when working with the schools to work with them, get to know them, and be accommodating." Since the reallocation of DHS cases to the patch area, all of the children on this worker's caseload lived in the patch and attended one of the two local elementary schools. This gave her the opportunity to get to know the teachers, school counselors, and social workers better and to visit the children more frequently.

Teamwork operated at several levels. In individual cases, the feedback of other team members made a decisive difference to a worker's actions. A DHS worker told the team of the strong pressure she was experiencing from teachers, service providers, and co-workers at DHS to recommend placement of a child whose mother was well known to professionals in the child welfare system. The mother, however, had asked the worker to give her a chance to show she was capable of caring for her child, and the DHS patch worker wanted to support her. After she presented the details of the case, including the mother's strengths, the patch team members concurred with the worker's view that the child should be with her mother. With her teammates' encouragement, the worker decided to stand up to her agency colleagues and other professionals and demonstrate her belief in the woman by not recommending removal. The DHS worker later noted that without her team's backing she probably would not have stood up to the pressure to place the child. Furthermore, it would have been difficult for both the worker and the mother to believe in their own abilities to improve the situation so that the family could stay together. The mother subsequently changed her behavior and proved that she was capable of caring for her child.

As a result of collaboration on the core team, workers were better able to respond to referrals, to conduct ecological assessments, and to access resources. They developed better understanding of each other's jobs, and their roles expanded and became more flexible. As a result of their interactions with the housing inspector, the other workers could recognize the dangerous living conditions of many of the families with whom they worked, make housing referrals, and work jointly with the housing inspector.

The housing inspector was very creative in expanding her own role. On one occasion, a woman with a developmental disability was having difficulty cleaning up the piles of clothes and other household items that had accumulated in the corners of every room. The housing inspector met with the woman to discuss the possibility of finding a friend or neighbor who might be willing to help. A woman who lived in the same building and was acquainted with the tenant agreed to assist her. After spending several days together cleaning the house, these women discovered they had much in common and a friendship began to form. In a similar way, the housing inspector put an isolated Chinese mother, with little command of English, in touch with another Chinese-speaking woman in the same street.

When the housing inspector went to check an apartment, in the early weeks of the team's existence, she found not only frayed electrical wiring, but also an isolated mother with two small children and no furniture except a sofa. The children slept on the sofa while their mother slept on the floor. In the past, the housing inspector would not have regarded the social situation as a professional concern, although she noticed such conditions and felt powerless to offer assistance. In this case she brought the matter back to the team. One worker then called several churches (with which the team had already established good relations) and located furniture, and another put the mother in touch with the Headstart program, which shared the same church basement as the Patch team. The mother was also invited to join a support group for young mothers that was just forming as a result of the team's discussion of its work in the neighborhood. In this case, the team responded proactively to a situation that more typically would have been ignored until it became a legally mandated case of child neglect some months or years later.

In this example, we see community social work, or community-centered practice, initiated by a worker who was not herself a social worker. The unit that engaged in community-centered practice was not an individual but the team. This work was part of the team's overall project of building partnerships with families, networks, and private, voluntary, and statutory organizations, an effort that operates at multiple system levels and at all points on the social work map.

Learning from Local People

In addition to the knowledge gained by its close relations with schools, churches, and neighborhood organizations, the team sought to learn from local residents in a variety of settings. They developed their projects and approaches so as to bring together their skills and resources with those of local people to address issues of concern. Team members learned from looking for patterns and talking to consumers about their common needs, as they shifted from solely assessing and targeting individuals for change to focusing on social situations and community networks. For example, in examining and discussing their formal caseloads, they found a pattern of isolated young mothers in the patch (which has a high proportion of renters, a low rate of housing stability, and the highest rate of school transfers in the district).

The workers thought that a group might be a way of bringing these women together. They tested the idea by speaking to women they thought might be interested, sending out invitations for a "Moms' Night Out," and recruiting community volunteers to provide child care. Six women attended the first meeting facilitated by two DHS patch workers. The group discussed the positive and negative aspects of being a mother in the neighborhood and the women decided to meet weekly.

The team also set out to learn from patch residents, whether or not they were service users at the time—about their perceptions of the needs and resources of the neighborhood and how the team could collaborate with them—by using the technique of "exchange meetings" learned from British patch trainers. Pairs of teammates began to meet with small groups of parents, neighbors, and others, such as residents at the homeless shelter and teens participating in a community support group, to exchange information about the perceptions, resources, and concerns of local people and team members.

From information shared at these meetings, the patch workers became involved in activities that residents felt were useful. When parents expressed their opinion that many of the problems in the area stemmed from lack of activities for children, the team responded by working with parents, the city council, and the elementary schools to set up a "tot lot" with supervised children's activities over the summer.

In another case, the team learned from the community's response to a team member who brought his skill in *tae kwon do* to his patch work. With the support of his teammates, the juvenile court, and the church that housed the team, the probation officer started teaching a *tae kwon do* class twice a week in the church gymnasium. A few of the participants were adolescents court-ordered to participate as a condition of their probation. The rest of the class (initially 30 students but later expanded to two classes) was made up of neighborhood children, teens, and a few adults.

This project played a crucial, but largely unanticipated, role in the patch team's relations with the neighborhood. During classes, parents of the participants would spend time in the patch office talking to each other and to team members about important issues in their lives, including parenting, substance abuse, health care, and relationships. The role of the workers in these encounters was often very marginal; parents shared information and supported each other. *Tae kwon do* became an important part of the team's relations with the community and even of the lives of particular children, youth, and families involved with the formal child welfare and juvenile justice systems.

The point here is not that *tae kwon do* in itself holds great potential to strengthen families and build communities, but that the team was able to take advantage of its own interests and capacities to lower the barriers between themselves as a group of professionals with wide legal powers over people's lives and the community they served. The workers began to gain credibility with area residents and to develop relationships with them. This also enabled the team to adapt, be flexible, and learn from the local people who increasingly became involved with the team in a range of activities and projects.

More formal mechanisms for engaging and learning from local residents, such as adding consumers and other local people to the advisory committee, and thereby involving them directly in the governance of the project, were less successful, for the usual reasons—in particular, the domination of such committees by professionals. Efforts to remedy this situation continue, but in relation to the team's day-to-day practice, the growing capacity to listen to and learn from consumers and other local people was decisive for the transition from conventional to community-oriented practice, to "going patch."

ISSUES AND CHALLENGES

Among the many issues and challenges facing those who wish to apply the lessons of patch to reinventing human services toward responsive, community-centered practice, two are of special importance to the functioning of a neighborhood-based team: the issue of patch as an add-on, and the need for an empowering approach to management.

There is sometimes a tendency to see patch as an add-on, as something workers do in addition to their mandated casework. It may even be seen as the province of certain team members, such as community or volunteer organizers, or students, while the statutory workers carry on in the traditional way. This cannot work and leads to a deep split within the team. To be effective, patch has to operate at every level. Patch workers bring to all their work, including statutory cases, their knowledge of the neighborhood, the relationships the team has developed with other formal and informal helpers, their strengths perspective, a willingness to share their work with the team and draw on its resources, and an approach to building partnerships with the other people involved.

Patch need take no more time than conventional practice, but it does require that time be used differently. Workers no longer take sole responsibility for the problem at hand. They recognize that most of the caring and monitoring is done informally in the family and neighborhood and work to build the caring capacity of the people and networks involved. Using their time to build partnerships with families and their networks, with agencies, schools, churches, and neighborhood groups, they and their team help interweave formal and informal caring. They spend less time doing to or for families and more time working with them, less time on crisis intervention and more on prevention and early identification.

Building partnerships implies that workers are in a position to negotiate in good faith with others in the neighborhood. This can lead to frustration and cynicism if line workers are frequently countermanded by those with the real decision making authority, far up the managerial line (Smale, Tuson, Biehal, & Marsh, 1993; Adams & Krauth, 1994). The patch approach requires that managers act on the principle espoused by Vice-President Gore's study on reinventing the federal government: "Empower employees to get results—decentralize authority and empower those who work on the front lines to make more of their own decisions and solve more of their own problems" (Gore, 1993).

At the same time, patch requires line staff to take ownership of the team's development and strategy. Staff in agencies operating in traditional, hierarchical settings may be unused to thinking about their relation to the community or to its formal and informal helping systems as a whole. Placed in a community-centered, interagency team, they may find it hard at first to respond to requests for statements such as the one produced by the Iowa team on the requirements and practices of team membership. Time and training are needed for this, as for all aspects of team development.

CONCLUSION

Patch is not another program, but a new approach to practice and human services. It can build on and support other attempts to achieve these goals, including services integration, decategorization, and family-based services. It brings to them a proactive stance at both case and community levels, an emphasis on teamworking, and a shared local knowledge. It translates the principles of services integration into a different practice on the ground.

Patch-based, community-centered practice involves some fundamental shifts, from reactive to preventive work; from individual casework to work that includes networks and the community; from services at arm's length, driven by bureaucratic and funding considerations, to services close to the community and responsive to its needs; from professional responsibility for the solution of problems to a responsibility shared with citizens and helping networks, interweaving formal and informal care and control; from service user as client and object of intervention to users and caregivers as partners in the planning and provision of services (Hadley, Cooper, Dale, & Stacy, 1987).

There is no one way to go patch. Patch offers not a blueprint for replication, but a body of principles and experience, a living tradition that includes knowledge, values, and skills. Citizens and professionals, in partnership with earlier reformers and innovators, need to reinvent the approach for themselves in their local context (Smale, 1993). It may be, as Hadley (1993) suggests, that the environment is currently more favorable for the development of responsive, community-centered services in the United States than in Britain. Certainly, the patch experience in Britain, and increasingly in the United States, offers a rich resource for those who want to reinvent human services.

APPENDIX

Patch Team Requirements: Team Membership/Practice

The patch team recently got together to articulate the characteristics of a patch team member and patch practice. Team membership includes:

1. designation as such by the employing agency and the team
2. attendance and active participation at weekly team meetings

3. for team members not permanently based in the office, frequent drop-in visits so as to be accessible to other team members and ongoing information
4. actively working to establish a professional relationship with other team members characterized by

   - collaboration and partnership
   - support, loyalty, and camaraderie
   - mutual learning and openness
   - a focus on strengths and positive outcomes

5. a willingness to share work by involving other team members with one's "assigned" families and being accessible to the families of other team members
6. a commitment to an approach to practice that stresses innovation, flexibility, vision, and creative problem solving
7. a commitment to documenting new avenues of practice and its effectiveness for evaluation and future funding purposes
8. a willingness to acknowledge and a commitment to working with the strengths of other team members
9. a willingness to address issues of concern about team member practice, the team as a whole, and the patch process/project with the team

   - a commitment to the principle that the team "consumes its own smoke"

10. a working understanding that at any given point in time team members may be at different stages in their development and demonstration of patch practice.

Working with families includes:

1. early, holistic intervention in order to be preventive
2. use of holistic assessment, with families' involvement via tools such as genograms and ecomaps
3. respect for families' past and present successes (acknowledgment and reinforcement of family strengths)
4. team consultation regarding families with concerns

   - a balance between individual family members' needs and the needs of the family
   - inclusion of families in consultations held to generate possible solutions regarding concerns

- use of team members within and outside their prescribed agency role (going outside prescribed job description without violating it) to utilize team members' special talents

5. use of family unity meetings to which a family extends the invitation, defines the concern(s), and chooses a course of action from among the options generated in the meeting

   - acknowledging, emphasizing, and promoting the informal support networks of families
   - use of the strengths and resources of the community to assist families in generating possible solutions regarding concerns, with workers remaining peripheral

6. working to establish relationships characterized by collaboration, partnership, support, mutual learning, and openness, with a focus on positive outcomes.

Working in the community includes:

1. a willingness to work with the designated patch population, which is diverse and tends toward lower socioeconomic status
2. knowledge of the entire patch

   - acknowledging, emphasizing, and promoting the informal support networks in the patch
   - sensitivity to and respect for diversity, as it affects life-style choices and related behavior
   - a focus on strengths and positive outcomes, working to establish relationships characterized by collaboration, partnership, support, mutual learning, and openness

3. accessibility and responsiveness to families with whom the team is directly working, and to other residents and institutions of the patch

   - acting as a team representative at community events or meetings

Working with the patch structure and the collaborative agencies includes:

1. meeting one's respective agency's statutory requirements in a timely manner
2. requesting and participating in inservice trainings to facilitate acquisition and strengthening of skills needed for effective practice
3. working toward effective consumer-driven practice by interfacing with the Work Group and Advisory Committee

4. sharing in a professional manner, formally and informally, successful practice with those in one's professional community

   - sharing "tools" developed within the context of patch practice with other professionals

5. hosting and scheduling meetings at the patch office as appropriate
6. continuing to work to establish professional relationships outside the team, characterized by collaboration, partnership, mutual learning, and openness, with a focus on strengths and positive outcomes.

ACKNOWLEDGMENTS

Research for this chapter was supported, in part, by grant number 90PD0196 from the Administration for Children and Families, Department of Health and Human Services, Washington, DC 20447.

REFERENCES

Adams, P., & Krauth, K. (1994). Empowering workers for empowerment-based practice. In P. Nurius & L. Gutierrez (Eds.), *Education and research for empowerment practice*. Seattle, WA: University of Washington School of Social Work.

Barclay, P.M. (1982). *Social workers: Their role and tasks*. London: Bedford Square Press for National Institute for Social Work.

Bayley, M., Seyd, R., & Tennant, A. (1989). *Local health and welfare*. Aldershot, UK: Gower.

Collins, A.H., & Pancoast, D.L. (1976). *Natural helping networks: A strategy for prevention*. Washington, DC: NASW Press.

Gore, A. (1993). *Creating a government that works better and costs less: From red tape to results*. Report of the National Performance Review. Executive Summary. Washington, DC: U.S. Government Printing Office.

Hadley, R. (1993). Decentralization, integration, and the search for responsive human services. In E.E. Martinez-Brawley (Ed.), *Transferring technology in the personal social services* (pp. 31–45). Washington, DC: NASW Press.

Hadley, R., Cooper, M., Dale, P., & Stacy, G. (1987). *A community social worker's handbook*. London: Tavistock.

Hadley, R., & McGrath, M. (1984). *When social services are local: The Normanton experiment*. London: Allen & Unwin.

Martinez-Brawley, E., & Brawley, E.A. (1992). Community care in a rural patch in Cumbria, England. *Social Services Review, 66*, 32–49.

Payne, M. (1982). *Working in teams*. London: Macmillan.

Peters, T.J., & Waterman, R.H. (1982). *In search of excellence: Lessons from America's best-run companies.* New York: Harper & Row.

Pincus, A., & Minahan, A. (1973). *Social work practice: Model and method.* Itasca, IL: Peacock.

Schorr, L.D. (1993). Keynote address. In National Association of Social Workers. *Effective strategies for increasing social program replication/adaptation: A review of the literature and summary of a seminar* (pp. 7–18). Washington, DC: NASW.

Schorr, L.D., with Schorr, D. (1988). *Within our reach: Breaking the cycle of disadvantage.* New York: Anchor/Doubleday.

Seebohm, F. (1968). *Report of the committee on local authority and allied personal social services* (Command No. 3703). London: Her Majesty's Stationery Office.

Sinclair, I., Crosbie, D., O'Connor, P., Stanforth, L., & Vickery, A. (1984). *Networks project: A study of informal care, services and social work for elderly clients living alone.* London: National Institute for Social Work Research Unit.

Smale, G.G. (1993). The nature of innovation and community-based practice. In E.E. Martinez-Brawley (Ed.), *Transferring technology in the personal social services* (pp. 14–26). Washington, DC: NASW Press.

Smale, G.G., & Tuson, G. (1988). *Learning for change: Developing staff and practice in social work teams.* London: National Institute for Social Work.

Smale, G., & Tuson, G., with Biehal, N. & Marsh, P. (1993). *Empowerment, assessment, care management and the skilled worker.* London: Her Majesty's Stationery Office.

Smale, G., Tuson, G., Cooper, M., Wardle, M., & Crosbie, D. (1988). *Community social work: A paradigm for change.* London: National Institute for Social Work.

U.S. Advisory Board on Child Abuse and Neglect. (1993). *Neighbors helping neighbors: A new national strategy for the protection of children* (Fourth Report). Washington, DC: U.S. Department of Health and Human Services, Administration for Children and Families.

5

Family-Centered Social Services: Moving Toward System Change

KRISTINE NELSON and MARCIA ALLEN

Faced with narrowly categorical and fragmented services, complex bureaucracies, and a tangle of legal mandates and constraints, child welfare agencies have responded by forging new practice models to better serve at-risk children and families. Dissatisfied with the lack of stability in the foster care system, reformers have looked for alternatives to provide more permanence in children's lives. With the development of new family-centered interventions, child welfare services now seek to avert placement whenever possible and to reunify children in placement with their families.

These new approaches evolved, however, at a time when the capacity of child welfare agencies to provide services to families was reduced by the sheer volume of child abuse and neglect reports (General Accounting Office, 1989; National Center on Child Abuse and Neglect, 1988). As a result, after a brief decline in the early 1980s, foster care placements started to increase again. In a context of rising caseloads and declining resources, "business as usual" is no longer possible and agencies are turning to family-centered services in an attempt to address increasingly complex family needs.

As developed in both public and private agencies over the past two decades, most of these innovative programs provided an alternative to the immediate placement of abused, neglected, or delinquent children. In the Child Welfare League of America's typology (1989), they fall within the category of "intensive family-centered crisis services," more commonly known as family preservation services. Intervention is brief (1 to 3 months), requires small caseloads (less than 10 families), and involves several hours of direct contact a week, usually in the families' own homes.

Although implemented initially as categorical programs, family-centered services are now the cornerstone of integrated human services systems in several states. Along with family support, family preservation has been recognized in new legislation as a fundamental component of child welfare services. In 1994, for the first time, states received federal funding earmarked for family-centered services.

THE HISTORY AND CONTEXT OF FAMILY-CENTERED SERVICES

Family-centered services represent a radical departure from the values and practices of the last 200 years in child welfare. Since their inception in the early part of the nineteenth century, child welfare agencies have focused primarily on placing children in institutions and foster families (McGowan, 1983). Starting in the 1970s, however, the permanency planning movement encouraged either rapid return of children from placement or, when reunification was not possible, termination of parental rights and adoption. The Adoption Assistance and Child Welfare Act of 1980 (P.L. 96-272) mandated that agencies make "reasonable efforts" to prevent placement and reunify families as a condition of federal aid, and provided funds for subsidized adoptions (Pecora, Whittaker, & Maluccio, 1992, pp. 21–29).

However, because of the large increase in reports of child abuse and neglect that followed the Child Abuse Prevention and Treatment Act of 1974, most of the scarce resources for social services have been diverted to investigation and substantiation of reports of child abuse and neglect (Pecora, Whittaker, & Maluccio, 1992, pp. 13–17; Stein, 1991, pp. 43–46). Although both the Child Abuse Prevention and Treatment Act and the Adoption Assistance and Child Welfare Act authorized money for services, neither has ever been fully funded (General Accounting Office [GAO], 1989). In contrast, there has been no limit on federal funding for out-of-home placement. Consequently, between 1981 and 1992 federal spending on placement grew from $2 to $8 for every $1 spent on other child welfare services. Federal spending on placement jumped 616% during this period; this represents only 47% of total spending, with states and localities contributing the rest (GAO, 1993).

At the same time federal dollars were going increasingly to support placement, voluntary agencies were experimenting with new methods to preserve families at risk of having a child placed in foster care. Building on earlier programs including the St. Paul Family Centered Project and the Mendota Mental Health Institute's Home and Community Treatment Team, programs such as Homebuilders in Tacoma, Washington, and Families, Inc., in West Branch, Iowa, developed innovative programs to provide an alternative to out-of-home placement (Cautley, 1979; Horejsi,

1981; Kinney, Haapala, Madsen, & Fleming, 1977; Nelson, Landsman, & Deutelbaum, 1990). In the early 1980s, encouraged by state and federal legislation, a variety of family-based prevention and reunification programs sprang up in several states (Nelson & Landsman, 1992).

COMMON CHARACTERISTICS OF FAMILY PRESERVATION PROGRAMS

Although they differ in structural features and theoretical orientation (Barth, 1990; Nelson, Landsman, & Deutelbaum, 1990), most family preservation programs share a common philosophy. Key assumptions are (1) that families should be maintained and supported whenever possible; (2) that most children are better off with their own families than in substitute care; (3) that services to avert placement should be funded at the same level as placement; (4) that services should be time limited, intensive, and comprehensive (including therapeutic, concrete, and supportive services); and (5) that services should be provided in accordance with the needs and priorities of individual families (Nelson & Landsman, 1992, p. 5).

As family preservation programs have developed over the past two decades, common practices have emerged, particularly in the way practitioners relate to families who use the services, in the way professional roles are defined, and in agency and community support for family-centered practice.

Relationships with Families

Although innovations occur at many levels within social agencies, none is as important as those that occur at the level of direct service. The most commonly shared feature among the different models of family preservation is a focus on reinventing services at the front line. Family preservation practice is, therefore

- strengths-oriented, identifying family competencies as well as issues of concern, and believing in the ability of families to change; and
- collaborative, with family members acting as the experts on their own situations and participating fully in setting goals and creating service plans.

Family participation in setting goals, the type of goals set, and goal achievement have all been found to be related to placement prevention in several studies of family preservation services (Fraser, Pecora, & Haapala, 1991; Nelson & Hunter, 1993; Nelson & Landsman, 1992; Reid, Kagan, & Schlosberg, 1988; Schwartz, AuClaire, & Harris, 1991).

In addition, "enabling" interventions that emphasize skill and self-esteem building and actively assist families to identify and access extended family support and community services have been found to be more effective than simply providing concrete services, or "doing for" families (Fraser, Pecora, & Haapala, 1991; Haapala, 1983; Nelson, Emlen, Landsman, & Hutchinson, 1988). Enabling interventions may range from teaching household or parenting skills, to helping parents communicate more effectively with school staff, to mediating strained relationships in natural support networks.

Professional Roles

Respect for family strengths and integrity requires a concomitant redefinition of professional roles so that they are more responsive to family needs. Professionals, no longer seen as the experts responsible for "fixing" families, use their skills and knowledge to increase the options families have for dealing with problems and help remove barriers to change. With a focus on the whole family and access to a comprehensive array of services and resources, professionals are freed from narrow role definitions and are able to be more creative in addressing family needs. And when they are part of a team of workers with complementary skills and resources, workers benefit from different perspectives and gain emotional support to cope with what otherwise could be an isolating and overwhelming job.

Changes in agency practice and procedures are needed to support new professional roles and relationships with families. These typically include smaller caseloads, usually between 2 and 12 cases, that enable workers to build family and team relationships and to access community resources. Smaller caseloads are made possible by time limits on service, usually of 1 to 3 months, although families with extensive service histories and multiple needs may receive services for as long as 6 months to 2 years. The structuring of service teams, whether they consist of professional workers only, include paraprofessional workers, or involve workers in other units and agencies, is also essential to supporting and maintaining new methods of practice. Finally, ongoing training, supervision, and consultation help workers sharpen their skills, learn new interventions, and maintain their enthusiasm.

Community Support for Family Preservation Services

Although family preservation programs commonly take an ecological perspective on families and their needs, the community context of the agency is often overlooked in establishing new programs. The availability of other resources in the community is crucial, especially when family preservation exists as a categorical program available to families only when placement is being considered. No social service program can be completely successful in helping families maintain their integrity and resolve their problems unless their basic needs for food, shelter, income, education, and health care are met. Meeting these needs requires both that resources exist in the community and that these resources work in collaboration with the family preservation program. In addition, many families need other resources such as day care, homemakers, flexible funds to meet emergency needs, and supportive groups concurrently with family preservation services. Counseling, concrete, and supportive services may also be required following termination for families to maintain gains achieved with family preservation services.

The experience of the state of Maryland illustrates the development of family preservation services as well as many of the characteristics commonly found in these programs.

Maryland Intensive Family Services

In 1984 the Maryland Department of Human Resources funded nine pilot projects to prevent out-of-home placement of children and expanded to five more sites the following year. Called Intensive Family Services (IFS), the program design followed the home-based, family systems approach developed by Families Inc. of West Branch, Iowa, in the 1970s (Nelson, Landsman, & Deutelbaum, 1990). The IFS program deploys teams of two workers, one professional and one paraprofessional, to work with caseloads of six families in their homes for a maximum of 90 days. Teams have flexible working hours, a 24-hour hotline, and flexible funds to purchase goods and services (Maryland Department of Human Resources, 1987).

The Maryland IFS program accepts families at risk of having a child placed within 6 months and focuses primarily on cases new to the child welfare system. They screen out caregivers with chronic mental health or substance abuse problems who have not sought or responded to treatment. Interventions include strategic and structural family therapy, parent education, skills training, supportive services, and concrete services. Usually services include individual counseling, family counseling, parent skills training, parent aide services, and transportation. An average of $681 to $795 per family in flexible funds is spent on furniture, household equipment, and rent, and smaller amounts are used for clothing, recreation, and other household necessities (Maryland Department of Human Resources, 1987).

Evaluation of the first 100 cases seen in the Maryland pilot programs found a placement rate of 10% and a decline in the number of foster care placements in the pilot counties. Data from standardized forms completed in all the sites showed improvement in caregiver support and home conditions. However, in this study, families with sexual and substance abuse problems did not improve (Maryland Department of Human Resources, 1987). A federally funded evaluation of the Maryland IFS program that compared IFS families with families who received traditional child protective services found lower rates of placement in the IFS program (18 and 33% respectively). Families receiving IFS services improved in terms of employment, housing, child protection, and support for the primary caregiver (Pearson & King, 1987).

In addition to significant improvement in child behavior and family functioning, studies have found that children are protected at least as well in family preservation as in other child welfare programs and that both families and workers are more satisfied with services (Feldman, 1991; Froelich, 1992; Henggeler et al., 1986; Institute for Social and Economic Development, 1993; McCroskey & Meezan, 1993; Nelson, Landsman, Tyler, & Richardson, 1995; Szykula & Fleischman, 1985).

Challenges Facing Family Preservation

Despite their many strengths, family preservation programs face a number of challenges. Although workers use an ecological approach and consider many system levels in assessing problems and planning interventions, most work is still done at the individual or family level and often consists of counseling. Although supportive and concrete services are typically offered and available, these are used less often and with fewer families than are clinical interventions. Crucial work linking families to community resources, overcoming barriers to the use of these services, and developing new resources is often left undone.

There is still much to discover about how the programs work and which elements are most effective. We also need to know more about the effectiveness of family preservation services with different kinds of families and problems (Bath & Haapala, 1994). Some programs have been found to be less effective with cases involving neglect and delinquency

(Berry, 1992; Fraser, Pecora, & Haapala, 1991; Nelson & Landsman, 1992; Nelson, Landsman, Tyler, & Richardson, 1995), but this may be because it is harder to engage the families in services (Nelson & Landsman, 1992).

We also need to clarify the type and degree of success that should be expected from family preservation programs. While it is clear that a few weeks or months of family preservation services cannot prevent the family having further problems in the future, the outcomes that can be reasonably expected, and for which programs should be held accountable, are still being debated. With little control over intake into the programs or decisions made after the case is closed, family preservation programs have found it hard to demonstrate impressive rates of placement prevention, when compared to other services currently available to families. Although family preservation services do not appear to place children at additional risk, neither do they guarantee a reduction in the rate of repeated maltreatment (Nelson & Landsman, 1992; Schuerman, Rzepnicki, & Littell, 1994; Yuan & Struckman-Johnson, 1991).

Perhaps the greatest difficulty facing family preservation programs, however, is surviving in inhospitable agency environments. Traditional child welfare services have a distinctly different orientation and way of working with families, which is sometimes directly at odds with family preservation programs. Large and rule-bound bureaucracies are difficult to change and often smother innovation and good practice. Workers in family preservation programs may face rigid personnel practices, tight budgets, and hostility from other workers in the agency who have large caseloads and little training or support. An ecological perspective and empowerment practices need to extend through all levels of the agency for family preservation services to survive and prosper in public social services.

EXPANDING THE VISION OF FAMILY PRESERVATION

Family preservation principles, practices, and values are spreading in several directions. Building on the success of well-defined program models, agencies are beginning to explore programs with varying lengths and intensity of service to meet families' differing needs. For example, the state of Maryland has expanded the Intensive Family Service model to include a continuum of child welfare services in its *Families Now* initiative.

Families Now

Families Now provides four levels of family preservation services that respond to different levels of family need. Level I, traditional IFS services, provides up to 3 months of service to caseloads of six families; Level II involves up to 6 months of service with caseloads of 10; Level III, continuing child protective services, can serve families for up to 1 year with caseloads of 15; and in Level IV, family reunification workers provide services to five families for an average of 6 months to return children or make another permanent plan (Jackson, 1993). Flexible funds are available to the professional/paraprofessional teams that work at each level.

The *Families Now* initiative also funds Family Support Centers in Maryland to provide more preventive, earlier intervention. The purpose of these centers is to help parents become self-sufficient and self-supporting through the development of life-planning and parenting skills and to access community resources before families reach a state of crisis (Jackson, 1993).

Family Unity

Building natural support networks in the community is also a focus of the Family Unity Model, developed from an audit of the "best practices" in child protective services in the state of Oregon. This search for strengths generated cooperation, positive energy, and creativity, and became a model for practice with families. The goal of Family Unity is to strengthen families and protect children while avoiding placement by engaging the resources and creativity of families, friends, relatives, and communities. Based on the values and beliefs of family preservation, the Family Unity Model is oriented toward strengths and solutions, focuses on "issues of concern" rather than "problems," and helps families develop choices and options (Graber & Nice, 1991). Workers' respect for different types of families and their traditions and the involvement of extended families and communities make this an especially appropriate model for working with families of color. It is similar to the method originally developed in New Zealand to work with Maori families and to Speck and Attneave's network intervention that incorporates the strengths of the tribe in Native American cultures (Halevy, 1993).

Originating in the context of deficit-oriented child protective services, the Family Unity meeting is the primary way services are provided in this model. Although implementation varies from program to program, the usual procedure when faced with a critical decision such as placement or reunification of a child is to call a meeting of the family and their support system. The family decides who is to be invited, bringing in neighbors, relatives, friends, and other service providers to help them come up with the best thinking to resolve the issues of concern (Graber & Nice, 1991).

In the meeting, each participant identifies what worries them about the situation and acknowledges what is going well in the family. If professionals are facilitating the meeting, they may help the group achieve consensus on the purpose of the meeting; listen for, clarify, and record concerns and strengths; and ask participants to identify possible resources and solutions. They may also, after asking permission from the group, offer options for them to consider. The outcome of the meeting, in addition to a decision about placement or reunification, is a Touchpoint agreement that records each person's part in helping the family and ensuring the safety of the child (Graber & Nice, 1991).

Because the plan resulting from a Family Unity meeting builds on family strengths, rather than uncovering and dwelling on problems, and reflects solutions chosen by the family, it evokes energy, creativity, and commitment and gives the family credit for positive results. The Family Unity Model is now used statewide and one county in Oregon has reported a 35% reduction in the number of children in foster care (Graber & Nice, 1991).

System-Wide Innovation

Perhaps the most exciting extension of the family preservation philosophy is the effort in several states to change the way they work with families throughout the human services system. Currently at least 16 states and jurisdictions are adopting a comprehensive, family-centered approach in their child welfare systems (Flint, 1993). This involves redirecting services toward the whole family, seeing families as allies with strengths and competencies, developing proactive and preventive services, and involving the community in protecting children and supporting families. These changes involve all aspects of agency functioning including mission, management, communications, policies and procedures, external relationships, and information systems (Flint, 1993).

The reforms instituted in Idaho illustrate the changes in philosophy and practice necessary to transform the current fragmented systems into an integrated family-centered system. In 1985, Idaho's poor performance on an audit of compliance with the Adoption Assistance and Child Welfare Act of 1980 precipitated a gradual shift from a "rescue"-based child protection and juvenile justice system to a family-centered model. Deciding to pursue system-wide reform rather than to add family preservation as another categorical program, the state integrated child protective, juvenile justice, child mental health, JOBS, adoption, and substance abuse services into a single family-centered practice model with a common administrative structure (Patterson, 1992).

The philosophical cornerstones of the new system are that

- all decisions must be based on client need;
- all clients have strengths, value, worth, and dignity that must be respected;
- staff are valued professionals with decision-making capability and power.

The agency treats staff the same way they are expected to treat families and children, including recognition and respect for individual strengths and values and for their ability to grow and change.

Seeking to redirect and retrain rather than replace existing staff, Idaho decided on a "bottom-up" process of change that engaged the creativity of line staff as well as management. Increased involvement of other service providers in treatment teams led to a sharing of clinical skills, innovations, and successes and of responsibility for the risks inherent in family preservation. Schools, police, churches, other agencies, and natural helping systems also helped communities to overcome their initial perception that the agency was abandoning its responsibility to protect children (Patterson, 1992). Whenever possible, the suggestions of community-based advisory groups that include advocates and consumers are implemented and full explanations are provided if they are not (DHHS, 1991, pp. 32, 38).

Extensive training and consultation from the National Resource Center for Family Centered Practice (formerly the National Resource Center on Family Based Services) and others assisted the agency in changing its practice. Management and supervisory staff received 2 weeks of training, direct service and supervisory staff attended a 50-hour course, and all new direct service staff complete a 4-week academy (Patterson, 1992). In addition, clinical consultation is available in all areas of the state. To reinforce the skills learned in training, consultants are hired directly as part of the service teams.

Work units now contain staff from all program areas (from JOBS to adoption) and apply a team approach to serving families. The type and level of services (i.e., intensity) are individualized to each family's needs and may be provided by anyone on the team. For the most part, the "mental health" staff provide the more intensive services commonly associated with family preservation. However, *all* staff, regardless of function, are grounded in the principles of a family-centered approach: an ecological and strengths-based perspective and collaborative relationships with families. In addition to extensive training and consultation, the state provides personal computers for every two line staff and maintains ongoing caseloads at about 15 families per worker. Workers can also authorize services without higher level signoffs and have access to flexible funds to meet family needs.

These changes in practice preceded administrative changes in rules and procedures. The system was allowed to evolve for several years before changes were codified in manual form. Policy and practice guidelines were deliberately avoided at the beginning so that once staff had developed substantive knowledge and skills through training, their experience could be incorporated into policy development. In addition, many agency procedures including payment systems, caseload standards, work hours, and supervision methods were radically modified. The developmental nature of the process accommodated differences in individuals' and work units' adaptation to the new practices. Gradual changes in client satisfaction, spending patterns, staff turnover, and dependence on placement were taken as indicators of progress.

In keeping with the collaborative relationships throughout the system, administrative reviews of local offices are directed toward solving problems and improving practice rather than enforcing procedures. Although reviews are required only every 18 months, local offices often request them more frequently (DHHS, 1991, p. 33). Management values staff input and tolerates mistakes without instilling fear of punishment. In return, management involvement is seen by staff as "helping to get us better at what we are supposed to be doing" rather than as intrusive or hierarchical (DHHS, 1991, p. 34). Less than 10% of the staff are located in the state office and they may be temporarily deployed to regional or local offices to cover cases, since meeting family needs takes priority over bureaucratic functions (DHHS, 1991, pp. 19–25).

Within the seven regional offices, Program Committees are the main planning, problem-solving, and decision-making bodies. The committees include regional program managers, bureau chiefs, and administrators and each appoints a liaison to the statewide Field Operations Council. The committees work on a consensus basis and continue discussion until all committee members can support and agree to implement a decision.

The overall success of these efforts can be measured by high staff morale, family satisfaction with services, and a decline in new placements from 2613 in 1985 to 929 in 1993, a period when most other states were experiencing increasing placement rates (K. Patterson, personal communication, August 1994). Staff report improved coordination, a more open work environment, increased flexibility and creativity, and a greater sense of accomplishment (DHHS, 1991, p. 3). Workers are held accountable for family involvement in decision making, which is seen as essential to empowerment and a contrast to previous practice. "Before, we would have said families don't want to be involved; now we realize we just didn't know how to do it." "If given an opportunity, families will participate" (DHHS, 1991, p. 14). Families can and do call for help after their case is closed and can receive services without becoming an active case again.

Despite these advances, staff shortages require that priority for services be given to the most serious situations: children who are suicidal, seriously mentally ill, sex offenders, in imminent danger, or in danger of being removed from their families. Less serious cases of abuse, neglect, or parent–child conflict are screened out. "It is not prevention or early intervention--not until Mom acts on her feelings does CPS intervene" (DHHS, 1991, p. 7). Although workers are active in developing services such as support groups and parenting classes, effective work with other providers, advocacy, and community groups is limited by staffing, time, and energy constraints (DHHS, 1991, p. 9). More extensive work with providers of contracted services who do not have a family-centered approach is an ongoing need. In particular, Court Appointed Special Advocates, who are charged with protecting the rights of children, disagree with the idea that child protection includes working to avoid out-of-home placement (DHHS, 1991, pp. 39, 51). Development of more adequate placement resources is recognized as another unmet but high priority need (DHHS, 1991, p. 11).

REPLICATING INNOVATIVE PRACTICE

Idaho's experience illustrates many aspects of successful replication of innovative practice. First, it involved replicating concepts, rather than specific programs. Most suited to changing large organizations, concept replication is also appropriate given limited new funding and the advantages of "bottom-up" innovations that promote consumer choice (Finney, 1993, p. 44). Idaho focused on adapting the general components and principles of family-centered practice to the local context, changing the organizational culture, and monitoring adherence to these principles (Finney, 1993, pp. 3, 10). This approach contrasts with the top-down "cookie cutter" method of replication, implemented by franchising programs or mandating the adoption of specific models.

Second, the innovative practice was introduced by an outside "champion" (Smale, 1993), the National Resource Center on Family Based Services (NRCFBS), which was involved in the creation of the new approach. NRCFBS training supported a widespread value orientation compatible with family-centered practice, provided examples of sites where these practices were successfully implemented, and promoted their adoption in Idaho. The actual decision to change to a family-centered model of practice, however, responded to a local need and was championed by top managers. Although change was not initiated by them, the managers were committed to the concepts and saw their role in creating change as extending beyond the usual expectations of their job (Finney, 1993, pp. 35, 42).

Other factors that promoted successful replication included an administrative structure that established a multisite network to share information and experience, a flexible and supportive field management staff who worked to maintain and improve standards of family-centered practice (Finney, 1993, pp. 16–17), and on-going training and technical assistance both at the state and local levels (Finney, 1993, pp. 19, 21).

Idaho also experienced some of the common barriers to concept replication. It takes a long time to successfully implant new concepts, and outcomes are seldom measurable. Limited funds and a lack of preparation and knowledge about the localities in which family-centered practice was introduced resulted in opposition to family-centered work by some organizations and communities (Finney, 1993, pp. 22–28, 32–33). Despite these barriers, Idaho has been successful in implementing the philosophy of family-centered work using "a sophisticated combination of central design and local choice, and useful training and technical assistance" (Finney, 1993, pp. ii, 39).

It is clear that creating a family-centered service delivery system is not an easy task for large state agencies. And yet, those agencies that have pursued such a change firmly believe that they are on the right track. Their only question is the best route to follow in accomplishing their goal. To quote Idaho's Ken Patterson (1992):

> Continual threats are present which can arrest or even reverse agency movement toward Family Centered Practice. These threats include child death or injury in a family receiving preservation services, crimes against others perpetrated by an adolescent..., and fiscal crisis. Top management must anticipate and strategically prepare for such threats. (p. 7)

As part of this preparation, administrators must work closely with the media, the legislature, the courts, and other human service providers, both public and private. They must continue to support and empower their staff to do good practice and they must ensure staff access to state-of-the-art training, supervision, and consultation in this process. Finally, agencies must begin to involve consumers in planning services for constructive feedback and a fresh perspective on program development.

CONCLUSION

The development of family-centered systems such as Idaho's provide considerable encouragement to others seeking new approaches to child welfare practice. These extensions of the family preservation model are also consonant with the goals of the new federal Family Preservation and Support Services Program established in 1993 "to promote family strength and stability, enhance parental functioning and protect children" through broadly defined family preservation and support services (Allen, Kakavas, & Zalenski, 1994, p. 1). The comprehensive, community-based planning process mandated in the legislation is expected to be a catalyst to create a "continuum of coordinated and integrated, culturally relevant, family focused services for children and families" (Allen, Kakavas, & Zalenski, 1994, p. 1).

The evolution of family preservation from its original focus on intensive services for at-risk families in the child welfare system to integration with community-based family support services has been remarkably rapid, enabled by many actors. Progress from the vaguely defined "reasonable efforts" provisions of the 1980 Adoption Assistance and Child Welfare Act to the comprehensive, community-based continuum of services for children and families envisioned by the Family Preservation and Support Services Program could be measured in centuries. Certainly within the context of child welfare history, this is a paradigm shift comparable to the development of child protection and foster family care in the nineteenth century. However, learning to build on the strengths of diverse families and communities and to avoid blaming and separating children from them will pose challenges for family-centered practice well into the next century.

REFERENCES

Allen, M., Kakavas, A., & Zalenski, J. (1994, Spring). Family preservation and support services: Omnibus Budget Reconciliation Act of 1993. *The Prevention Report*, pp. 1–3.

Barth, R.P. (1990). Theories guiding home-based intensive family preservation services. In J. K. Whittaker, Kinney, J., Tracy E. M., & Booth, C. (Eds.), *Reaching high risk families: Intensive family preservation services in human services* (pp. 89–112). Hawthorne, NY: Aldine de Gruyter.

Bath, H.I., & Haapala, D.A. (1994). Family preservation services: What does the outcome research *really* tell us? *Social Service Review, 68*, 386–403.

Berry, M. (1992). An evaluation of family preservation services: Fitting agency services to family needs. *Social Work, 37*, 314–321.

Cautley, P.W. (1979). *The home and community treatment process: A look at four groups providing intensive in-home services.* Unpublished manuscript, Wisconsin Department of Health and Social Services, Madison.

Child Welfare League of America. (1989). *Standards for service to strengthen and preserve families with children*. Washington, DC: Child Welfare League of America.

Department of Health and Human Services [DHHS]. (1991). *Child welfare services program review: Idaho*. Region X. Washington, DC: Author.

Feldman, L.H. (1991). Evaluating the impact of intensive family preservation services in New Jersey. In K. Wells & D. A. Biegel (Eds.), *Family preservation services: Research and evaluation* (pp. 47–71). Newbury Park, CA: Sage.

Finney, G.S. (1993). *Building from strength: Replication as a strategy for expanding social programs that work.* Philadelphia, PA: The Conservation Company.

Flint, S. (1993). *Family-centered child welfare services: A national overview of jurisdictions that have adopted a systemic family centered approach.* Prepared for the Vermont Department of Social and Rehabilitation Services. New England Association of Child Welfare Commissioners and Directors.

Fraser, M.W., Pecora, P.J., & Haapala, D.A. (1991). *Families in crisis: The impact of intensive family preservation services*. Hawthorne, NY: Aldine de Gruyter.

Froelich, P.K. (1992). *An analysis of change in placements and investigations associated with home based services*. South Dakota Department of Social Services.

General Accounting Office [GAO]. (1989). *Foster care: Incomplete implementation of the reforms and unknown effectiveness*. Washington, DC: United States General Accounting Office.

General Accounting Office [GAO]. (1993). *Foster care: Services to prevent out-of-home placements are limited by funding barriers*. Washington, DC: United States General Accounting Office.

Graber, L., & Nice, J. (1991, Fall). The Family Unity Model: The advanced skill of looking for and building on strengths. *Prevention Report*, pp. 3–4.

Haapala, D. (1983). *Perceived helpfulness, attributed critical incident responsibility, and a discrimination of home-based family therapy treatment outcomes: Homebuilders model*. Final Report prepared for the Department of Health and Human Services, Administration for Children, Youth and Families.

Halevy, J. (1993). Bigger can be better: Social network intervention with families in acute distress. In M. Forgy & J. Zamosky (Eds.), *Empowering families: Papers from the Sixth Annual Conference on Family-Based Services* (pp. 37–49). Cedar Rapids, IA: National Association for Family-Based Services.

Henggeler, S.W., Rodick, J.D., Borduin, C.M., Hanson, C.L., Watson, S.M., & Urey, J.R. (1986). Multisystemic treatment of juvenile offenders: Effects on adolescent behavior and family interactions. *Developmental Psychology, 58*, 336–344.

Horejsi, C.R. (1981). The St. Paul Family-Centered Project revisited: Exploring an old gold mine. In M. Bryce & J. Lloyd (Eds.), *Treating families in the home: An alternative to placement* (pp. 12–23). Springfield, IL: Charles C Thomas.

Institute for Social and Economic Development. (1993). *An evaluation of Families First of Minnesota*. Iowa City, IA: Author.

Jackson, S.M. (1993, November). *Families now! Expanding the family preservation model*. Paper presented at the 7th Annual National Association for Family-Based Services Conference, Fort Lauderdale, FL.

Kinney, J., Haapala, D., Madsen, B., & Fleming, T. (1977). Homebuilders: Keeping families together. *Journal of Counseling and Consulting Psychology, 14*, 209–213.

Maryland Department of Human Resources. (1987). *Intensive family services: A family preservation service delivery model*. Baltimore: Author.

McCroskey, J., & Meezan, W. (1993). *Outcomes of home based services: Effects on family functioning, child behavior, and child placement*. Los Angeles, CA: University of Southern California, School of Social Work.

McGowan, B.G. (1983). Historical evolution of child welfare services: An examination of the sources of current problems and dilemmas. In B.G. McGowan & W. Meezan (Eds.), *Child welfare: Current dilemmas, future directions* (pp. 45–92). Itasca, IL: Peacock.

National Center on Child Abuse and Neglect. (1988). *Study of national incidence and prevalence of child abuse and neglect: 1988*. Washington, DC: U.S. Department of Health and Human Services.

Nelson, K., Emlen, A., Landsman, M., & Hutchinson, J. (1988). *Factors contributing to success and failure in family-based child welfare services*. Iowa City, IA: The University of Iowa, National Resource Center on Family Based Services.

Nelson, K.E., & Hunter, R.W. (1993, October). *Empowering families through home-based services*. Paper presented at the Education and Research for Empowerment Conference, Seattle, WA.

Nelson, K.E., & Landsman, M.J. (1992). *Alternative models of family preservation: Family-based services in context*. Springfield, IL: Charles C Thomas.

Nelson, K., Landsman, M., & Deutelbaum, W. (1990). Three models of family-centered placement prevention services. *Child Welfare, 69*, 3–21.

Nelson, K.E., Landsman, M.J., Tyler, M., & Richardson, B. (1995). *Costs and outcomes in two intensive family services programs*. Iowa City, IA: The University of Iowa, National Resource Center for Family Centered Practice.

Patterson, K. (1992, Spring). Investing in an agency's "work family": Idaho's experience in implementing a family-centered practice model. *Prevention Report*, pp. 6–7.

Pearson, C.L., & King, P.A. (1987). *Intensive family services: Evaluation of foster care in Maryland*. Baltimore, MD: Maryland Department of Human Resources.

Pecora, P.J., Whittaker, J.K., & Maluccio, A.N. (1992). *The child welfare challenge: Policy, practice, and research*. Hawthorne, NY: Aldine de Gruyter.

Reid, W.J., Kagan, R.M., & Schlosberg, S.B. (1988). Prevention of placement: Critical factors in program success. *Child Welfare, 67*, 25–88.

Schuerman, J.R., Rzepnicki, T.L., & Littell, J.H. (1994). *Putting families first: An experiment in family preservation*. Hawthorne, NY: Aldine de Gruyter.

Schwartz, I.M., AuClaire, P., & Harris, L.J. (1991). Family preservation services an alternative to the out-of-home placement of adolescents. In K. Wells & D.E. Biegel (Eds.), *Family preservation services: Research and evaluation* (pp. 33–46). Newbury Park, CA: Sage.

Smale, G.G. (1993). The nature of innovation and community-based practice. In E.E. Brawley (Ed.), *Transferring technology in the personal social services* (pp. 14–26). Washington, DC: NASW.

Stein, T.J. (1991). *Child welfare and the law.* New York: Longman.

Szykula, S.A., & Fleischman, M.J. (1985). Reducing out-of-home placements of abused children: Two controlled field studies. *Child Abuse and Neglect, 9,* 277–283.

University Associates. (1993). *Evaluation of Michigan's Families First program: Summary report.* Lansing, MI: Author.

Yuan, Y.T., & Struckman-Johnson, D.L. (1991). Placement outcomes for neglected children with prior placements in family preservation programs. In K. Wells & D.E. Biegel (Eds.), *Family preservation services: Research and evaluation* (pp. 92–120). Newbury Park, CA: Sage.

6

Self-Employment Training and Family Development: An Integrated Strategy for Family Empowerment

SALOME RAHEIM

Helping families and communities meet the needs of their members has become the primary goal of a number of human service programs. Many human services agencies have adopted empowerment principles to guide their interventions and empowerment practice has become a subject of increasing interest among the helping professions.

Many of these human service programs focus on the economic context of empowerment, as the goal of recent welfare reform efforts is to help poor families achieve economic self-sufficiency. However, conventional social welfare programs rely primarily on education and job training to promote economic self-sufficiency. These types of programs are limited to microlevel interventions and, while they may provide new knowledge and skills for program participants, they do not address any of the structural issues (e.g., lack of jobs in a community and high rates of underemployment) that obstruct the efforts of poor families striving for economic self-sufficiency. Therefore, strategies to create economic opportunities must be used in tandem with more traditional interventions.

While usually considered to be outside the domain of human service agencies, economic development interventions can operate on both the microlevel and the macrolevel to help poor families develop new competencies while creating economic opportunities. One strategy that operates on both levels is self-employment development. This chapter describes the Small Enterprise and Family Development Project (SEFaD) that combines self-employment development with family-centered services to promote economic self-sufficiency in poor families.

Before discussing this project, the concept that provides its philosophical framework, empowerment, is examined.

EMPOWERMENT THEORY

A number of theorists and practitioners in a variety of fields have sought to define empowerment and to identify general practice principles (Dunst, Trivette, & Lapointe, 1992; Gutierrez, 1989, 1990; Hegar & Hunzeker, 1988; Kieffer, 1984; Parsons, 1991; Zimmerman, 1990). Many have focused on empowerment with specific populations, such as African-Americans (Solomon, 1976), Latinos (Gutierrez & Ortega, 1991), women (Gutierrez, 1987), women of color (Gutierrez, 1990), citizens with disabilities (Checkoway & Norsman, 1986), adolescent girls (Simmons & Parsons, 1983a; 1983b), and senior citizens (McDermott, 1989; Parsons & Cox, 1989). These efforts have resulted in a variety of definitions.

While the literature commonly discusses empowerment as a principle, a process, and an outcome, a useful framework for understanding the many aspects of empowerment is presented by Dunst, Trivette, and Lapointe (1992). Their framework, based on an extensive review of the literature, includes six dimensions: (1) philosophy, (2) paradigm, (3) process, (4) partnership, (5) performance, and (6) perception. These dimensions are summarized in Table 6.1.

From the vantage point of practice, this framework suggests that philosophy and paradigm determine the guiding principles and perspective of an intervention. The philosophy and paradigm are evidenced in the nature of the client–worker relationship (partnership) and in the types

Table 6.1. Major Dimensions, Key Elements, and Exemplars of Empowerment

Dimensions	*Key Elements*	*Exemplars*
Philosophy	Principles	Presumed capabilities of people, valuing diversity
Paradigm	Properties	Strengths-based, proactive, mastery orientation
Process	Enabling experiences	Learning opportunities and events
Partnership	Collaboration	Mutual respect, shared decision-making, cooperation
Performance	Behaviors/capacities	Knowledge, skills, personal growth, affiliate behavior
Perceptions	Attributions	Self-efficacy, personal control, self-esteem, locus-of-control, political efficacy

From Dunst, C.J., Trivette, C.M., & Lapointe, N., 1992. Toward clarification of the meaning and key elements of empowerment. *Family Science Review*, 5(1&2), 119. Copyright 1992 by *Family Science Review*. Reprinted with permission.

of experiences the intervention makes available to the client (process). The desired outcomes of an empowerment intervention are an increase in knowledge, skills, and proficiencies and in clients' perceptions of self-efficacy. Thus, Dunst, Trivette, and Lapointe's (1992) framework refines the broad conceptualization of empowerment as principle, process, and outcome found in the literature.

In addition to identifying these six dimensions of empowerment and the elements of each, Dunst, Trivette, and Lapointe (1992) discuss the importance of level of analysis and context in conceptualizing empowerment. They contend that the application of empowerment principles involves different participatory activities and outcome indicators at each level of analysis (i.e., individual, group, organization, community). They also assert that empowerment is context specific, achieved in particular arenas of human affairs, rather than in a generalized way. Therefore, to increase our understanding of empowerment, we must consider empowerment in specific realms of human activity.

The social work literature identifies several strategies that are central to empowering interventions applicable at various system levels (i.e., individuals, groups, communities, organizations) and in a variety of contexts including human services (Hasenfeld & Chesler, 1989), public schools (Gruber & Trickett, 1987), and nursing homes (McDermott, 1989). These strategies and their corresponding dimensions from Dunst, Trivette, and Lapointe's (1992) framework are listed:

- creating a helping relationship based on trust, mutual respect, and shared power (partnership);
- recognizing the client systems' abilities to know what they need and to choose adequate solutions for themselves (philosophy and paradigm);
- identifying and building upon existing strengths (paradigm and process);
- engaging in critical thinking with client systems (process);
- teaching specific knowledge and skills (process);
- creating a group context for mutual support and mutual aid (process); and
- mobilizing resources and advocating for client systems (paradigm).

These strategies are an integral part of the interventions in the SEFaD. The next section discusses the origins of the project's interventions and examines the empowerment dimensions of these interventions.

THE FAMILY DEVELOPMENT MODEL

Family development is an intensive case management model that emerged out of the field of family-based services. It was pioneered by Mid-Iowa Community Action (MICA), a community action agency in east central Iowa. Family development is designed to help low-income families build on their strengths and achieve economic independence. This model of working with families focuses on mastery and optimization as opposed to treatment and prevention. Hence, the principles of family development are congruent with empowerment philosophy (Dunst, Trivette, & Thompson, 1991).

Participation in family development programs is voluntary, and programs may be sponsored by social service, mental health, or educational organizations. Services are provided by family development specialists who use a family systems theoretical framework to assist families in identifying their strengths, setting goals, removing obstacles, and developing the competencies they need to achieve their goals. Toward these ends, family development specialists work in partnership with families. This model of intervention involves (1) engaging in an assessment with families of their needs and strengths, including preparing ecomaps and genograms, and (2) working with families to build their vision of the future, develop specific goals, identify the tasks and resources required to achieve them, and outline a time line for task completion. The intervention may take place in families' homes, groups, or agency-based activities.

The family development model was expanded statewide in 1987 when the Iowa General Assembly established a Family Development and Self-Sufficiency Grant Program and funded 10 project sites. Using family development as the primary intervention, these projects were designed to help families receiving Aid to Families with Dependent Children (AFDC) and "at risk" of long-term welfare receipt to achieve greater self-sufficiency. Factors that were used to identify families as "at risk" included (1) the head of household had less than 8 years of education; (2) the head of household was female or had three or more children with at least one preschool age child; (3) the head of household was a teenager at the birth of her first child; (4) the family had multiple episodes of welfare assistance or had received welfare for 3 years or more. The selection of these factors, as well as much of the philosophy and design of these projects, was based on the findings of three bodies of research: Bane and Ellwood's (1985) characteristics of families receiving AFDC, Gueron and Pauley's (1991) evaluation of welfare-to-work programs, and Schorr's (1988) analysis of exemplary programs that have been successful in helping disadvantaged families and children (Bruner, Berryhill, & Lambert, 1992).

Use of the family development model expanded nationally when the University of Iowa School of Social Work's National Resource Center on Family Based Services, in cooperation with MICA and other Iowa community action agencies, developed a curriculum to certify family development specialists. The National Resource Center has trained more than 1,500 family development specialists in 16 states over the past 7 years.

SELF-EMPLOYMENT DEVELOPMENT IN THE UNITED STATES

Self-employment development in the United States was inspired by the long and successful history of microenterprise in developing countries. Newer initiatives in Europe have also met with much success (Balkin, 1989). Self-employment or microenterprise development has proven to be a viable approach to creating economic opportunity for many low-income and unemployed people in the United States (Else & Raheim, 1992). Currently, there are over 200 organizations that operate self-employment development programs in the United States. These include community action agencies, community development corporations, women's organizations, refugee organizations, and single-purpose microenterprise groups. Seventy-one percent serve low-income and unemployed persons in general, while others are targeted at more specific groups (e.g., moderate to low-income women, Native Americans, AFDC recipients, displaced homemakers, dislocated workers, Southeast Asian refugees) (Clark & Huston, 1994).

Many self-employment programs include both business training and lending components, while others have only one of these program elements. Among programs that provide training, there is a great deal of diversity. The training may include business plan preparation, business management, self-esteem training, and personal financial management. The training may be in formal classroom settings, in peer lending groups (described below), and/or in internship and mentoring programs.

Lending programs also operate in a variety of ways. Most microenterprise lending organizations maintain their own revolving loan fund. Some programs provide loans to individuals. Others provide loans only through self-selected peer-lending groups modeled after the Grameen Bank in Bangladesh, an innovative, government-owned, grass-roots controlled bank organized specifically to encourage microenterprise by making small business loans (Yunus, 1988). Peer lending substitutes accountability to one's peers for collateral, since most low-income individuals have no assets to serve as collateral. In organizations such as the Lakota Fund in South Dakota, peer group members must co-sign each other's loans and one group member must begin repaying the loan before other group members are eligible to borrow funds. Other peer lending programs include the Women's Self-Employment Project in Chicago, Working Capital in New Hampshire, the Coalition for Women's Economic Development (CWED) in Los Angeles, and the Good Faith Fund in Arkansas (Clark, Huston, & Meister, 1994).

Self-employment programs in the United States were initiated by several types of agencies using funding from diverse sources. As early as 1986, community action agencies in New York and Vermont began operating self-employment programs for low-income people with funding under the Demonstration Partnership Program of the Office of Community Services, Department of Health and Human Services. The success of these demonstration projects supports the viability of self-employment programs for public assistance recipients (U.S. Department of Health and Human Services, 1990).

Similarly, some of the most innovative Community Development Corporations (CDCs) started small enterprise development programs for low-income citizens, also with funding from the Office of Community Services. CDCs are neighborhood or regionally based economic development organizations formed in the 1960s as part of the antipoverty program. CDCs in many states, including Indiana, Ohio, and Maine, developed small enterprise programs as an extension of their traditional focus on housing and physical development of business districts in impoverished neighborhoods (Puls, 1988).

Women's economic development organizations emerged in the 1980s to encourage female business ownership by providing access to credit, business training, and technical assistance with sensitivity to the concerns and needs of women. Among these organizations are WomenVenture (formerly the Women's Economic Development Corporation) in St. Paul, Women's Self-Employment Project in Chicago, Women's Initiative for Self-Employment in San Francisco, the Entrepreneurial Center for Women in Hartford, and CWED in Los Angeles. Some of these organizations serve women of all economic levels, while others focus on assisting low-income women. Many were started with funding from foundations and corporations, such as the Stanley Foundation, the Mott Foundation, and the Ms. Foundation.

The first U.S. program to use transfer payments to fund self-employment was the Self-Employment and Enterprise Development Demonstration (SEED) Project modeled after its European predecessor, the

British Enterprise Allowance Scheme. With funding of $2.75 million from the U.S. Department of Labor, Washington State Employment Security and the Department of Trade and Economic Development sponsored SEED in 1989. Individuals eligible to receive unemployment insurance who volunteered to participate in this program were randomly assigned to a treatment or control group. The treatment group was given business training and, after completing all training requirements, group members were given the option to receive their remaining unemployment insurance benefits in a lump sum payment to finance their business. Preliminary results indicate that of the 755 (60%) treatment group members, 451 started 350 businesses and generated 113 new jobs in addition to their own (Benus, Johnson, & Wood, 1994; Johnson & Leonard, 1991). The results of this demonstration and a similar one in Massachusetts are encouraging and have stimulated calls for legislative changes in unemployment insurance regulations.

The first national, publicly funded microenterprise program for low-income people initiated in the United States was the Self-Employment Investment Demonstration (SEID) Program. The program was a result of the efforts of the Corporation for Enterprise Development to bring to the United States some of the benefits of microenterprise programs for low-income people that had been successfully implemented in other countries (Guy, Doolittle, & Fink, 1991). Specifically, it was designed to (1) test the viability of self-employment as an economic self-sufficiency strategy for AFDC recipients, and (2) remove the policy barriers that prevent AFDC recipients from moving to economic independence, using, for example, income waivers to prevent reduction of participants' AFDC grants due to income generated during their first year of business operation.

Five states participated in this demonstration program—Iowa, Michigan, Minnesota, Mississippi, and Maryland. Programs in the five states were implemented by various types of local program operators including a small business development center, a community college, a community action organization, and self-employment development organizations. These local program operators provided self-employment training, counseling, technical assistance, direct loans or aid in gaining access to credit, as well as assistance in getting waivers of the AFDC rules to allow program participants to keep their business income without jeopardizing their AFDC grants for the first year of operation of their businesses.

In Iowa, SEID was operated by the Institute for Social and Economic Development (ISED), a nonprofit corporation founded in 1987 with a mission to facilitate the empowerment of disadvantaged persons through the integration of social and economic development strategies.

ISED piloted SEID in 12 Iowa counties that included both urban and rural areas. Some have argued that self-employment training programs for AFDC recipients merely "skim," i.e., reach those who are already better off, who have been on welfare for a short time, and who are likely to get off on their own. The opposite proved to be true for ISED. Whereas 11% of the AFDC population in the 12-county pilot area had received benefits for more than 2 years, 64% of ISED's participants had received AFDC benefits for at least 2 years, nearly six times their representation in the general AFDC population (Else, 1991).

ISED's participants were predominantly divorced women in their 30s with high school diplomas or equivalents. Most had three or more children and would have been eligible for AFDC for at least 5 more years because the oldest child was 13 years old or younger. The proportion of minority participants was slightly higher than their representation in the AFDC population in the pilot areas. In short, most participants in the ISED self-employment program were not individuals who were better off than the general AFDC population.

During the implementation of SEID, it became clear that families experienced many problems associated with poverty that had to be overcome for them to become economically self-sufficient through self-employment. According to the interim evaluation of SEID conducted by the Manpower Demonstration Research Corporation, many clients needed support services, such as child care and transportation, to complete the training program. Unlike members of higher income groups who are interested in pursuing self-employment, these participants had to overcome the disempowering effects of receiving public assistance to complete the training program and launch their own business ventures (Guy, Doolittle, & Fink, 1991).

In response to the lessons learned from SEID, ISED, and MICA, Southeast Iowa Community Action Organization (SEICAO) designed an integrated strategy to provide both self-employment training and family development to AFDC recipients. SEFaD was the result of this partnership.

AN INTEGRATED STRATEGY FOR ECONOMIC EMPOWERMENT

SEFaD was a 2-year demonstration project, implemented in 1990 with federal funding from the Department of Health and Human Services, Administration for Children and Families, Demonstration Partnership Program. The purpose of the project was to assist AFDC recipients in nine Iowa counties to attain economic self-sufficiency by providing self-employment and family development services. The project defined self-sufficiency as earned self-employment income in an amount that made the family ineligible for AFDC. This project was the first in the nation to integrate the strategies of family development and small enterprise development (Yarbrough, 1993). An important feature of this project was that AFDC waivers were granted to program participants so that business loans they received, business income they generated, or assets they accumulated would not make them ineligible for AFDC during the first year of business operation. Without these waivers, most participants who started businesses would have been immediately ineligible for AFDC, although they could not have used their business loans, income, and assets to support their families and simultaneously build a successful business. The family development and self-employment development interventions occurred simultaneously. The family development intervention began early in participants' contact with the project and continued until the demonstration was completed. The self-employment training intervention had five distinct components: (1) recruitment and orientation, (2) assessment, (3) business plan preparation, (4) loan acquisition and business opening, and (5) on-going monitoring and technical assistance. Various techniques for facilitating the personal empowerment of participants were employed throughout all components.

Recruitment and Orientation

Potential participants were recruited for the program through mailings sent by the Iowa Department of Human Services, referrals from local JOBS programs, articles and advertisements in local news media, and referrals from education, training, economic development, and social service organizations. Interested individuals attended a 6-hour informational meeting in which a business trainer explained how the program worked, as well as the risks, the demands, and the rewards of small business ownership. The business trainers had owned their own businesses and were familiar with the business communities in which the participants would establish their businesses. After the informational meeting, participants decided whether self-employment was a viable option for them.

The self-selection process marked the beginning of the empowerment intervention during the training program. Allowing participants to self-select, rather than having staff determine their appropriateness for the program, reinforced participants' abilities to make choices and to determine what course of action was appropriate for them.

During the initial phase of self-employment training, family development specialists explained the family development services and arranged individual meetings with participating families. The family development specialists were employed by the two partner community action agencies, MICA and SEICAO, and had completed family development certification training through the National Resource Center on Family Based Services.

Assessment

Participants who decided to pursue the training attended 3 weeks of business development workshops (four 6-hour days) and had weekly individual meetings with business trainers to work on issues specific to each business idea. Staff did not recommend business ideas for participants. Rather, participants pursued their own business ideas with the assistance of staff.

Participants learned how to conduct a feasibility study of their business idea to determine operating costs, potential markets, advertising needs, pricing strategies, location, inventory, and loan needs. During this and subsequent phases of the program, financial management and self-esteem building were integral parts of the training. The knowledge and skills acquired through the business development workshops (1) built upon the knowledge and skills participants had, (2) reinforced critical thinking skills, (3) taught new skills, and (4) increased participants' ability to make decisions about their economic well-being. The curriculum required a great deal of work outside of the classroom (e.g., interviewing business competitors in their communities or researching product information at the library) and affirmed participants' abilities to be independent and self-directed.

Once participants completed the feasibility study, they were invited to "enroll" in the next phase of the training program. At this point they had collected sufficient information to make an informed decision about the advisability of starting their own businesses. Although business trainers gave participants feedback about their business ideas, the decision to enroll was made by individual participants rather than staff. In this way, the trainers communicated respect, shared power with participants, and affirmed their competence to make decisions affecting their lives.

During the assessment phase of the business training, family development specialists met with participant families in their homes to engage in a broader assessment. At the first several family meetings, family development specialists helped members complete assessment tools, including a genogram, an ecomap, and a time line that outlined pertinent events in the participant's history. Once the assessment process was complete, the family development specialists engaged families in "vision building," during which families identified 3- to 5-year goals. Subsequently, they completed a goal sheet, established a timetable for completing subgoals, and identified the resources needed to accomplish these goals.

Most of the elements required for an empowerment intervention are incorporated in these family development services. The joint assessment and goal setting process helps to create a relationship of trust, mutual respect, and shared power, while it recognizes families' abilities to know what they need and to choose appropriate solutions for themselves. This process also helps families to identify and build upon their strengths and engages them in critical thinking. This problem-solving process teaches the families new skills, as well as identifying the resources they may need to acquire additional knowledge and skills. To gain access to these and other resources, family development specialists may advocate for families or help them advocate for themselves.

Business Plan Preparation

Over the next 10-week period, participants attended weekly 6-hour training workshops in which they learned the various components of a business plan. Each week they conducted a segment of their research and drafted a section of the plan to share with other participants in the classroom and with the trainer in weekly individual conferences. By the end of the 10 weeks, participants had prepared a draft business plan for their proposed enterprise and had opportunities to practice presenting it to others. Over the next 2 to 3 months, the business plan was refined.

The process of business plan preparation and presentation to peers is another important aspect of the empowerment intervention. Participants' self-efficacy is increased by developing a detailed business plan that they are able to articulate and defend. Their sense of power is increased by having developed the plan themselves and their sense of control is increased by having a blueprint that indicates how to move from where they are economically to where they want to be.

The group context in which this process takes place is also significant to the empowerment process. Although participants are focusing on their individual business plans, the program is structured so that they have opportunities to discuss their ideas with peers and get feedback from them. The mutual support developed during training has been of such importance to participants that some have initiated an on-going mutual support group subsequent to their training.

Loan Acquisition and Business Opening

ISED facilitates participant access to loan funds to begin their businesses. There are four types of loan sources: banks, a state low-income loan fund, ISED's loan guarantee fund, and private sources (e.g., participants' families and friends).

Banks. One aspect of ISED's success in promoting self-employment of AFDC recipients has been its ability to involve traditional financial institutions. Whereas many self-employment programs have relied primarily on their own revolving loan funds, ISED's approach to financing has been to encourage its trainees to operate like any other entrepreneur. They are encouraged to establish relationships with commercial lending institutions. AFDC recipients learn how the lending process works and how to work with traditional lenders. Iowa banks have been very responsive to this approach. Of the $380,000 in loans acquired by AFDC recipients in ISED's pilot region, 61% have come from commercial banks. Several banks have established loan pools specifically for program participants. Current commitments of loan pool set-asides total $1.6 million.

State low-income loan fund. The second loan source available to participants is a state-sponsored loan fund for low-income Iowans, administered by the Department of Economic Development. The maximum amount available has recently been increased from $5,000 to $10,000 at an interest rate of 5.25%.

ISED's loan guarantee fund. ISED created a separate, nonprofit corporation, the Self-Employment Fund of Iowa (SEFI), to make partial business loan guarantees available for ISED participants who are unable to get bank loans on the strength of their business plan alone. SEFI is administered by a Board of Trustees composed of individuals from the community, and funds were raised from foundations, businesses, churches, and civic organizations. Decisions to approve SEFI loan guarantees are made by regional advisory committees representing banks, businesses, economic development organizations, and educational, training, and social service organizations. When an advisory committee approves an SEFI loan guarantee, ISED staff negotiate with a local bank for a partial loan guarantee, that is, the local bank takes part of the loan risk and agrees to administer the entire loan. This approach has been very successful in involving traditional financial institutions, stretching SEFI funds, and avoiding the high cost of loan administration.

Private sources. On a national level, many new businesses are financed by family members or friends. ISED encourages its participants to explore this resource for financing. About 10% of participants' business loans come from this source.

On-Going Monitoring and Technical Assistance

Once a business was opened, ISED business trainers maintained contact with these new business owners and provided on-going technical assistance. Affirming participants' ability to know what they need and to choose adequate solutions for themselves, trainers respected their autonomy and offered assistance when it was requested, but did not insist that their recommendations be implemented. If requested, trainers provided information and support regarding financial management, personnel management, advertising and marketing, inventory control, identification of suppliers, and problem solving.

Similar to the partnership between business trainers and the participants, family development specialists maintained their relationships with participants throughout the project. Unlike the business trainer, family development specialists had more intense relationships with participants and focused on a wide variety of issues not directly related to operating the business. Family development specialists continued to support participants in accessing the resources they needed and completing the tasks required to achieve the goals they had developed.

Upon completion of the program, participants have the knowledge and skills needed to start their own businesses, access to capital, and a plan for continued goal attainment for themselves and their families. These are the primary tools they need to exert more control over their economic circumstances as well as other aspects of their lives. In tandem, self-employment training and family development assist families to overcome the debilitating social effects of poverty, while they increase their control over the economic circumstances of their lives.

Third-party evaluation of SEFD revealed that 50 participants completed the program. At the conclusion of the project, 13 participants were in the process of starting businesses and an additional 12 had completed a business plan. Twenty-eight of the 50 started 23 businesses, and two expanded their previously owned, nonprofitable businesses. Twelve of those who had started businesses received loans, ranging from $500 to $14,000 (Yarbrough, 1993). Most participant businesses were service or retail sole proprietorships. These businesses varied greatly and included lawn care and landscaping, janitorial services, food vending, antique and consignment shops, automobile detailing and repair, as well as others.

These outcomes document the ability of this intervention to facilitate the performance dimension of empowerment, allowing participants an opportunity to master new skills and participate in the economy in a way they have selected. Further, participants reported an increase in their knowledge and skills as a result of completing the business training. In both surveys and in-depth interviews conducted by the third-party evaluator, participants reported that the training (1) got them to produce a good business plan and (2) allowed them to learn about all aspects of operating a small business (Yarbrough, 1993). Participant evaluations of their experiences, the business plans completed, and the businesses started all support the utility of this intervention for enhancing the performance dimension of empowerment in an economic context.

Another important outcome of SEFD was an increased sense of self-efficacy, which corresponds to the perception dimension of the Dunst, Trivette, and Lapointe (1992) empowerment framework. In in-depth, open-ended interviews conducted by the third-party evaluator, participants reported an increased sense of self-respect, self-esteem, and sense of being able to contribute to the community. In their words:

> It has helped us know how to get grants and how to apply for loans.
> I respect myself more. I found myself through this program. I feel more confident.
> It's given a lot of self-esteem back to me--I feel I can contribute to the community. (Yarbrough, 1993, p. 13)

Participants' evaluations also support the value of this intervention in facilitating the perception of empowerment among economically disadvantaged families.

CONCLUSION

This integrated strategy of self-employment development and family development illustrates how an empowerment philosophy and paradigm can be used to shape an intervention to facilitate the empowerment of economically disadvantaged families. Although this was a small demonstration project, the findings are encouraging. SEFD documented that self-employment and family development can be integrated to promote both the performance and perception dimensions of empowerment in an economic context.

With shrinking economic opportunities available to low income families due to unemployment and underemployment (U.S. Bureau of the Census, 1992; U.S. Department of Commerce, 1991), the use of microenterprise development as an economic development strategy is growing in the United States. Programs that promote microenterprise development for low-income people help people create economic opportunities for themselves. While not a panacea for the poor, self-employment is an important option for some low-income people. Existing self-employment development programs are using a variety of strategies to assist individuals and families overcome the disempowering effects of poverty and increase their ability to influence their economic circumstances through self-employment. For those interested in family empowerment, self-employment development programs, particularly when combined with family development, provide a rich opportunity to build knowledge about how to help economically disadvantaged families.

REFERENCES

Balkin, S. (1989). *Self-employment for low-income people*. New York: Praeger.

Bane, M.J., & Ellwood, D.T. (1986). Slipping into and out of poverty: The dynamics of spells. *Journal of Human Resources, 21* (Winter), 1–23.

Benus, J.M., Johnson, T.R., & Wood, M. (1994). *First impact analysis of the Washington State Self-Employment Enterprise (SEED) demonstration*. Unemployment Insurance Occasional Paper 94-1. Washington, DC: U.S. Department of Labor Employment and Training Administration Unemployment Insurance Service.

Bruner, C., Berryhill, M., & Lambert, M. (1992). *Making welfare work: A family approach*. Des Moines, IA: Child and Family Policy Center.

Checkoway, B., & Norsman, A. (1986). Empowering citizens with disabilities. *Community Development Journal, 21*, 270–277.

Clark, P., & Huston, T. (1993). *Assisting the smallest businesses: Assessing microenterprise development as a strategy for boosting poor communities*. Washington, DC: Aspen Institute for Humanistic Studies, Self-Employment Learning Project.

Clark, P., Huston, T., & Meister, B. (1994). *1994 directory of micro-enterprise programs*. Washington, DC: Aspen Institute for Humanistic Studies, Self-Employment Learning Project.

Dunst, C.J., Trivette, C.M., & Lapointe, N. (1992). Toward clarification of the meaning and key elements of empowerment. *Family Science Review, 5*(1&2), 111–130.

Dunst, C.J., Trivette, C.M., & Thompson, R.L. (1991). Supporting and strengthening family functioning: Toward a congruence between principles and practice. In D. Unger & D. Powells (Eds.), *Families as nurturing systems: Support across the life span* (pp. 19–44). New York: Haworth Press.

Else, J.F. (1991, December). *Testimony to the Subcommittee on Human Resources, Committee on Ways and Means, U.S. House of Representatives*. Washington, DC

Else, J.F., & Raheim, S. (1992). AFDC clients as entrepreneurs: Self-employment offers an important option. *Public Welfare, 50*, 36–41.

Gruber, J., & Trickett, E.J. (1987). Can we empower others? The paradox of empowerment in the governing of an alternative public school. *American Journal of Community Psychology, 15*, 353–371.

Gueron, J.M., & Pauley, E. (1991). *From welfare to work*. New York: Russell Sage.

Gutierrez, L.M. (1987). Social work theories and practice with battered women: A conflict of values analysis. *Affilia: Journal of Women and Social Work, 2*, 36–52.

Gutierrez, L.M. (1989, March). *Empowerment in social work practice: Considerations for practice and education*. Paper presented at the annual program meeting of the Council on Social Work Education, Chicago, IL.

Gutierrez, L.M. (1990). Working with women of color: An empowerment perspective. *Social Work, 35*, 149–153.

Gutierrez, L.M., & Ortega, R. (1991). Developing methods to empower Latinos: The importance of groups. *Social Work with Groups, 14*, 23–45.

Guy, C., Doolittle, F., & Fink, B. (1991). *Self-employment for welfare recipients: Implementation of the SEID program*. New York: Manpower Demonstration Research Corporation.

Hasenfeld, Y., & Chesler, M.A. (1989). Client empowerment in the human services: Personal and professional agenda. *Journal of Applied Behavioral Science, 24*, 499–521.

Hegar, R., & Hunzeker, J. (1988). Moving toward empowerment-based practice in public child welfare. *Social Work, 33*, 499–501.

Johnson, T., & Leonard, J. (1991). *Washington State Self-Employment and Enterprise Development Demonstration interim report: Implementation and process analysis*. Seattle, WA: Battelle Memorial Institute.

Kieffer, C.H. (1984). Citizen empowerment: A developmental perspective. *Prevention in Human Services, 3* (Winter/Spring), 9–36.

McDermott, C.J. (1989). Empowering the elderly nursing home resident: The resident rights campaign. *Social Work, 34*, 155–157.

Parsons, R.J. (1991). Empowerment: Purpose and practice principle in social work. *Social Work with Groups, 14*, 7–21.

Parsons, R.J., & Cox, E.O. (1989). Family mediation in elder caregiving decisions: An empowerment intervention. *Social Work, 34*, 122–126.

Puls, B. (1988). *From unemployed to self-employed: A program analysis*. Washington, DC: National Conference of State Legislatures.

Schorr, L. B., with Schorr, D. (1988). *Within our reach: Breaking the cycle of disadvantage*. New York: Anchor Press (Doubleday).

Simmons, C., & Parsons, R. (1983a). Developing internality and perceived competence: The empowerment of adolescent girls. *Adolescence, 18*, 917–922.

Simmons, C., & Parsons, R. (1983b). Empowerment for role alternatives in adolescence. *Adolescence, 18*, 193–200.

Solomon, B. (1976). *Black empowerment: Social work in oppressed communities*. New York: Columbia University Press.

U.S. Bureau of the Census. (1992). *Workers with low earnings: 1964–1990*. Current Population Reports, Series P-60, No. 178. Washington, DC: U.S. Government Printing Office.

U.S. Department of Commerce. (1991). *Statistical abstract of the United States* (111th ed.). Washington, DC: U.S. Government Printing Office.

U.S. Department of Health and Human Services, Office of Community Services, Family Support Administration. (1990). *Demonstration Partnership Program: Summaries and findings, FY 1987 Demonstration Partnership Program projects*. Washington, DC: Author.

Yarbrough, D. (1993). *Final evaluation report: The small enterprise and family development project*. Washington, DC: Administration for Children and Families, Office of Financial Management, Division of Discretionary Grants.

Yunus, M. (1988). *Grameen bank: Organization and operations*. Prepared for the Microenterprise Conference, U.S. Agency for International Development. Washington, DC: Agency for International Development.

Zimmerman, M.A. (1990). Taking aim on empowerment research: On the distinction between individual and psychological conceptions. *American Journal of Community Psychology, 18*, 169–177.

7

School-Based Comprehensive Services: An Example of Interagency Collaboration

JO M. HENDRICKSON and DONNA OMER

In a climate of fiscal austerity, changing family structure, increasing ethnic and cultural diversity, and a myriad of other changing social conditions, the comprehensive service school (CSS) has emerged as a promising approach to school reform. The school-based CSS concept expands the mission of the public schools from education to include the organization, coordination, and delivery of services for children and families. In this chapter we use the term CSS or full-service school (FSS) to refer to a school-based service center for children, families, and, when appropriate, people in the surrounding community. By way of example, a CSS/FSS developed in Alachua County, Florida, will be described.

CSS models represent a relatively new strategy for providing services to children and families at the neighborhood or community level (Groves, 1992). According to the past Commissioner of Education for the State of Florida, the FSS is primarily implemented in schools geographically accessible to at-risk children and families.

A major assumption underlying the CSS/FSS concept is that integrated, interdisciplinary, interagency services are critical for positive, lasting outcomes for children, and that public schools are the logical sites through which such services should flow. Through interagency collaboration and coordination, services are to be coplanned and codelivered, thus reducing or completely eliminating duplication and fragmentation of services.

The CSS concept also embodies the notion that each school changes across time, that partnerships are dynamic, and that adjustments and modifications are a natural consequence of self-evaluation, overcoming barriers, reallocating resources, identifying new resources, and problem solving in different ways. Kochan (1992) contends, "[The]. . . full service school is not something we do. It's something we become" (p. 97). Support and commitment of school administrators, faculty, families, and the community are prerequisites to realizing the CSS concept.

To date, few school districts have fully implemented the CSS concept, and these districts differ in terms of priorities, children and families served, funding sources, numbers and types of partnerships, as well as local resources. Systematic evaluation of CSS remains to be undertaken, and summative data for assessing the merit and/or relative effectiveness of the CSS model and its component parts are not available. Nonetheless, the full service school model is viewed favorably by many legislators, educators, social service personnel, and health providers. CSS is rapidly gaining favor as a promising alternative for preventing and remediating conditions that place children and families at risk.

CHILDREN AT RISK, FAMILIES AT RISK, A NATION AT RISK

Krist (1991), a California policy analyst, graphically portrays factors placing children at risk:

> The risks add up: Johnny can't read because he needs glasses and breakfast and encouragement from his absent father; Maria doesn't pay attention in class because she can't understand English very well and she's worried about her mother's drinking and she's tired from trying to sleep in the car. Dick is flunking because he's frequently absent. His mother doesn't get him to school because she's depressed because she lost her job. She missed too much work because she was sick and could not afford medical care. (p. 615)

Variables such as problem behaviors (e.g., aggression, severe withdrawal), poor school performance, pregnancy or teen parenthood, special education needs, homelessness, a medically complex condition, truancy and/or delinquency, high absenteeism, suspension/expulsion, and substance abuse are risk factors for school-age children. Children in families who (1) are eligible for public assistance, Medicaid, or free/reduced school lunches, (2) need adult literacy training, employment assistance, job training, parenting education, adult education, or mental health services, and/or (3) are single-parent families, recent immigrants with complex health and/or social service needs, or who speak English as a second language may be at risk for poor social, physical, and educational outcomes. That is, children from such family circumstances experience higher rates of school drop-out, illiteracy, arrest, under- and unemployment, and poverty.

Schools are a natural means for positively affecting the lives of such children and families. More than any other agency, schools are involved in the daily lives of children 9 to 10 months each year until the child is

16 years old. Consequently, educators are expected to help redress these negative emotional, behavioral, and learning outcomes. Recent demographic data from Florida foreshadow nationwide population shifts that will require creative approaches to meet the challenges facing families. In Florida 62% of mothers of children under age 6 work outside the home; 13% of the population were born outside the United States; 66% of young children experience biological risk (e.g., HIV, fetal alcohol syndrome, inadequate prenatal care, physical disabilities, chronic illnesses), and 49% of these children are threatened by environmental risk factors (mainly poverty) (Interagency Work Group on Full Service Schools, 1991).

Resnick and his colleagues (1992) in a long-term follow-up study of newborns discovered that over 70% of infants born into poverty experienced severe academic problems in the early elementary grades. Poverty and the educational level of mothers proved to be better predictors of poor school performance than low birth weight. When gender and race were added to Resnick's regression analysis, poor African-American males were by far the most likely to be developmentally delayed. These data have important educational implications. At-risk children are more likely to evidence poor cognitive development, decreased language ability, inadequate social skills, reduced abstract reasoning ability, deficient problem-solving skills, reduced self-esteem, shortened attention spans, and little impulse control.

During the school years, a large proportion of at-risk children will receive very expensive compensatory or special education services. In Florida the annual cost of special education teachers is over $1 billion. Each student who repeats a grade draws an additional $2350 from the education budget. Every student dropout prevention program costs an additional $1700. English as a second language programs require an extra $1000 per student. Such high costs mean that schools and other agencies must develop new approaches to address the needs of at-risk children. Creative, cost-effective use of funds is mandatory, as student growth almost entirely absorbs new money (Interagency Work Group on Full Service Schools, 1991).

SCHOOL REFORM AND RESTRUCTURING

The 1980s saw a deluge of calls for school reform with many new models and approaches. In general, school reform enthusiasts held a common view that promoted restructuring schools, decentralizing power, installing site-based management, and shared responsibility. Teachers, parents, and children were to be involved in the management of schools in meaningful ways. Participatory decision making introduced a new optimism for the future of public education. Cobb (1992) proposed that schools should be communities with a shared vision and close personal interactions.

However, Hodgkinson (1991) points out, "educators alone cannot 'fix' the problems of education because dealing with the root cause of poverty must involve health-care, housing, transportation, job training, and social welfare bureaucracies" (p. 16). For example, the lives of homeless and neglected children are marked by continual moving—which deprives them of a sense of roots, personal space, or ownership; frequent changes of schools—which severely inhibits the development of friendships, leads to fragmented learning, and hinders cognitive development; and, overcrowded living arrangements—which reduce physical activity, increase the probability of conflict, destroy privacy, intensify stress, and foster the skill of "tuning others out." Reflecting further on the conditions that homeless and neglected children face, it is apparent that the expertise of the most dedicated educator is only one of many resources that will be necessary to reduce risk.

All too frequently homeless individuals and other at-risk groups receive limited services because agencies offer limited services. Once engaged, individuals tend to stay with an agency, even if other services they desperately require are available just down the street (Hodgkinson, 1991). This means that any given service may be under- or overutilized simply as a result of how an individual or family was referred and where the agency is located.

School-Based Services and the Comprehensive Service School (CSS)

As a natural outgrowth of the school reform movement of the past decade, two concepts for the restructuring of schools have emerged: school-based services and school-linked services. For the most part, the school-based service model includes a variety of services at the school site. School-linked services tend to be located at community organizations, youth centers, places of employment, the offices of other service providers, and even in the homes of youngsters. In both models the school plays a pivotal role in linking or integrating services to ensure optimal use of community facilities, resources, and funding.

The CSS approach, as discussed in this chapter, is predicated on the assumption that co-location of services (e.g., education, health, social services, recreation, mental health, cultural activities, child care) is particularly advantageous to at-risk children and families. In the CSS approach, great effort is exerted to locate different services at the school or in close proximity to the school. In cases where co-location is not feasible, families are referred to appropriate programs and supported (generally in the form of "case management") in procuring off-site services (Crowell, 1994). Co-location requires extensive interagency communication as well as the fostering of intraagency collaboration. A common location is only the starting point for effective coplanning and coimplementation of services, as discussed later in the chapter.

Within the CSS, the child cannot be educated in isolation from the family, which is integral to realizing the child's educational potential. Similarly, the family's concerns and needs are issues that must be addressed if the child is to flourish. The CSS takes an ecological perspective in assessing relationships between and among students, families, institutions, and communities to design a unified family plan. As seen in Figure 7.1, from an ecological perspective there are nested connections between individuals, larger groups, and organizations (Bronfrenbrenner, 1986; Hobbs, 1966). Although CSS participants seldom describe their approach as ecological, the CSS model attempts to influence multiple environmental variables that affect children and families. Substantial attention and energy may need to be focused on laws, policies, and procedures at different levels of government (e.g., city, county, state) that affect collaboration at the local level. Consequently, the ecological perspective necessarily includes assessment and intervention across a wide spectrum of issues.

EVOLUTION OF ONE FULL SERVICE SCHOOL MODEL

The Family Service Center (FSC), a key component of the School Board of Alachua County (SBAC) comprehensive service school model, is located in Gainesville, Florida. The FSC operates on the premise that a child cannot be educated in isolation from his or her family. The FSC concept was developed as a vehicle for meeting Goal 1 of Florida's "Blueprint 2000: Initial Recommendations for a System of School Improvement and Accountability" to ensure the physical, emotional, and educational readiness of all young children to begin school and to succeed in school.

Alachua County, located in north central Florida, ranked 97th of 150 hunger and poverty counties cited in the 1986 Physicians' Task Force on Hunger in America. The Gainesville Metropolitan Statistical Area has the fourth lowest family income in the United States. Twenty-three percent of all families in Alachua County live below the poverty level and many rely on public assistance. Although the school system has made repeated and innovative attempts to address the educational needs of at-risk children, these initiatives have realized limited success, mainly because factors outside the school setting exert a strong influence on

Broad Ecological Bands

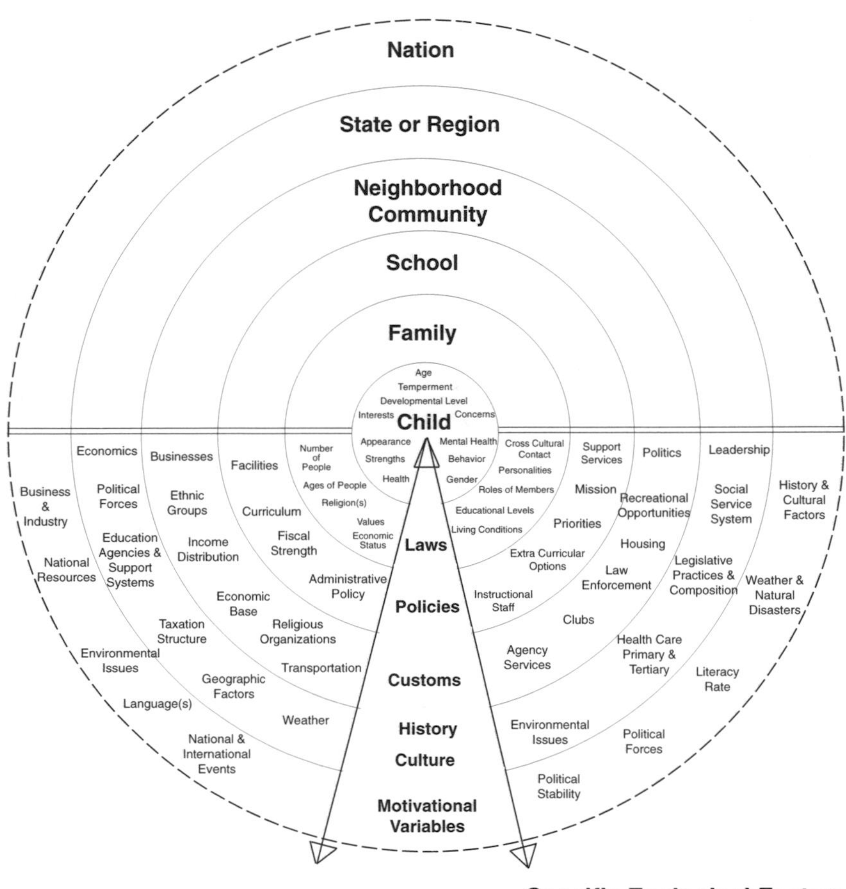

Figure 7.1. Sample of broad and specific ecological factors affecting the child.

program outcomes. In recognition of this reality, and the many ways agencies were failing to assist and empower at-risk families, a local initiative to coordinate services was begun in 1982.

Program Development

At the outset, the Superintendent of Schools initiated mutual planning sessions with health and human service agencies to reduce duplication of services and to establish a mechanism for communication and cooperation among agencies. The goal was to create a functional continuum of health, education, and social services. An essential dimension of the term "functional" was "accessible." While these planning sessions led to better interagency understanding and communication, regulations on the expenditure of program funds, job descriptions, confidentiality, and other barriers impeded the establishment of a comprehensive service system.

In 1986 a new Health and Rehabilitative Services (HRS) regional director brought renewed commitment to coordinating cross-agency services to at-risk families. HRS worked with SBAC, the City of Gainesville, Santa Fe Community College, and, eventually, the University of Florida School of Nursing among others, to develop the FSC concept for young children and their families. Based on this fledgling effort, in 1990 interagency funds primarily targeting at-risk middle school children enabled the school district to locate portable units on the school grounds of a district middle school. These units housed the personnel and equipment that constituted the first FSC. Included at the FSC were a health clinic, education classes, parenting classes, employability services, mental health services, and child care services.

Three staff from the local community college were outposted at the FSC, as well as various mental health and HRS personnel. In 1991 federal money enabled Even Start (children birth–5) to be added to the roster of programs located at the FSC. By the 1993–1994 school year, overall FSS funding had increased from around $100,000 to over $350,000 in Alachua County. As of spring 1994, nine full-time family liaison workers were serving 22 elementary schools, and the district was planning to expand to the high school level. Recently, the state committed $2.5 million for building a permanent FSC on the grounds of an elementary school.

Current Program

The goal of the SBAC FSS is family self-sufficiency, empowering families to control their lives and set a positive direction for their children. The FSS approach fosters the belief that to help children develop socially, emotionally, physically, and academically, schools should be involved in helping families provide the basic necessities of a healthy home environment.

Before a family receives services, staff work with them to create a plan that reflects their short- and long-term goals. The family liaison then helps coordinate the needed services. A case management approach eliminates duplication in planning and service delivery.

Presently, the SBAC FSS is funded by a complex web of sources, both state and federal, including but not limited to Chapter 2, Even Start,

Florida First Start, Full Service Schools, Head Start, a Head Start Demonstration grant, Head Start Family Day Care Homes, HRS, the Supplemental School Health Program, and Medicaid. Services viewed as basic to the FSS are described in brief below:

> *Adult Education and Career Development* includes GED (high school equivalency exam) and employability skill classes. Held in a computer lab, these classes provide opportunities for parents to learn about computers, job interviewing, and job opportunities.
>
> *Child Care Activities* are available on-site for children 0-5 whose parents are involved in activities at the FSC. Eligible children are enrolled in the Head Start Program. Child care is also contracted through Alachua County's Child Care Resources.
>
> *Economic and Social Services* process AFDC and food stamp eligibility on-site. Some FSC participants are enrolled in Project Independence, a welfare-to-work program. A family liaison specialist coordinates child care to enable the parents to be at the activities and gain a GED or work-related skills. The family liaison also helps families find housing, employment, emergency food assistance, utilities, and so on.
>
> *Family Support Services*, available through a variety of grant sources, include support groups, parenting classes, and social and recreational activities. Parents discuss issues such as discipline, homework, and age-appropriate activities. Parent education also focuses on budgeting, employment, and nutrition.
>
> *Health Services* are contracted to HRS. A clinic is available to program participants and Medicaid eligible families. It is staffed by an advanced registered nurse practitioner.
>
> *Mental Health Counseling* is provided by psychologists contracted from Mental Health Services. They are outposted at the FSC. Individual and group counseling sessions are available, as well as parent support groups.

Program Outcomes

The CSS approach appears to have had a dramatic impact on many program participants. Interviews with FSC Even Start participants (Roth, 1992), for instance, have indicated a number of recurrent themes and positive outcomes. As one parent stated:

> Coming back to school has given me confidence. . . . I do have the ability to still learn. . . . I'm not beyond learning new things. It gave me the idea of not wanting to give up.

Several of the respondents contrasted their current excitement at the prospect of coming to class with their recent past in which "nothing" was happening:

> I didn't have nothing to do. I don't mix and mingle with a lot of people. So it was just me and these small kids, home all the time.

One of the indirect benefits of adult education classes, therefore, is the companionship it offers isolated women. In reporting what they have learned in parenting class, FSC parents stressed communication, self-control, and better disciplining of their children:

> I learned when you get angry, when you have something on your mind and your children is distracting you, don't just yell at the child, more like just take your child and put them in another room until you get whatever's on your mind off.

More recent evaluations indicate increased confidence on the part of parents in dealing with their children's school issues, pride in themselves, and appreciation of their children's unique personalities. Early evidence shows children who had little interest in schoolwork are beginning to do homework side by side with their mothers. Mothers also stated they were spending more time with their children in enjoyable activities (Crowell, 1994).

According to direct service personnel and parents, on-site child care is one of the most important features of FSS. In addition, transportation is a highly valued component, and transportation expenses and/or vehicles are now part of each annual budget. Personnel who have been active in the development of Alachua County's FSC are convinced that *all* potential players (e.g., agencies, consumers) must be involved and committed to the FSS concept at the beginning. Furthermore, top level management involvement from all agencies and written cooperative agreements are necessary if the FSS approach is to succeed.

In summary, at this time the SBAC FSS appears to be having a positive impact on the school lives of children, family functioning, and family aspirations. Many lessons have been learned through establishment of the FSS. In the remaining sections of this chapter three broad issues found to be central to the FSS—the collaborative process, interagency collaboration, and accountability—are discussed.

THE COLLABORATIVE PROCESS

Bruner's (1991) generic definition of collaboration can be applied to interagency collaboration. He views collaboration as a process to reach goals that cannot be achieved acting singly (or, at least not achieved as efficiently). Collaboration is a *process*, a means to an end, not an end in itself, and communication and coordination are essential to all collaboration. Mutual goals and shared missions should guide the behavior and priorities of collaborators.

In relation to the CSS, collaborative strategies first and foremost are aimed at accessing more appropriate assistance for families already being served by different systems. Collaboration may be viewed as a quality control mechanism—a process by which the type and quality of services can be assessed. Second, collaboration within the CSS aims at preventing students from "falling through the cracks." Students and families, especially those ineligible for categorical programs (e.g., Medicaid, special education), are caught in the CSS safety net. Meeting student and family needs goes beyond traditionally funded programs. Third, CSS collaboration efforts should reduce environmental risks that affect all children in a given neighborhood or community.

On a cautionary note, Gardner (1993) warns that a potential tendency of collaboration resulting from the desire to "fix" the child is the creation of new projects or programs. Vigilance is required to avoid "projectitis" and an add-a-new-program mentality. Adding new programs can inadvertently reinforce traditional agency boundaries and further entrench institutions.

For most children, Bruner (1991) points out, the family is the mechanism by which services are identified, coordinated, and integrated in today's society. Families with complex medical, social, and personal needs often require someone from outside to assist with what may be an overwhelming job at that point in the family's life. Developing a unified plan with the family is a common goal in CSS collaboration.

Consonant with an ecological perspective, collaboration must occur at every level within and across agencies. Understanding the organizational demands of each agency fosters trust and good will and enhances the problem-solving process. Collaboration at high levels often involves the redesign of agency policies, responsibilities, and procedures that may lead to or be driven by legislative action. At the intermediate organizational level, collaboration focuses on local resources and getting to know community and agency people who have the authority to take action. At both the top levels of agency management and intermediate levels, funding and monetary issues need to be addressed.

Collaborators must learn about the historical precedents within different agencies, the traditional roles of each agency's workers, and potential professional turf problems. In interagency collaboration the question of who (i.e., which agency and which person) has responsibility for what (i.e., tasks and timelines) must be agreed upon and articulated in a manner understood by everyone. Direct service providers also must know who is responsible for what, especially when working with support staff and direct service providers from outside agencies. The responsibility and authority of staff should be balanced in a manner that enables frontline providers to collaborate effectively with families (e.g., make informed, authorized decisions that facilitate the delivery of services) and to support families in functioning as independently as possible. Table 7.1 contains 10 action steps to facilitate the development of partnerships. The action steps presented are based on guidelines developed by the Education and Human Services Consortium (Melaville & Blank, 1991).

A wide array of services may characterize any given CSS: crisis intervention, mental health counseling, child care, transportation, immunization and primary health care services, prenatal care, law enforcement

Table 7.1. Action Steps for Successful Collaboration

1. *Involve key players at every level*—from the highest administrator to child and parent representatives. Assist them in finding ways to show their commitment to the partnership.
2. *Choose realistic goals*—at first simply coordinating services among agencies may be the most achievable goal that demonstrates progress in the right direction. Remember that it takes time to establish trust and understanding.
3. *Identify priority goals*—goals of critical players (e.g., parents, policymakers, and the public) should be factored into the process of goal selection. Keep the number of goals small.
4. *Establish a shared vision*—shared visions are based on projected outcomes for shared service recipients. Further, the greater familiarity collaborators have with the perspectives and priorities of each other, the better the chance of establishing a mutual mission.
5. *Set attainable objectives*—it is important to build momentum and create a successful experience for all participants early in the collaboration process.
6. *Keep focused on the objectives*—it is easy to become bogged down in day-to-day operations and distracted by frustrations and disappointments that are part of the process of learning to work together.
7. *Aim for the stars*—ambitious collaboration efforts require the active support of systems level leadership. Keep top management updated and involved in the collaborative process to the greatest extent possible. Never underestimate the value of positive recognition of the partnership by the community, policymakers, and other VIPs.
8. *Avoid "red herrings"*—implementation difficulties may arise from policies or operating procedures (both of which can be changed) or statutory regulations that must maintained. Misunderstandings regarding the source of an obstacle should not be allowed to derail the partnership.
9. *Institutionalize change*—the most useful and best designed interagency initiatives will dissolve if the innovations do not become part of the system. Partnership objectives need to be incorporated into each agency's budget and resources adequate for sustaining joint efforts should be earmarked annually.
10. *Publicize success*—well-publicized results that document consistent attainment of objectives count heavily in the never-ending pursuit of funds.

and legal services, parent education, adult literacy, vocational training, support groups, and recreational programs, to name the most common. By co-locating services, experience has shown that crisis response time will be reduced, direct service time increased, cost per hour lowered, parent and community involvement promoted, and prevention viewed as a legitimate role for agency personnel.

We want to emphasize that the term "service delivery" can be misleading if not archaic in that families must be active partners with service agencies. The words "delivery" and "providers" mistakenly can imply that a service is dropped off (or given away) to passive recipients. Such a notion is contrary to the mission and functions of the CSS.

THE DEVELOPMENT OF INTERAGENCY COLLABORATION

Bruner (1991) describes first, second, and third generation strategies in the development of interagency collaboration strategies. It should be emphasized, however, that a bottom-up movement should coexist with this top-down process. Along with Bruner's model, we describe the evolution of collaboration and the emergence of the CSS in Florida.

First-generation strategies for collaboration, according to Bruner (1991), are initiated from the top down and usually involve the establishment of interagency task forces, councils, commissions, or committees. A crucial body formed in Florida was the State Coordinating Council (SCC) whose membership included key stakeholders, representatives of a wide range of service agencies and disciplines, as well as parents, private agencies, business persons, political activists, and representatives from institutions of higher education. Individuals with high status within their respective agencies and organizations were appointed to the SCC (and local councils) as a strategy for gaining the commitment of the agencies and bringing expertise to the councils.

The primary mission of the SCC was to provide oversight to HRS and the Department of Education (DOE) in their collaboration efforts in behalf of young children and their families, establish communication and collaborative links with local interagency councils, and provide technical assistance to local programs. As the SCC became more knowledgeable about the operation and mission of HRS and DOE, it made recommendations for enhancing collaboration, met with legislators to underscore the plight of at-risk children and families, and worked to shape policy that promoted collaboration, that is, coplanning, resource and revenue sharing, and even coimplementation. Presently the SCC meets bimonthly and has established procedures for facilitating vertical and horizontal communication among its membership as well as formal procedures for conduct of its 2-day meetings in which a tremendous volume of business is covered.

When SCCs or similar state level interagency groups are formed, Bruner (1991) recommends addressing several questions that have a direct bearing on the productivity and impact of the group. There are five questions to resolve: (1) Is there a clearly defined problem that the interagency group is commissioned to address? (2) Are all key stakeholders represented in the group? (3) Does the mission require the development of specific goals related to children and families, and are action steps and time frames for achieving those goals required? (4) Is the group accorded sufficient status, authority, technical assistance, support, and staffing? (5) Is there a way to enlist meaningful participation by families and feedback from local and frontline staff?

Second-generation strategies include state-supported technical assistance to localities and may also involve state initiatives to encourage local interagency collaboration. At this stage, members of Florida's SCC provided technical assistance to local districts and attended local interagency council meetings. Each local interagency council also had a representative on the SCC. Several demonstration projects began to develop FSS approaches. Teen parent programs and programs for preschool children with disabilities have had the longest history of interagency coordination and advanced most rapidly toward collaboration once incentives were offered.

As second-generation strategies are put into action and mutual goals identified, agency authority structures and professional assumptions are challenged; previous rules of decision making no longer fully apply. Actions cannot be justified by pointing to regulations, but instead must be assessed by their impact on children and families (Bruner, 1991). At this stage, the collaborative process can be extremely tedious as participants strive to become familiar and comfortable with one another. Individuals are tempted to ask, "Wouldn't it be easier for me to do this myself?" Second-generation strategies call for new measures of accountability, but there are no set guidelines for documenting accountability. Administrative rules and professional practice standards are no longer valid guideposts. Program evaluation within the context of interagency collaboration is driven by outcome measures (i.e., was the problem solved? the shared vision achieved? the primary goal attained?).

During this stage the rigidity of categorically funded programs often leaves workers frustrated and somewhat demoralized as they try repeatedly to find acceptable routes around regulatory barriers. Because of the magnitude of funding attached to categorical, federally funded programs such as Chapter 1 (compensatory education), AFDC (Aid to Families with Dependent Children), and Medicaid, these regulations cannot be ignored or taken lightly.

Service providers who once embraced the concept of collaboration enthusiastically may be at the edge of despair, having sorely underestimated potential obstacles. Two additional challenges—getting the agendas of different participants on the table and getting each participant to concede that the goal of collaboration is not to persuade someone else to change—can be time-consuming and laborious. At this stage of collaboration, it is important that the salaries, support, and training of workers collaborating on the frontlines are commensurate with the skills required of them.

In the final stage of collaboration, or when *third-generation strategies* are implemented, the goal is to promote collaboration across the entire state, that is, within all jurisdictions (Bruner, 1991). The challenge of third-generation strategies is to involve communities that up to this time have not been receptive to interagency collaboration. Leadership development in local communities is prerequisite to adoption of a collaborative approach, especially in noninvolved communities.

In Florida third-generation collaboration activities are in an embryonic stage with many communities still resisting goals and strategies associated with interagency collaboration. It is especially important that expert technical assistance and guidance are available to local districts at this stage. As collaborative efforts multiply across the state, it becomes important to define FSS models that embody the collaborative philosophy, models that can be exported, replicated, or adapted. For replication to be possible, the most salient elements of the collaborative model must be articulated clearly. Strategies that are useful in developing these crucial elements of the model should be detailed in writing to facilitate replication.

Across the three generations of strategies, the skills and knowledge of every individual participant influence the collaborative process—positively or negatively. Although the focus has been on agency representatives, it is assumed that families are an integral part of each step. For each individual, parent, professional, or interested party, a number of skills are desirable before the collaborative venture begins, although many skills will be learned in the process of coplanning and coimplementation. Good communication skills (e.g., active listening, clarification skills, paraphrasing skills), effective time-management, group problem-solving, decision-making, and goal setting strategies, leadership ability, and skills in conducting and participating in meetings are important. There is an abundance of resources available for developing these skills including self-help books, audio and video tapes, professional seminars, university and community college courses, and staff development activities, to name a few. Prior experience working in multidisciplinary programs, on interdisciplinary teams, or sharing job responsibilities often proves useful.

Collaboration may have negative consequences. For example, the authority of service providers may be increased, problems of confidentiality can arise, and the family's ability to determine the care their children receive may be compromised. A given "case manager" simply may not get along with a given child or family or not have the requisite skills to perform the role of liaison effectively. These and related issues must be anticipated, discussed, and potential solutions designed.

Special Issues for Interagency Collaboration

Adjustment of the social welfare and educational systems to match the needs of children and families requires public and private sector collaboration. The likelihood of successful interagency and cross-organizational collaboration can be enhanced if collaborators are aware of how present systems operate. A recent publication of the Education and Human Services Consortium (Melaville & Blank, 1991) identifies five underlying reasons service systems have failed. Each of the five reasons is paraphrased below. We believe the recognition of these issues is important when establishing CSSs and have provided one recommendation to illustrate each guideline:

1. Most present-day services are crisis-oriented and attempt to remediate or ameliorate events that already have transpired, that is, they are reactive in nature. *Collaborative groups should prioritize CSS goals with extra weight given to prevention, that is, proactive student and family assistance.*

2. Current programs are categorical, divide problems of children and families into distinct entities, and have rigidly defined rules for service eligibility. *CSS collaborators should seek waivers to existing rules and be especially careful not to create add-on programs or programs that isolate family problems.*

3. To date agencies have been negligent in communicating with each other in a timely and accurate manner. Occasionally, agencies withhold information. *While confidentiality must be ensured, a priority of the CSS should be to improve communication within and between agencies, work to change conditions that impede information sharing, and monitor the communication process continuously.*

4. Specialized agencies are not able to readily craft comprehensive solutions to conditions that place children and families at risk. *Specialized*

support programs should be assessed carefully and replaced by or linked in a systematic manner with the CSS.

5. Existing services are insufficiently funded. *Every effort should be made to identify and analyze the types of available local services with the explicit goal of eliminating duplication and redirecting funds to areas in which there are service gaps.*

Finally, it is essential that the impact of prevention, intervention, and support services be measured and assessed and services redesigned, if necessary. Clear, written specification of mutually agreed upon goals and objectives, activities and timelines for reaching them, designation of who is responsible for what actions, and identification of strategies for measuring outcomes are essential.

THE QUESTION OF ACCOUNTABILITY

As expressed previously, CSSs should be evaluated according to their effect on the lives of children and families. Effects may be assessed by measuring attitudes as well as behavior of professional collaborators (i.e., service providers), children, and families. Often outcomes are measured by counting the number of goals and objectives achieved and assessing the relevance and importance of those particular goals and objectives (usually by a third party). Certainly multiple measures or a multimodal approach to assessment will be needed so that the broad range of potential effects can be tapped. In addition to examining the quality of services, issues of efficiency of service delivery and cost are likely to be important.

Historically, educational and social service agencies have not had to be particularly concerned with outcome measures. Rather evaluation has entailed assessment of adherence to procedures, rules, and regulations, and examination of documentation to confirm that funds were expended appropriately. This system of accountability is outdated. On the other hand, if accountability is tied directly to program goals, certain other problems can arise. For example, if program goals are narrow, measurement tends to foster specialization and fragmentation of services. If program goals are broad and ambiguous, it is difficult to reach agreement about whether the goals have been met. This lack of agreement occurs when various participants (e.g., the family, the nurse, the social worker) and other interested parties (e.g., politicians) arrive at different interpretations of what constitutes "a healthier family life" or "being ready for school."

Organizations are likely to pay closest attention to the goals espoused by the agency on which they depend upon for funding. Thus, there is a risk that goals in partnership will reflect the agency supporting the "case manager" or other primary service provider. This potential problem must be recognized with goals and evaluation strategies selected based on child and family needs, not agency mission.

In addition, the CSS by definition relies on the coarticulation of multiple and different services for each child/family. Consequently, the effect of a "weak link" in the chain of services is difficult to assess. Eventually we may be able to determine the relative influence of CSS component services; however, at this time identifying the contribution of each element of the CSS to the whole remains a task for future evaluators. These assessments should be both formative and summative in nature, include qualitative and quantitative measures, and assist agencies in improving specific intervention components (e.g., parent education and day care) as well as affecting broader ecological variables (e.g., a legislative act, a new school discipline policy). Finally, both short-term and long-range outcomes measures will be needed. Typically, evaluation has been a much lower priority than service provision. However, for long-term positive change, a commitment to outcome evaluation is mandatory. Otherwise the CSS will become another "quick fix" strategy driven by politics and popular myth.

REFERENCES

Bronfrenbrenner, U. (1986). Ecology of the family as a context for human development: Research perspectives. *Developmental Psychology, 22,* 723–742.

Bruner, C. (1991). *Thinking collaboratively: Ten questions and answers to help policy makers improve children's services* (pp. 4–31). Washington, DC: Education and Human Services Consortium.

Cobb, C.W. (1992). *Responsive schools, renewed communities.* San Francisco: ICS Press.

Gardner, S.L. (1993). Key issues in developing school-linked, integrated services. *Education and Urban Society, 25,* 141–152.

Groves, L. (1992). Preface. [Summary]. *Proceedings of the Florida Full Service Schools Training Conference* (pp. iii–v). Tallahassee, FL: Department of Education.

Hobbs, N. (1966). Helping disturbed children: Psychological and ecological strategies. *American Psychologist, 21,* 1105–1115.

Hodgkinson, H. (1991). Reform versus reality. *Phi Delta Kappan, 72,* 16.

Interagency Work Group on Full Service Schools. (1991). Full service schools: Concept paper. [Summary]. *Proceedings of the Florida Full Service Schools Training Conference* (pp. 101–110). Tallahassee, FL: Department of Education.

Kochan, F. (1992). Becoming full service schools. [Summary]. *Proceedings of the Florida Full Service Schools Training Conference* (pp. 97–98). Tallahassee, FL: Department of Education.

Krist, M.W. (1991). Improving children's services: Overcoming barriers, creating new opportunities. *Phi Delta Kappan, 72*, 615–622.

Melaville, A.I., & Blank, M.J. (1991). *What it takes: Structuring interagency partnerships to connect children and families with comprehensive services*. Washington, DC: Education and Human Services Consortium.

Resnick, M., Roth, J., Ariet, M., Carter, R., Emerson, J., Hendrickson, J., Packer, A., Larsen, J., Wolking, W., Lucas, M., Schenck, B., Fearnside, B., & Bucciarelli, R. (1992). Educational outcomes of neonatal intensive care graduates. *Pediatrics, 38*, 373–378.

Roth, J. (1992). *Even Start Family Services Center: Results of first case study interviews*. Gainesville, FL: School Board of Alachua County.

8

Linking Schools with Family- and Community-Centered Services

MARY R. LEWIS

This chapter examines service models being developed in other countries to bring schools into collaborative networks on behalf of children and families. These efforts reflect growing concern in industrial countries about the extent of underachievement and early school leaving by youth with normal abilities, especially as secondary school completion is generally required for entry-level jobs. One strategy for combating such educational disadvantage involves bringing educational systems into closer coordination with social and health systems.

Similar concerns are found in the United States. The U.S. National Commission on Children (USNCC) (1991) described the educational status of children in the United States:

> Almost 30 percent of ninth graders in the United States do not graduate four years later. Among young people age 16 through 24, 12.6 percent, about 4 million, have not completed high school and are not currently enrolled in school. Dropout rates vary by race and ethnicity—12 percent of white, 14 percent of black, and 33 percent of Hispanic 16 to 24-year-olds have dropped out of high school. Dropout rates are particularly pronounced in many of the nation's major cities: for example, Chicago's rate was approximately 40 percent. (p. 180)

> Fewer than half of American 17-year-olds who are in school possess the skills and basic knowledge required for college and many entry-level jobs.... Many are so limited in their command of written English that they are unable to communicate a reasoned point of view. (p. 179)

In the United States a study of factors that contributed to dropping out of school concluded that add-on programs for failing or at-risk children and youth have not prevented dropping out, especially if they involve labeling students. An examination of successful efforts led to the recommendation that "dropout strategies should actively collaborate with community-based human service agencies to provide services for students at risk" (Massachusetts Advocacy Center, 1988, p. 64).

Many public policy experts in the United States and other countries argue that schools have been too narrowly focused on educational tasks and that they have not given sufficient attention to family, neighborhood, or community circumstances contributing to the failure or underachievement of children. Current trends to change this include school-linked service provision (School-linked services, 1992), school-based services (Dryfoos, 1994), and other models of collaboration between education, health, and social service professionals and organizations (Melaville & Blank, 1993). A central distinction between school-based and school-linked services is whether the education system is in charge of collaborative efforts or whether interorganizational, community-based entities share leadership responsibility.

WHO ARE THE EDUCATIONALLY DISADVANTAGED CHILDREN?

A 3-year project on service integration for educationally disadvantaged children that includes 12 highly industrialized countries has identified risk factors that contribute to educational disadvantage in the participating countries. In the United States, factors that place a child at educational risk include being poor, belonging to a racial or ethnic minority group, having limited English proficiency, having only one parent or poorly educated parents, and having a disability (USNCC, 1991). However, when socioeconomic status is held constant, school drop-out rates between black and white students are about the same (Massachusetts Advocacy Center, 1988).

Based upon study visits to six European countries, Lewis (1993) concluded that cultural deprivation created higher risk of school failure than financial deprivation in countries that have comprehensive welfare and health benefits cushioning the impact of low income or parental unemployment. Cultural deprivation is found in families that lack communication skills and in which reading or other activities supporting cultural identity and expression are minimal.

When ethnic minority or immigrant group status is coupled with low income, the risks seem to accelerate in all countries. Which ethnic minorities are most vulnerable varies from country to country, depending upon immigration patterns, language, and other cultural dimensions. Inadequate proficiency in the dominant language is recognized in all countries as a barrier to accessing education, health, and social welfare benefits.

One community-based networking program in Amsterdam serves a largely Moroccan, Turkish, and Surinamese population with the goal of enhancing children's success in school. Despite illiteracy and severe restrictions on women's roles, 3 months of careful community work enabled mothers to participate outside the home in a planned activity. Initially, a health program for newborns was used as a base to contact mothers and eventually to organize small groups, one reaching 24 Turkish and another 18 Moroccan mothers. Both materials and information were provided. For example, mothers were given a spoon for 3-month-old babies along with information about feeding them solid food. After learning more about the possibilities of play, mothers requested a supervised play group. School settings are being used in a similar way for linking families, neighborhood, and schools. Many Moslem parents do not allow their adolescent girls to attend mixed schools, so a separate school program for Islamic girls ages 12 to 16 was established, as well as a center to offer activities just for girls.

WHY SERVICE INTEGRATION?

Even the nations with the highest literacy rates and most comprehensive health and welfare systems, such as Finland and Sweden, are taking steps to promote community-based, family-focused service integration in reaction to the inflexibility and rigidity of large formal organizations administering welfare and health programs. A "stovepipe mentality" or vertical orientation to functional specializations such as health and education leads service providers to emphasize hierarchical thinking and organizational priorities. Therefore, reforms seek a holistic approach to serving individuals, groups, and families through interdisciplinary teams that can respond to differences between neighborhoods and communities. Even in countries where benefits are comprehensive and available without means testing, citizens do not have adequate information about how and where to access them.

A second motivation for service integration is the belief that costs can be reduced while services become more effective. Yet research on previous service integration efforts in the United States revealed that they required more money and resources to establish basic service integration mechanisms such as client information systems and co-located services (Kusserow, 1991). Nevertheless, on a multinational scale, there are major initiatives to promote neighborhood and/or community-based interagency and multidisciplinary service provision to children and families, many of which are school-linked.

ALBERTA, CANADA'S CHILDREN'S INITIATIVE[1]

An example of a collaborative effort in Canada was chosen for this chapter because it illustrates linkages between policy, administration, and practice. These linkages are essential to institutionalize family-centered, school-linked, community-based services. The convergence of grass-roots or bottom-up collaborative innovations with top-down policies and strategies is also necessary to support, disseminate, and institutionalize successful community-based initiatives.

The Province of Alberta began a Children's Initiative in response to several pressures including a very critical analysis of the child welfare system. Government deficits and economic recession are also forcing major new directions in government operations. In addition, bottom-up efforts in some local communities to develop neighborhood-based, family-focused collaborative teams among health, education, welfare, and other community organizations were already underway. The Provincial Government's Coordination of Services for Children's Initiative was formed in partnership with communities to identify, understand, and support the most promising of these collaborative projects to facilitate interagency and cross-disciplinary fertilization and the formulation of policies to more effectively serve children and families. Five communities were chosen to participate in this initiative with four provincial departments: Health, Education, Family and Social Services, and Justice.

A Working Committee (WC) consists of two representatives from each department at the Director or Program Planner level. This committee reports directly to an Assistant Deputy Ministers' Steering Committee. Each member of the WC has connections to some of the community sites to develop procedures in support of community initiatives, to keep Ministers informed, and to seek to remove barriers to effective program coordination. Two people in the WC from different departments provide links with each of the five community projects, not as representatives of their departments but as resources. One person attends the planning meetings of the project. The other focuses on evaluation issues. Each pair is backed up by a lead Assistant Deputy Minister.

Working in this way required representatives of different departments to develop understanding of the unique culture, administrative structure, and language of each other's agencies. For example, concepts of client groups vary. Health views the whole community as the client in contrast to Child Welfare Services, which focuses upon a narrower, mandated group.

Confidentiality issues appeared to pose major barriers to collaboration at first, but after trust and more understanding of direct service operations developed, policies did not seem to be as rigid as first perceived. More sharing and flexibility within existing policies was possible.

The designated pairs from the WC sit on the local steering committees of the five projects. In the beginning, their role was to bring issues back to the Assistant Deputy Ministers level. In fact, members of the WC often became advocates for the local projects. To function effectively, WC members had to learn the language of the community and of direct service personnel. Voting rights have not become an issue because most of the local committees agree on plans and policies by consensus.

THE OPENING DOORS INITIATIVE IN CALGARY

The Opening Doors Initiative in Calgary is one of the five exemplary programs in the Coordination of Services for Children's Initiative. It illustrates both ways of involving direct service, supervisory, and management levels of the community-based agencies in the change process and some of the issues confronting a community that initiates a collaborative effort on behalf of children and families.

Calgary is the business center and largest multicultural community in Alberta. Collaboration initiatives have mushroomed throughout the city during the past 10 years, some of which focused upon fighting educational disadvantage. In 1985 the Alberta Education Department and Calgary Board of Education prepared a report enumerating the large number of agencies that served the same children and families. A community liaison worker was employed to improve collaborative relationships between agencies. The community worker initiated regular meetings between management personnel of key agencies and the chief executive officers of the Calgary Family and Social Services Department, a public agency that both provides direct services and contracts for services from voluntary agencies. One tangible outcome was the creation of an Interagency Intake Workers Group that includes 15 agencies in a high-risk area of town. The intake workers meet monthly to learn more about each others' services.

Another outcome was the decision to support a neighborhood-based, interagency, multidisciplinary collaboration that would include schools as major partners. One goal was to find a way to merge bottom-up and top-down efforts to achieve better service integration. The Opening Doors Steering Committee selected a community site based on need as identified by relevant data, agency willingness to participate, and community willingness to be involved. In this neighborhood there are nine schools attempting to provide services to individual students, some of whom have complex needs.

The Opening Doors plan called for a community-based direct services team called the Professional Resources Group (PRG), a Supervisors' Group consisting of the PRG workers' agency supervisors, and a Community Resource Group that brings together all potential participant agencies, both governmental and nongovernmental. A Steering Committee consisting of management level personnel representing the participating agencies orchestrates all levels of participants. The Steering Committee includes representatives of the government agencies providing citywide services, including Education, Social Services, Health, and Justice.

The PRG includes a public health nurse, a police officer, a mental health worker, a public school itinerant behavioral resource teacher, a child welfare worker, a financial benefits and client support services worker from the Alberta Family and Social Services Department, and a single parent worker from the City of Calgary Social Services Department. The individuals were selected before their PRG roles and team protocols were completed. This made it possible for them to evolve their roles and protocols as a team with the support and involvement of their agency supervisors.

The individuals chosen were, for the most part, already involved in the community. For example, the police officer was selected because of his innovative community police work and good relationship with the schools. Instead of waiting at the police station to be called after an incident occurred, he spent his time walking in the community, getting to know the people, and gaining their trust. This enabled him to become involved in the resolution of neighborhood disputes and family conflicts before they emerged into full-blown law enforcement issues. It had been noted that when he took vacations, the crime rate went up in the neighborhood. In this style of work, he learned much about the welfare of the community that he could use to function as a proactive member of the PRG.

In the beginning phase, while developing mutual understanding and protocols, the PRG related closely to the Student Resource Group (SRG) of the school, almost as an extension of it. The SRG is the school's administrative team that focuses upon academic and behavior problems of children. It includes the school's administrators, and, when a particular child is being discussed, the teacher. Other school service providers such as the counselor or school nurse may participate. The public health nurse and the police officer in the PRG have often been invited to participate. The SRG deals primarily with situations involving only one outside agency and has more difficulty coping with many agencies or with many families facing the same problem, such as violence. The PRG works with families with complex problems and multiple agency involvement.

In concept the Opening Doors Initiative is community-based, although the PRG began its operations in close relationship to children and families in one elementary school. The decision to be community-based rather than school-based was made to encourage broader accessibility. Since there are nine schools in the residential area, having a community base rather than a one school-base makes it possible to enlarge the operation to include the other schools as the project matures. With the resources available it was not possible to provide a separate program at each school.

Referrals to the Opening Doors Initiative can be received from any source. A family may be invited to meet with the PRG depending upon their situation and their interest. The PRG meets once a week for a half day. In their first meetings, the PRG developed the norms by which they would operate. This meant learning about each other's agency mandates and resources, and the professional roles, styles, preferences, and views of each member in order to develop trust and become a team.

When the PRG began, each member tended to function according to their training and usual practice, but over time there has been some blurring of roles. However, there is no intent to dilute the positive and unique contributions of different professional competencies and perspectives. The examples described below indicate the kind of changes that take place in a well-functioning community-based team.

Whereas previously, there were four or more child welfare workers assigned to the school, now the child welfare worker assigned to the PRG is the only one serving children in this school. Her agency has allowed her more flexibility in her role than in her former agency-based work. Through relationships with the SRG and the PRG, she becomes more aware of families in the community and their needs before formal referrals are made to the child welfare agency. She can open cases for intensive preventive services and spend time with families in order to avert a formal referral to the agency. She has shifted from being primarily agency-focused to being community-focused, and, as a result, the community's and families' images of her are becoming more positive.

The nurse still performs regular school health work, but as a result of her involvement with the SRG and the PRG, becomes involved with children in crisis in other ways, for example, by talking with a child who has been disruptive in a class. Also, she may be asked to make a home visit for assessment by the PRG, since a visit from a public health nurse is less threatening than a visit by a child welfare worker.

The mental health worker began as the therapist on the team, working with individuals, families, and groups. What changed for him was seeing people in the community rather than in an agency office. He is also providing consultation to the PRG and to community groups about how to develop more mental health services in the area.

The Client and Support Services Worker from the Alberta Family and Social Services Department deals with applications for financial aid and can also access other support services such as counseling, crisis intervention, parent aide, employment, or job training services.

The single parent worker from the City of Calgary Social Services Department provides supportive counseling regarding the child care subsidy, advocacy, and housing to single parents who have recently separated or divorced. She organizes support or drop-in groups for single parents, introduces resources on how to deal with legal and custody issues, and provides information on effective parenting. She also engages in community development activities, such as setting up a Food Bank Depot using volunteers and supervising a university student who started a social skills program for children in grades 5 and 6, which focused on issues such as developing self-esteem and knowledge about safety.

In one example a PRG action averted foster placement of a newborn child. The parents' competence to meet the baby's basic needs was questioned by several nurses in the hospital where the child was born and the case had been formally referred to the public health and child welfare agencies. The PRG assessed possible ways to approach the situation. The child welfare worker believed that, according to the usual standards and operating procedures of her agency, the child would be placed in foster care while further study of the situation continued. However, she agreed that working together, the PRG would attempt to prevent foster placement.

The public health nurse made a home visit while the child welfare worker explored the availability of extended family and other community resources that might provide a support system for the family. A sister of the child's mother offered to take the child home from the hospital so that foster placement would not be needed, at least immediately. The services of a Parent Outreach Service in the neighborhood were obtained. The parents were allowed to take the baby home during the day while an outreach worker was in the home to provide role modeling and other support services. In several weeks it was decided that it would be safe for the baby to live at home with wrap-around support services.

Other changes have been initiated in the Supervisors' Group, which meets once a month. Prominent on their agenda have been administrative issues such as confidentiality, meshing of agency priorities, the mandates of different agencies, waiting lists, involving the voluntary sector, and evaluation, particularly of personnel on the PRG.

Staff development for current PRG members includes the possibility that they would provide training for other agency personnel. Possible issues for this training include how to get collaboration started, making group rules for teams, mutual expectations of PRG team members and their agencies, and various approaches to casework, conflict management, and confidentiality.

The supervisors are becoming aware that supervising the PRG team is different from regular agency-based supervision. Informally, they are logging effects on children and families to advocate for the PRG and to enable their agencies to change. The PRG and the Supervisors' Group meet jointly every 6 weeks and both rotate leadership roles such as chairing meetings and taking minutes.

The supervisors identified the most important issues that they face in this new mode of practice. The nurse's supervisor said that confidentiality issues inhibit the PRG work. The mental health worker's supervisor thought that workload issues were paramount. Other issues were defining and working with the community, marketing the initiative so that clients are aware and make use of it, communication, space for service providers based outside the neighborhood, and the development of an integrated, multidisciplinary client record. In some agencies blockages between supervisors and chief executive officers are an issue, especially in large organizations.

The child welfare worker's supervisor observed that the child welfare worker was becoming somewhat alienated from the other workers in the home agency, feeling that she is now in a more supportive environment for her work with families. She has more job satisfaction than when working in traditional child welfare, despite the fact that the work is "messier" (i.e., less routinized and predictable). Another child welfare worker will be added to the project to assist with investigations of alleged abuse and neglect, since the first one has become very involved in preventive work. The Opening Doors Initiative is in the neighborhood with the heaviest demand for child welfare investigations. The supervisor believes that the preventive child welfare work is positively viewed by the community and that it is having the desired effect in work with families.

All of the supervisors expressed doubts about whether every qualified person would be able to work in this new way. Also, they believe that teamwork requires more personnel time than the traditional agency methods of work. The supervisors' work on the Initiative has been added on to regular responsibilities. Because the goal is to expand the initiative into other communities, consideration is being given to employing a coordinator for the entire initiative.

CONCLUSION

The Opening Doors Initiative in Calgary addresses the important issue of creating links among direct practitioners, their supervisors, and agency administrators as a community attempts to break down hierarchical approaches to serving children and families. The Provincial Government's style of relating to the five communities also models the cross-fertilization among agencies and professions that is essential at top policy and executive levels in order to create a reasoned and sustained process of system change.

This chapter has presented an example of family-focused, community-based, integrated service development, linking policy and practice to create and sustain both good multidisciplinary practice and the necessary support systems. The United States has legislation that encourages education systems to develop stronger links to health and welfare institutions. Several states have initiatives to promote community-based practices. But new practice models, as well as models for changing systems are rare. Alberta, Canada, and the Opening Doors Initiative offer a model for the beginning phase of finding new practice models and creating supportive policy and administrative systems.

NOTE

1. The Organization for Economic Cooperation and Development, Paris, France, provided support for this research. Information reported about Alberta, Canada, was obtained through interviews with Assistant Deputy Ministers and members of the Working Group on May 24, 1994, in Edmonton, Alberta. Information about the Opening Doors Initiative was obtained through interviews with the Chief Executive Officers of Education, Welfare, and Health Departments, the Community Resource Group, the Supervisors' Group, and the Professional Resource Group on May 24 and 25, 1994, in Calgary, Alberta.

REFERENCES

Dryfoos, J.G. (1994). *Full-service schools.* San Francisco: Jossey-Bass.

Kusserow, R.P. (1991). *Services integration: A twenty-year retrospective.* Washington, DC: Department of Health and Human Services, Office of the Inspector General.

Lewis, M.R. (1993). European policy responses to school truancy and dropout. In R. Page & J. Baldock (Eds.), *Social Policy Review 5.* Canterbury, Kent, UK: University of Kent and the Social Policy Association.

Massachusetts Advocacy Center. (1988). *Before it's too late: Dropout prevention in the middle grades.* Boston, MA: Author.

Melaville, A.I., & Blank, M.J. (1993). *Together we can.* Washington, DC: U.S. Government Printing Office.

School-linked services. (1992). *The Future of Children, 2* (1). Los Altos, CA: Center for the Future of Children, The David and Lucile Packard Foundation.

U. S. National Commission on Children. (1991). *Beyond rhetoric, a new American agenda for children and families, Final report of the National Commission on Children.* Washington, DC: U. S. Government Printing Office.

9

Community Policing: The Police as a Community Resource

QUINT C. THURMAN

In a provocative look inside America's police forces, the author of *The Police Mystique*, Anthony Bouza, a recently retired Minneapolis Police Chief, writes (1990, p. 225) that "[Police] Chiefs might well strengthen their agencies' operations by eschewing the offers of more cops while insisting that the resources be spent for such ancillary purposes as detox centers, mental-health-care facilities, and shelters." While it seems relatively easy to capture the attention of taxpayers by sensationalizing violence on the streets and the need for better protection, as Bouza adds, attacking highly visible symptoms with short-term fixes fails to address the causes of social problems and provides bleak prospects for long-term gains:

> Nobody wants to look at the upstream questions of family, education, income, jobs, teenage pregnancy, or any of the other numberless disabilities visited upon our underclass. We've lost our passion for the huddled masses and the tempest-tossed. In our myopia we focus on crack, the variable, and ignore the constant, the need for the underclass to escape awful realities of their daily lives. (p. 227)

Police agencies in the United States, as well as elsewhere in the world, typically provide law enforcement and related duties 24 hours a day every day of the year and, as such, play an important role in maintaining the quality of life of a community. However, in addition to being one of the few public service agencies on call around the clock, the police are poised to be effective problem solvers as well, especially when they work in concert with other social service organizations and volunteers who are similarly committed to improving the social well-being of a community.

This chapter explores some promising developments that suggest that modern police forces are entering a new era of social services delivery—one in which it is expected that police agencies imbued with a philosophy of community-oriented policing will do much in the future to help facilitate community based problem-solving.

AN ABBREVIATED HISTORY OF AMERICAN POLICING

Since the early 1900s, American policing has emphasized "crime fighting" as the basis of its public service role. Viewed from this perspective, the "war on crime" would best be fought with greater numbers of personnel, better training, and more sophisticated weaponry and communications. While it was unavoidable that "civilians" would be caught up in the fray as victims/casualties, a more direct role for the public in resolving the social problem of crime was neither asked for nor wanted.

More recently, however, police organizations nationwide have begun to question the relevance of early strategies of crime control. For example, Bouza writes (1990, p. 227):

> The Criminal Justice System is collapsing. In its confusion and tawdriness, it resembles nothing so much as an oriental bazaar. Yet the insistent call for more cops, tougher judges, bigger jails, and more macho prosecutors grows shriller. Our Praetorian Guards have never been bigger, stronger, or more efficient, but they're losing, in ways precisely analogous to the Vietnam war, and with the same official silences, body counts, and promises of victory.

Frequent headlines depicting gang violence, carjackings, and drug deals gone bad suggest to both the public and police executives that traditional, reactive approaches to law enforcement are not winning the crime war. More has to be done to proactively address the root causes of crime and, thus, prevent crime from happening in the first place (cf. Currie, 1993).

While effective policing still requires professionally trained personnel, the lesson learned since the 1930s is that the key to solving social problems is the "co-production of order" (Brudney & England, 1983; Curtis, Thurman, & Nice, 1991). Regardless of their preparedness, the police cannot do the job alone—the public must be effectively involved as co-producers of social order by enlisting their voluntary support for reporting crime and actively engaging in community-based problem solving. Ultimately for police forces, the public good is best served when present-day police services promote future-oriented crime prevention.

Within the realm of law enforcement, the co-production of order is referred to as community-oriented policing (COP), or, more simply, in the remainder of this chapter, community policing. In line with this view, law enforcement should give ground to peace keeping (mediation within interpersonal relationships) and service (problem solving in the broader environment). As Langworthy (1992) suggests, it is this kind of "organic" organization that allows the agency flexibility in solving the problems of the public by asking "How can we help?," rather than responding mechanistically and reactively to only those situations where the enforcement of criminal statutes is prescribed.

COMMUNITY POLICING: WHAT IS IT?

Herman Goldstein (1987) has identified four elements common to agencies that adopt a community policing philosophy. First, the police mission is expanded to include order maintenance. Second, the police are seen as being an integral part of a community's well being. Third, the police become proactive problem solvers. Finally, line officers are given greater freedom to identify community problems and develop solutions to these problems.

Goldstein believes that the success of community policing hinges upon access to a setting in which the police and the community (citizens, schools, social and public service agencies, etc.) are encouraged to work closely with local residents and other interested parties in problem identification and resolution. Similarly, Trojanowicz and Bucqueroux (1990, p. ix) define community policing as

> an organizational strategy that challenges police officers to solve community problems in new ways. It says that the police must form a partnership with people in the community, allowing average citizens the opportunity to have input into the police process, in exchange for their support and participation.... Freed from the isolation of the patrol car and the incessant demands of the police radio, Community Policing Officers operate as full fledged law enforcement officers, but their expanded mission allows them the flexibility and autonomy to develop short- and long-term, community-based efforts to improve the safety and quality of life in the communities they serve.

While the tactics of community policing vary, Goldstein suggests that the most common are (1) increased police–citizen accessibility, (2) the use of problem-oriented policing, (3) order maintenance strategies that require police intervention even without a complaint, (4) increased contact between the police and community organizations or police support for the development of such organizations when they do not already exist, (5) strengthening of community cohesion and the willingness of citizens to take control of their neighborhoods, and (6) sponsoring community crime prevention activities.

SWITCHING FROM TRADITIONAL POLICING TO COMMUNITY POLICING

At a glance, community policing may not appear all that different from its predecessors. After all, criminals and their actions still require a traditional police response from men and women in uniform. But beyond the relatively infrequent occasions when the police are required to use legitimate force, agencies that adhere to a community policing philosophy will commit a greater portion of their resources to crime prevention and less to maintaining a strictly enforcement-oriented police presence.

Mobilizing resources to proactively reduce crime and head-off human tragedies before they materialize is, in effect, smarter policing. Furthermore, engaging capable people to do such work with the realization that they can make a difference within a community is not only smarter policing, but makes better use of police personnel than just their mouths and their muscles; community policing adds to the organization the use of the minds and the hearts of those in uniform.

The institutional image of the police is in need of change when a large segment of the population that police agencies target for services believes that the police are neither effective nor trustworthy. However, agencies are warned not to do this superficially as some departments attempted in the 1970s. More is needed than just a public relations ploy to improve public perceptions of local police (or to try to indoctrinate the public into seeing crime control problems from the police point of view). Instead, agencies will have to sincerely commit to a philosophical change if the public is going to support them and help "co-produce order" and, in turn, if any real progress is to be made in resolving crime and related social problems within a community.

At least partly, a more progressive, second-generation police organization will have to overcome a police subculture inherently resistant to change by hiring, and then training, different types of people to do law enforcement than have been relied upon in the past. Police executives need to develop recruitment programs to attract personnel who can perform at higher levels—individuals who will respect diversity, tolerate civil disobedience, and generally uphold the rights of all citizens as spelled out in the U.S. Constitution. Talking and working *with* the public must become the order of the day rather than talking *to* and working *around* them.

On a par with hiring those persons best suited for incorporating a community-centered approach to police services is education and in-service training. For some time police executives have stressed the need to hire well-rounded, liberally educated individuals with good personal communication skills. Theoretically, such persons will see virtue in the equal protection of all persons regardless of economic, political, or ethnic origin. College-level coursework in criminal justice and law-related fields may be important for informing prospective employees about the careers they have chosen. However, courses in the sociology of the family, criminology, social psychology, political science, social work, and public administration will promote familiarity with the full range of human behavior, provide a broad appreciation of the context of social problems, and lead to a better understanding of the complexities of problem solving in the abstract.

Similarly, in-service training that stresses a sensitivity to cultural diversity as well as opportunities for observing social service delivery at its best is crucial for two reasons. First, given the notoriety of the police subculture, it is to be expected that many (but not all) veteran officers will resist adopting a more service-oriented image. Second, since the nature of the job continually exposes even the most altruistic personalities to the worst side of human behavior, the police, if they are to change, have to be continually reminded that their efforts are highly valued by a worthy public that needs them. From this view, both intrinsic and extrinsic rewards commensurate with an expanded police role are necessary for conveying to police officers the importance of their new mission.

OPERATIONALIZING COMMUNITY POLICING

While many police departments in the United States are making an effort to switch to community policing as an organizational strategy, Moore (1992) notes that there is no definitive evidence to suggest that any police agencies have done so entirely.[1] Nevertheless, Manning (1988, p. 36) suggests that as police organizations move closer to this philosophy, outcomes of community policing will likely include both positive external and internal effects (Table 9.1).

Promising community policing innovations underway in the state of Washington suggest the form that police executives envision when they attempt to operationalize community policing. For example, efforts in Spokane to expand police services into schools to create a community-based link with middle school teachers, students, and local residents have recently been documented (Thurman, Bogen, & Giacomazzi, 1993). This intervention, as well as a second one involving organized interactions with youth from economically disadvantaged neighborhoods (Thurman, Giacomazzi, & Bogen, 1993), have gained recognition in the state and throughout the Pacific Northwest, and suggest one reason that Spokane has been identified as a model community policing city.[2]

Table 9.1. Expected Outcomes of Community Policing

External Effects

1. Police activities in the community (various programs are included in this generalization) increase police job satisfaction.
2. Police actions—positive, proactive, or initiatory—in the community promote community integration and satisfaction.
3. Community policing reduces posited psychological distance between the police and the public.
4. Community policing provides reassurance to citizens.
5. Increased visibility of foot officers increases citizen satisfaction.
6. Increased access to police and "personal" contact with police increases citizen satisfaction.
7. The police foot officer is a surrogate for the community at large, functioning as communal eyes and ears, and acting as a moral and political force on behalf of the community.
8. Community policing reduces the fear of crime.
9. Community policing reduces physical disorder (dirt, abandoned cars, etc.).
10. Community policing increases the security of target groups (the aged, women, and children).

Internal Effects

1. Community policing increases the psychological involvement of officers in the community.
2. Community policing officers develop new skills and roles; for example, they serve as mediators of disputes, as well as being channels through which citizens can contact schools, local social services, and government.
3. Community policing reduces demand upon police time as indicated by changes in the number of calls made to the police.
4. Community policing facilitates police information-gathering.

Adapted from Manning (1988, p. 36).

Community Police Officers (CPOs) in Spokane

The first innovation began in 1992 and involved the assignment of community police officers (CPOs) to East Central and West Central Spokane, the city's two most economically disadvantaged areas. From a list of patrol officers who had volunteered for this assignment, these CPOs were selected for their communication skills, as well as their appeal to local community leaders, and specially trained concerning local public services that might be used in community-centered problem solving.

Input from area residents was sought to identify problems and develop solutions. One goal was an improvement in police–community relations through increased accessibility of police officers and better communication and understanding of the needs of each neighborhood. In addition, the CPO demonstration project sought to actively target "at-risk" children and their parents for intervention.[3] However, in so doing the CPOs were expected to be sensitive to parental authority and, therefore, quick to explain their presence to parents with whom they came into contact. Finally, the CPOs also were expected to provide information on other agencies' resources and initiate assistance whenever appropriate.

In East Central Spokane approximately 17% of the neighborhood's 11,500 residents were minorities, in comparison with the city-wide average of about 5%.[4] Minority groups represented included African-Americans, Southeast Asians, and Native Americans. About 25% of the families were identified as single-parent households, and 41% were considered low income.

The East Central CPO was principally assigned to the local community center, which offered residents a variety of community-based resources, including a library, after school sports and study activities, and workshops on pregnancy prevention, self-esteem, drug prevention, and parenting. Three days each week, part of the CPO's time was spent in the community center and part was spent patrolling the surrounding neighborhood interacting with local residents; the other 2 days were committed to service with the local middle school.

The East Central CPO's duties also included taking responsibility for surveying the East Central area for obvious code violations (e.g., abandoned cars, dangerous nuisances, boarded-up buildings that might invite exploration by children and accommodation for transients, areas in need of sidewalks, and streets and alleys in need of repair or lighting). Once problems were identified, the appropriate city officials were notified. Requests for services then were tracked over time to verify that improvements had occurred.

West Central Spokane also was noted for having a high concentration of families of color, in addition to high resident turnover, physical deterioration, low levels of resident attachment to and identification with the neighborhood, and a significant number of families receiving public assistance (42% live below the poverty level). Furthermore, Spokane's West Central neighborhood had produced a disproportionately high number of adults and children at risk of criminal and/or delinquent involvement, as well as disproportionately high drug use, domestic violence, victimization of elderly residents, robberies, and residential burglaries.

The West Central CPO was assigned directly to the local middle school. Three days each week the West Central CPO provided instruction in the school curriculum, including such courses as Life Sciences, Social Studies, and Language Arts as well as instruction at the Learning Opportunity Center. Prior to his assignment, there were no antidrug programs offered in Spokane schools beyond the AWARE programs for grades 3–5 and the DARE program for all sixth-grade classes. At the time when youth moved from elementary schools to middle school, support programs involving drug refusal skills, recognition of choices, and the strengthening of self-esteem all ceased. The CPO was expected to provide at least partial reinforcement of the lessons learned from AWARE and DARE curriculum, and, in addition, was asked to continue the drug resistance education the students received in the sixth grade.

The West Central CPO spent additional time after school hours and 2 days during the week working in the community contacting parents of seventh graders identified by the officer and the school staff as "at-risk," among various other tasks similarly undertaken by his East Central CPO counterpart.[5]

Both CPOs garnered considerable support for their efforts among teachers, counselors, and students. Teachers viewed the CPOs as educational resources who could be used to promote refusal skills relating to the temptations of gang affiliation, drugs, and alcohol. Counselors also welcomed CPO involvement when dealing with the parents of at-risk youth since the presence of a CPO seemed to increase parental awareness of a youth's problems and the need for working together to arrive at solutions.

Both CPOs were expected to anticipate the needs of at-risk children in their assigned neighborhoods, as determined by contacts with middle school staff and community center personnel, calls for police services, and the officer's own personal observations. In this respect, each officer was viewed as a resource agent charged with determining what course of action would best serve an individual family and either taking action or referring the family to another area agency for drug/alcohol treatment, mental health or public health services, education or job training, marriage/family counseling, or public assistance.

COPY Kids

A second noteworthy innovation, the Community Opportunities Program for Youth (otherwise known as the COPY Kids program) developed by the Spokane Police Department was administered during the Summer of 1992 as an 8-week demonstration project designed to target 11- to 15-year-old children from economically disadvantaged neighborhoods. Each week, program staff (which included police personnel as well as unpaid volunteers) worked in small groups with youths at local sites where they were offered the opportunity to participate in community service projects. The day continued with lunch at a park, followed by recreational activities, and a tour of a local business or municipal organization.

A process evaluation (Thurman, Giacomazzi, & Bogen, 1993) indicated that COPY Kids helped the youths develop a sense of responsibility through participation in community service assignments and suggested that the youths' view of police officers as positive role models was enhanced through close interactions with police department personnel in an informal setting. Research also suggested that a small monetary award of $40 was sufficient to communicate community appreciation for the work each youth had accomplished.

In sum, COPY Kids youths credited the program with helping them learn responsibility, how to work hard with others, how to cooperate, how to be polite, how to make friends, and the importance of staying in school. Other indirect benefits that were observed included a favorable response to the program and its sponsors from the parents of participating youths, as well as benefits to COPY Kids staff in the form of improved images of the young citizens that they serve and protect.

While these evaluations cannot confirm that the Spokane Police Department succeeded in making a philosophical switch to community policing, these and other operational changes suggest that the police in Spokane have in fact moved closer to such an orientation. For example, other innovations that help to better connect the Department with the people of Spokane include a "Responsible Students Are Responsible and Sober" (STARS) program for high school students that was initiated by a patrol officer who saw a need for more involvement with Spokane youths. Also, three community policing substations staffed with local volunteers trained by the police are currently in operation (with plans to open two more) and two unstaffed "storefront" substations made available to officers by local residents and businesses recently opened.

Other relevant programs supported by the Spokane Police Department include speakers bureaus, city-wide DARE/AWARE instruction, a liquor law/nuisance abatement team, an academy for citizen volunteers, a "Neighbors on Patrol" program, a "Parents on Patrol" program, a crime prevention center, a neighborhood block watch coordinator, a volunteer services program, and SHOCAP (Serious Habitual Offender Comprehensive Action Program).

Additionally, an abandoned vehicle team to combat what Wilson and Kelling (1982) refer to as the "broken windows problem" also is in place in Spokane. Wilson and Kelling's widely cited thesis posits that neighborhood signs of unmanaged physical decay and disorderly behavior lead inexorably to fear of public places among law-abiding citizens, followed by their eventual withdrawal, and then the domination of the streets by the disorderly and criminal (cf. Felson, 1987).

OTHER IMPLICATIONS FOR COMMUNITY-CENTERED SERVICES

Anthony Bouza (1990, p. 273) notes that "A nation full of zest and vigor, growing under values that emphasize 'us' rather than 'me,' altruism over hedonism, sacrifice over pleasure, and service over self, will provide for a much safer society than the one we have today." It seems that as they exist today many institutions in the United States, including the police, suffer from the same tendencies toward isolation and drift as many middle-class citizens. To overcome this, the police, like the citizens they serve, have to become interconnected.

This chapter suggests a new direction for contemporary police forces, one that will not only make U.S. streets safer but allow police personnel to significantly contribute to the betterment of social conditions. Some agencies already have made such a commitment, while many others wait, unsure of how to proceed.

Long-term solutions in tight economic times require immediate, short-term sacrifices. Police administrators in a position to take advantage of the fear of crime and chaos by persuading city officials to commit scarce funds to hiring more police personnel for traditional enforcement duties ought first to reexamine the needs of the communities they serve. While the temptation always will be to expand in terms of equipment, personnel, and salaries, the primary responsibility of a police executive is to protect and serve the community. In many cases, using funds to create more humane jail conditions, hiring support staff to assess and then refer nonviolent offenders for treatment, or rehabilitating chronic offenders may be the most cost-effective criminal justice system response.

Similarly, police unions are challenged to consider the public good in negotiations involving the allocation of human resources. For example, more flexibility may be needed in creating meaningful duty assignments. Police chiefs and other criminal justice executives can do little without the support of powerful unions that must decide the form that their contribution to community policing will take.

For both groups, co-producing order with the public will sow the seeds of its own rewards and allow them to make the best use of their minds and hearts while serving the public good. Bellah, Madsen, Sullivan, Swidler, and Tipton (1985) note that

> Undoubtedly, the satisfaction of work well done, indeed 'the pursuit of excellence,' is a permanent and positive human motive. Where its reward is the approbation of one's fellows more than the accumulation of great private wealth, it can contribute to what the founders of our republic called civic virtue. Indeed, in a revived social ecology, it would be a primary form of civic virtue. And from it would flow a number of positive consequences. For one thing, the split between private and public, work and family, that has grown for over a century, might begin to be mended. (p. 288)

CONCLUSION

Social problems persist over time because many of them ultimately may not prove solvable. Complex and complicated questions cannot be resolved with simplistic answers. Many might place the problems of crime and its correlates in this domain. While proponents of community policing offer hope that under proper conditions the successful application of this philosophy can produce desirable benefits, Weisburd and McElroy (1988) remind us that when community policing is confronted with severely disorganized social settings and asked to "make a difference" the result will fall short of the rhetoric. However, it is in just such an environment that change is most crucial. Co-producing solutions to crime and related social problems seems the best means at hand for bringing together human resources and the police for mutual benefit, while at the same time respecting the ability of residents to make important contributions to solving their community's problems.

NOTES

1. The most formal development of a community policing model seems traceable to the foot patrol programs in Flint, Michigan (Trojanowicz & Bucqueroux, 1990) and the Executive Session on Policing at Harvard University (e.g., Kelling & Moore, 1988; Wasserman & Moore, 1988).

2. The U.S. Bureau of Justice Assistance (BJA) recently awarded the Spokane Police Department $200,000 for documenting their efforts to promote Spokane as a model COP city. Only three other cities and one county sheriff's department in the United States have been similarly recognized for their efforts.

3. The determination of whether or not a student was "at-risk" was made in consultation with the CPO and relevant school officials (e.g., counselors, teachers, and staff).

4. Proponents of community policing acknowledge that the people most vulnerable to predation—minorities and the underclass—routinely are ignored in decisions about the most appropriate strategies for controlling crime and disorder and that rediscovery of the community role is instrumental for ameliorating crime and disorder (see Reiss & Tonry, 1986).

5. In addition to contacting parents, the West Central CPO also worked with the community at large to identify abandoned vehicles, settle neighbor-to-neighbor disputes, etc.

REFERENCES

Bellah, R.N., Madsen, R., Sullivan, W.M., Swidler, A., & Tipton, S.M. (1985). *Habits of the heart: Individualism and commitment in American life*. Berkeley, CA: University of California Press.

Bouza, A.V. (1990). *The police mystique: An insider's look at cops, crime, and the criminal justice system*. New York: Plenum Press.

Brudney, J.L., & England, R.E. (1983). Toward a definition of the coproduction concept. *Public Administration Review, 43*, 59–64.

Currie, E. (1993). *Reckoning: Drugs, the cities, and the American future*. New York: Hill and Wang.

Curtis, C., Thurman, Q., & Nice, D.C. (1991). Improving legal compliance by noncoercive means: Coproducing order in Washington State. *Social Science Quarterly, 72*, 645–660.

Felson, M. (1987). Routine activities and crime prevention in the developing metropolis. *Criminology, 25*, 911–931.

Goldstein, H. (1987). Toward community-oriented policing: Potential, basic requirements and threshold questions. *Crime and Delinquency, 33*, 6–30.

Kelling, G.L., & Moore, M.H. (1988). The evolving strategy of policing. *Perspectives on Policing*, No. 4. Washington, DC: National Institute of Justice, U.S. Department of Justice, and Harvard University.

Langworthy, R.H. (1992). Organizational structure. In G.W. Cordner & D.C. Hale (Eds.), *What works in policing: Operations and administration examined* (pp. 87–105). Cincinnati, OH: Anderson Publishing.

Manning, P.K. (1988). Community policing as a drama of control. In J.R. Greene & S.D. Mastrofski (Eds.), *Community policing: Rhetoric or reality* (pp. 27–45). New York: Praeger.

Moore, M.H. (1992). Problem-solving and community policing. In M. Tonry & N. Morris (Eds.), *Modern policing* (pp. 99–158). Chicago, IL: University of Chicago Press.

Reiss, A.J., Jr., & Tonry, M. (Eds.). (1986). *Communities and crime*. Chicago, IL: University of Chicago Press.

Thurman, Q., Bogen, P., & Giacomazzi, A. (1993). Program monitoring and community policing: A process evaluation of community policing officers in Spokane, Washington. *American Journal of Police, 12*, 89–114.

Thurman, Q., Giacomazzi, A., & Bogen, P. (1993). Research note: Cops, kids, and community policing—An assessment of a community policing demonstration project. *Crime and Delinquency, 39*, 554–564.

Trojanowicz, R., & Bucqueroux, B. (1990). *Community policing: A contemporary perspective*. Cincinnati, OH: Anderson Publishing.

Wasserman, R., & Moore, M.H. (1988). Values in policing. *Perspectives on Policing*, No. 8. Washington, DC: National Institute of Justice, U.S. Department of Justice, and Harvard University.

Weisburd, D., & McElroy, J.E. (1988). Enacting the CPO role: Findings from the New York City Pilot Program in Community Policing. In J.R. Greene & S.D. Mastrofski (Eds.), *Community policing: Rhetoric or reality* (pp. 89–101). New York: Praeger.

Wilson, J.Q., & Kelling, G.L. (1982). Broken windows: The police and neighborhood safety. *The Atlantic Monthly, 249*, 29–38.

10

Young People as Community Resources: New Forms of Participation

BARRY CHECKOWAY, JANET FINN, and KAMESHWARI POTHUKUCHI

Human service workers have traditionally viewed youths as problems to be solved, pathologies to be cured, even threats to be feared. In the nineteenth century, youth were often viewed as "little adults" and treated like other workers on farms and in factories (Aries, 1962). Early twentieth-century reformers viewed young people as victims of urban–industrial society and sought measures to protect them from neglect and abuse by adults. Today, there is a growing recognition of "youth as resources" (Kurth-Schai, 1988). The notion is that young people have roles as citizens—with rights to participate and responsibilities to serve—and that adults are allies in the process. This changing conception of youth promises to benefit young people and their communities—in addition to human services.

Young people are proving their resourcefulness in communities nationwide. In Indianapolis, they are assessing community needs and reviewing youth proposals for local improvements. In New York City, they are rehabilitating housing for homeless families. In Selma, Alabama, they are formulating strategies for civil rights and social change. In Albuquerque, New Mexico, they are taking steps against toxic waste and environmental hazards. And in South Dakota, they are setting priorities for small town community development. These efforts vary from place to place, but together demonstrate that young people can plan programs, take action, and create change.

Human service workers are strategically situated to involve young people as resources. Professional mandates and organizational missions in the human services obligate those who work with young people, from school social workers to youth court counselors, to employ empowerment concepts and techniques. For example, the Code of Ethics of the National Association of Social Workers states that "the social worker should make every effort to foster maximum self determination on the part of clients," and that "the social worker should act to expand choice and opportunity for all persons, with special regard for disadvantaged or oppressed groups" (National Association of Social Workers, 1979). Presumably, this extends to young people.

However, human service workers have an uneven record in their promotion of youth participation. Many service providers organize themselves around segments of service delivery that address particular problems, rather than developing methods of participation that build on the strengths of youth. They often view youth as passive recipients of services who are separate from society, rather than as competent citizens with active roles to play. Some seek the representation of young people on committees or boards of youth-serving agencies, whereas others encourage the involvement of youth as mentors and peer counselors in the process of service delivery. Such efforts are not typical in the field, and even these efforts seldom promote the full participation of youth in organizational and community decision making.

This chapter provides a perspective of young people as community resources. It identifies various forms of youth participation, describes some of their benefits, and relates these to the human services. It draws upon extensive work in the field, including a national study of innovative program planning for community-based youth programs (Checkoway & Finn, 1992). It is based on the belief that young people are valuable community resources, and that human service workers should promote youth participation. Further, new knowledge indicates youth participation can strengthen community.

WHAT IS YOUTH PARTICIPATION?

Youth participation is a process of involving young people in the institutions and decisions that affect their lives. It includes initiatives to organize groups for social action, plan programs at the community level, and develop community-based services and resources. It includes efforts to enhance education, employment, environment, housing, health care, or other community systems. It is not a form of adult advocacy for local youth or token representation of youth in committees and meetings of agencies. It is a process through which young people solve problems and carry out plans that provide tangible benefits and increase their involvement in the community.

Youth participation has diverse origins and covers a range of activities. Participation may originate with public agencies or private institutions involving young people as problem solvers, as when a church youth group helps clean up a neighborhood. Or young people themselves may plan a new program of their own, as when a community youth group decides to rebuild a neighborhood center or register voters in political elections. Youth participation is a process of community-based leadership development. Through participation, young people develop as critical actors able to reflect on, act upon, and change their situations.

FORMS OF PARTICIPATION

Youth participation can take various forms, which can be distinguished in order to clarify domains in the field. The following are not the only forms, but they are among the most important.

Social Action

These initiatives involve youth who organize groups for social action. Individuals identify issues of common concern, organize themselves into a group, and take action to create change. Issues include environmental protection, racial discrimination, and neighborhood revitalization. When youth join together for social action, they increase their collective capacity, a lesson that powerful adult groups have known for years.

In Selma, Alabama, for example, youth from the 21st Century Youth Leadership Network organized against tracking African-American students into lower levels in the public schools. They organized protest demonstrations, called a citywide boycott, conducted a sit-in in the high school cafeteria, and influenced change in educational practice. Since then, they have marched against toxic waste dumps, conducted tours of houses whose landlords refused to make needed improvements, and mobilized residents against drug abuse in public housing projects (Sanders, 1991). These efforts are exceptional, but there are also other examples of young people organizing to stop water pollution, win seats for students on local school boards, and conduct letter writing campaigns to public officials.

Community Planning

These initiatives include efforts to plan programs at the community level. Planning may include assessing local conditions, formulating action plans, and building support for implementation.

Some planning is in reaction to issues in the community. In Massachusetts, young people learned about solid wastes that violated air quality standards, researched the causes of the problem, and submitted a proposal to city planners who adopted some of their solutions. In North Carolina, they heard merchants' complaints about teenagers, surveyed students about the situation, and formulated a plan to relocate youth activities. In California, youth assessed neighborhood needs, prepared plans for housing and transportation improvements, and made recommendations to the Redevelopment Planning Board that were incorporated into later decisions (Crabbe, 1989; Lewis, 1991).

Young people proactively plan programs of their own choosing. In Indianapolis, for example, Youth as Resources members form planning committees, assess community needs, invite proposals for programs that involve and benefit youth, and allocate funds for implementation according to established criteria (O'Neil, 1990). In Ann Arbor, Youth Advisory Council members survey their peers, issue requests for proposals, and award grants for programs that address priorities such as race relations, cultural diversity, and teenage stress. They are among 35 youth councils supported by community foundations statewide that assess community needs, set priorities, and award grants to programs that involve youth in the planning process.

Public Advocacy

These initiatives provide representation for young people in legislative, administrative, and other established institutional arenas. Advocates communicate with legislators about policy proposals that affect youth, hold agencies accountable for administrative compliance with existing regulations, and build coalitions to support the interests of youth.

For example, the Youth Action Program of East Harlem rehabilitated their first building for the homeless and wanted to share the experience with others in the city. They formed a coalition of youth groups and social agencies and conducted a city-wide campaign to raise municipal funds for this purpose. They lobbied the city council, testified in public hearings, and responded to announced public municipal cutbacks, holding a 48-hour vigil during the final budget deliberations at city hall (Stoneman, 1988).

Latin American Youth Center youth leaders also responded to announced municipal cutbacks in programs serving youth in the community. They circulated petitions, testified at public hearings, and demonstrated against the Mayor at city hall. They staged theater productions in front of the city council chambers, visited council members in their offices, and presented them with T-shirts with the Center's emblem and helped convince them to restore the funds (Checkoway & Finn, 1992).

Community Education

These initiatives strengthen the consciousness, competence, and confidence of youth to "transform the world." In contrast to situations in which young people sit in silence rather than raise questions, or accept the roles that others attribute to them rather than develop their own, these initiatives encourage them to reflect, act upon, and change their situation. In a low-income neighborhood in Salt Lake City, for example, elementary school students identified a hazardous waste site near the school—a barrel recycling plan with a stockpile of drums that contained hazardous chemicals. Ignoring health officials who had tried to discourage them, they studied the situation and decided to remove the barrels from the neighborhood. They conducted community surveys, spoke out at meetings, and wrote resolutions that stimulated state legislation. Young people also present educational programs to school children, sociodramas to popular audiences, and demonstrations in community centers. They publish newspapers with critical perspectives on social issues, and conduct programs that analyze racism and discrimination in society (Lewis, 1991).

Local Services Development

These initiatives involve youth in efforts to develop community-based services for themselves and the community. This may produce programs responsive to needs such as education, employment, healthcare, housing, and economic development in urban (Lewis, 1991) and rural (Heartland Center, 1988) areas.

In Washington, for example, the Latin American Youth Center promotes social and economic development in a Latino neighborhood. They have a facility for cultural events and a drop-in center for recreational activities. They provide employment and training opportunities, several social services, and multicultural activities. They conduct seminars on youth issues, publish a bilingual youth newspaper, and involve youth in the political process of the community.

Also, the Youth Action Program of East Harlem rehabilitates abandoned housing for the homeless, while completing their education and preparing for employment. They operate a resource center and "safe haven" on East 103rd Street and form citywide coalitions to set priorities and formulate a youth agenda for the city. Each project is governed by an activist core of young people who serve on the governing body and make policy and budgetary decisions for the program overall. This program was a model for congressional legislation that authorizes federal agencies to support counterpart programs in low-income communities nationwide (Stoneman, 1988).

BENEFITS OF YOUTH PARTICIPATION

What are the benefits of youth participation at the individual, organizational, and community levels? The following are some of the benefits on which researchers and practitioners tend to agree.

Individual Involvement

Youth participation provides opportunities for individuals to meet others and build support in ways that produce positive psychosocial results. Studies show that participation can have positive effects on openmindedness (Wilson, 1974), personal responsibility (Conrad & Hedin, 1982; Rutter & Newmann, 1989), social competence (Newmann & Rutter, 1988), moral and ego development, and sense of efficacy and self-esteem (Zimmerman, 1995). In contrast to the pattern of frustration and alienation in which youth withdraw from participation, these initiatives reduce isolation and increase their interaction in the community (Calabrese & Schumer, 1986; Sutton, 1992).

Youth participants report personal benefits as a result of their participation. "The center has never let me down and gives me a feeling of security and unity," said one youth reflecting on her experience at a community youth center. "Because of the center I have been able to accomplish many things and have been part of many leadership activities which have helped me be a better leader, listener, and friend," said another. "We got a sense of pride and importance, something teenagers don't get anywhere else," said another. "The program gave me a reason to live, something I didn't have before" (Checkoway & Finn, 1992).

Participation can enhance experiential education and skills development. Consistent with the theories of John Dewey (1938) on learning as a form of interaction with the environment, studies show that participation can strengthen student motivation and academic achievement in the classroom and increase their substantive knowledge and problem-solving capacity in the community (Checkoway & Cahill, 1981; Conrad & Hedin, 1991; Crabbe, 1989). Indeed youth report that community service often teaches them more than they learn in the classroom (Conrad & Hedin, 1982; Nathan & Kielsmeier, 1991; Newmann & Rutter, 1988; Sheat & Beer, 1989).

In contrast to those who accept their social situation as given, youth participants are more likely to think critically and actively challenge their circumstances. They include youth who challenge the conditions that perpetuate poverty, analyze the causes of racism, and critically reflect on important issues. They show a personal and political transformation that contrasts with their peers. It has been observed that group problem solving in a public environment leads to the development of better citizenship skills than participation in isolated projects (Boyte, 1991).

Psychosocial benefits of youth participation may have particular importance for at-risk or socially oppressed youth. In Chicago's Cabrini-Green housing project, for example, the Jesse White Tumbling Team performs in the community, offering young males alternatives to the gangs in the neighborhood (Irby, 1991; Irby & McLaughlin, 1990). Community participation provides structures and discipline, a sense of personal identity, and social supports unavailable elsewhere. Studies document the special benefits of participation for at-risk groups in Boston, Detroit, Chicago, Los Angeles, and other cities (Heath & McLaughlin, 1991).

Organizational Development

Youth participation can contribute to organizational development. It is difficult for young people to plan programs when they lack consciousness of themselves as competent community builders or when adults promote practices that foster their dependence. Young people are often unaware of their rights as citizens in society or hesitant to intrude in matters that seem beyond reach. They may accept the notion of adult control over youth services, even when these are intended to meet their special needs, or defer to adult advocates who represent their interests without involving them in the process.

However, youth participation can build formal and informal organizational structure. Formal organization includes intentional efforts to set priorities, formulate plans, and implement programs. Participants develop skills in forming committees, conducting meetings, making decisions, and completing tasks. Informal organization includes personal relationships that provide social supports and, in some cases, surrogate family functions. Heath and McLaughlin (1991), in their study of participation in Chicago, document young people's capacity to build organizations. Part of this strength stems from the benefit of "organization as family" where supportive intergenerational ties for mutual teaching and learning are cultivated.

For example, Students Educating Eachother about Discrimination (SEED) is a group of teenagers who educate themselves and young children about discrimination. SEED started as an informal group of friends who assessed racial attitudes in the schools, formulated an action plan, and built community support for its program. It has a core of people who recruit members and train more than 100 facilitators for work in the middle schools. Their organizational structure permits them to formulate plans and implement programs without adult intervention in a nonhierarchical dialogical process, while also developing the capacity to deal with the hierarchical institutional systems of adults (Polakow-Suransky & Ulaby, 1990; Winn, Morado, & West, 1992).

Community Development

Youth participation can contribute to community development. In New York, for example, young people plan programs that rehabilitate abandoned buildings while also completing their education and preparing for employment. When construction is complete, the buildings become permanent housing for the homeless, program participants graduate to nonsubsidized jobs, and the neighborhood is improved as a result (Stoneman, 1988).

In rural North Carolina, young people plan programs that turn initiative into economic development. The program includes an educational component in which youth take courses in entrepreneurship and business management, a planning component in which they develop their own businesses in cooperation with local institutions, and an implementation component in which they operate their own enterprises that enhance the economy. As young people become entrepreneurs, they contribute to community development (Heartland Center, 1988).

Youth participation can also contribute to political development. Public policy issues affecting young people operate in an imbalanced political arena. First, interest groups concerned with adult issues mobilize more political resources than do representatives of youth. Second, child welfare advocates concerned with problems affecting youth—such as substance abuse, teen pregnancy, and juvenile delinquency—mobilize more resources than those who concern themselves with building the capacity of young people to influence policies and plan programs on their own.

However, youth participation can involve young people in the policy process. There are young people who effectively participate in public proceedings, conduct voter registration campaigns, serve on organizational boards and committees, and act as leaders in the community. They persuade public officials to allocate resources for programs and pressure agency staff to comply with administrative regulations (Lewis, 1991). Several publications promote youth participation in public policy (Schine & Harrington, 1982; Crabbe, 1989) and develop citizenship skills for political democracy (Boyte, 1991; Drews, 1992; Hamilton & Zeldin, 1989; Newmann, 1975).

YOUTH PARTICIPATION AND HUMAN SERVICE WORKERS

Human service workers have a long history of commitment to youth, but the voices of young people have been largely silent in planning, delivery, and evaluation of programs and services. Professional social work journals address important issues on family preservation, child abuse prevention, and a comprehensive continuum of care for children and youth. However, concepts and techniques of youth participation are usually absent from these debates.

How do we account for this uneven record? There are three common ways to explain the gap between promise and practice in youth participation. First is to attribute the gap to the characteristics of the participants. It is difficult to involve young people when the issues do not capture their imagination or when they do not view themselves as a group that should participate in the process. Young people are socialized into a subservient orientation in which an acceptance of the adult monopoly in the family or society is transferred to human service delivery. It is no surprise that young people may question their own role or show symptoms of alienation from the community. Strengthening their skills for collective action would encourage participation, according to this view.

The second view attributes the performance gap to human service workers and their agencies. It is difficult to involve young people when human service workers do not recognize them as a legitimate constituent group or when organizations lack the resources to make participation work. Human service professionals often perceive laypersons as uninformed amateurs. They may emphasize professional expertise, technical efficiency, and administrative control, which are antithetical to participation. Agencies often select safe methods—such as public hearings—designed to provide public relations and serve administrative ends without transfer of power to ordinary citizens. If workers had an alternative vision of their role as collaborators and partners rather than "experts" or agents of social control, and if they had the resources for the purpose, they would promote participation, according to this view (Checkoway, 1982; Checkoway & Finn, 1992).

The third view contends that the performance gap is the direct result of the community context in which human services operate. Simply stated, adults perceive that they, not youth, should control the decision-making process. For example, child welfare advocates view young people as vulnerable members of society who are too often neglected or abused by adults or victimized by forces beyond their control. Advocates seek to strengthen services for youth, but usually without their participation, thus relegating them to secondary or tertiary roles rather than allowing them primary roles in decision-making processes. To the extent that the process is—or should be—reflective of the community, it is no surprise that human service workers favor adults rather than young people. Human service workers respond to the most powerful inputs they receive and these come from adults, not children. To promote the participation of youth, it first would be necessary to alter the community context in which it occurs, according to this view.

NEW ROLES FOR HUMAN SERVICE WORKERS?

What could human service workers do to promote youth participation? The following are a few suggestions.

First is to help develop the capacity of young people as participants in the community. People cannot be expected to participate effectively if they lack knowledge, skills, and attitudes necessary to the task. By adopting a strengths perspective, human service workers can recognize and foster the capacities of young people (Saleebey, 1992; Cowger, 1994). As young people and adults recognize one another as resources, they open themselves to learn from one another and to strengthen the bonds of friendship and collaboration. For example, at Indianapolis Youth as Resources, young people constitute one-third of the board of directors' membership. The board operates on a partnership principle that promotes close working relationships among younger and older members.

New initiatives are needed for education and training to enable human service providers—and the young citizens whom they serve—to develop knowledge and skills to assess community conditions, to set priorities, make decisions, develop action plans, and formulate strategies to implement programs. These skills are basic to community problem solving. There is no a priori reason why citizens should not have them. By reinventing their roles as allies with youth, human service providers could think of their knowledge and skills as something to be shared with young people rather than to be used on them. As young people are given meaningful consultant roles, they will develop confidence as participants, which is particularly important in working with people who experience oppression.

There is evidence that training can alter the quality of community participation and that some people desire such training and benefit from it (Checkoway, Pothukuchi, & Purnell, 1992). For example, in a community education program for substance abuse prevention in Detroit, service providers, community members, and researchers collaborated to organize and train youth, parents, and community residents to serve as counselors, community surveyors, and educators. The program has demonstrated that community members, especially youth, can be successfully involved in identifying community needs and implementing change-oriented activities (Sarri, Mogane, & Schwab, 1991).

Leadership development could be a central focus of education and training for young people. In addition to the basic knowledge of problem solving, they would learn about the political economy of human service systems, the ideologies of principal actors, the distribution of community power, and the special problems of young people. Lessons would include ways to recognize adult discrimination, counteract oppression, and organize youth to have an impact on the community. For example, young people of Belle Fourche, South Dakota, have learned important civics lessons as they made the community their classroom. They have taken an active role in understanding and changing the course of community decision making (Checkoway & Finn, 1992). Through participation, young people develop competence as community leaders (Stoneman, 1988).

New initiatives are needed to increase public awareness of the importance of youth participation. Awareness building can take various forms. For example, Gordon (1978) formulates strategies for using newspapers, radio, and television media for social change. Brawley (1983) presents ways in which agencies can use mass media to communicate their message. Lauffer (1984) analyzes marketing methods for social agencies that produce popular publications for mass distribution. Youth themselves have proven their effectiveness as critical analysts of the issues that affect their lives and have taken their messages to the streets. Young people around the country are starting their own newspapers, radio stations, and television shows, with adults as allies (Checkoway & Finn, 1992). National youth news services connect young journalists with youth audiences around the country. These organizational networks provide conduits for collaboration among young people and adults in promoting youth participation.

CONCLUSION

Youth participation in human services can increase involvement of individuals, contribute to organizational development, and create community change. It can represent an important, ignored constituency, promote their leadership development, and make human services more responsive to their interests. Despite the benefits, human service workers have an uneven record in the promotion of youth participation as competent citizens and community builders. There are exceptional efforts by some human service workers to promote youth participation, but they are not typical in the field. New initiatives are needed to increase the knowledge and capacity of young people, increase youth involvement in the decisions that affect their lives, and increase public awareness and raise community consciousness. Human service workers are strategically situated for such work. And if only a few of them were to promote participation of young people, it might make a difference.

ACKNOWLEDGMENTS

Some of the research on which this chapter is based was supported by a grant from the W.K. Kellogg Foundation.

REFERENCES

Aries, P. (1962). *Centuries of childhood: A social history of family life.* New York: Alfred Knopf.

Boyte, H. (1991). Community service and civic education. *Phi Delta Kappan, 72,* 765–767.

Brawley, E.A. (1983). *Mass media and human services: Getting the message across.* Beverly Hills, CA: Sage Publications.

Calabrese, R.L., & Schumer, H. (1986). The effect of service activities on adolescent alienation. *Adolescence, 21,* 675–687.

Checkoway, B. (1982). Public participation in health planning agencies: Promise and practice. *Journal of Health Politics, Policy and Law, 7*, 722–733.

Checkoway, B., & Cahill, W. (1981). Student workshops and neighborhood revitalization. *Journal of Alternative Higher Education, 6*, 96–110.

Checkoway, B., & Finn, J. (1992). *Young people as community builders*. Ann Arbor, MI: University of Michigan, Center for the Study of Youth Policy.

Checkoway, B., Pothukuchi, K., & Purnell, R. (1992). *Training materials for community youth programs*. Ann Arbor, MI: University of Michigan, Center for the Study of Youth Policy.

Conrad, D., & Hedin, D. (1982). The impact of experiential education on adolescent development. *Child and Youth Services, 4*, 57–76.

Cowger, C. (1994). Assessing client strengths: Clinical assessment for client empowerment. *Social Work, 39*, 262–268.

Crabbe, A.B. (1989). The future problem-solving program. *Educational Leadership, 47*, 27–29.

Dewey, J. (1938). *Experience and education*. New York: Collier.

Drews, N. (1992). *Learning the skills of peacemaking: An activity guide for elementary-age children on communicating, cooperating, resolving conflict*. Minneapolis, MN: Free Spirit Publishing.

Gordon, R. (1978). *We interrupt this program... A citizen's guide to using the media for social change*. Amherst, MA: Citizen Involvement Training Project.

Hamilton, S.F., & Zeldin, L.M. (1989). The impact of volunteer experience on adolescent social development: Evidence of program effects. *Journal of Adolescent Research, 3*, 65–80.

Heath, S.B., & McLaughlin, M.W. (1991). Community organizations as family: Endeavors that engage and support adolescents. *Phi Delta Kappan, 72*, 623–627.

Heartland Center. (1988). *Schools as entrepreneurs: Helping small towns survive*. Lincoln, NE: Heartland Center.

Irby, M.A. (1991, Spring). Black with an eager mind: The design of diversity in a neighborhood-based organization. *Future Choices, 2*, 107–110.

Irby, M.A., & McLaughlin, M.W. (1990, Fall). When is a gang not a gang? When it is a tumbling team. *Future Choices, 1*, 31–39.

Kurth-Schai, R. (1988). The roles of youth in society: A reconceptualization. *The Educational Forum, 53*, 113–132.

Lauffer, A. (1984). *Strategic marketing for not-for-profit organizations*. New York: Free Press.

Lewis, B.A. (1991). *The kid's guide to social action: How to solve the social problems you choose—and turn creative thinking into positive action*. Minneapolis, MN: Free Spirit Publishing.

Nathan, J., & Kielsmeier, J. (1991). The sleeping giant of school reform. *Phi Delta Kappan, 72*, 739–742.

National Association of Social Workers. (1979). *1979 Code of Ethics for the National Association of Social Workers*. Washington, DC: Author.

Newmann, F.M. (1975). *Education for citizen action: Challenge for secondary curriculum*. Berkeley, CA: McCutchan.

Newmann, F.M., & Rutter, R.A. (1988). The effects of high school community service programs on adolescent social development: Evidence of program effects. *Journal of Adolescent Research, 3*, 65–80.

O'Neil, J. (1990). *Changing perspectives: Youth as resources.* Washington DC: National Crime Prevention Council.

Polakow-Suransky, S., & Ulaby, N. (1990). Students take action to combat racism. *Phi Delta Kappan, 71*, 601–606.

Rosener, J.B. (1975). Citizen participation: Tying strategy into function. *Public Management, 21*, 16–19.

Rutter, R.A., & Newmann, F. (1989). The potential of community service to enhance civic responsibility. *Social Education, 53*, 372–374.

Saleebey, D. (Ed.). (1992). The strengths perspective in social work practice. New York: Longman.

Sanders, R.M. (1991, Winter). 21st century leaders: A model program in the Black community. *Future Choices, 2*, 74–82.

Sarri, R., Mogane, M., & Schwab, G. (1991). *Community education for substance abuse prevention: Evaluation of the Wolverine Human Services Program in Detroit, Michigan.* Ann Arbor, MI: University of Michigan, Institute for Social Research.

Schine, J.G., & Harrington, D. (1982). *Youth participation for early adolescents: Learning and serving in the community.* Bloomington, IN: Phi Delta Kappa Educational Foundation.

Sheat, L., & Beer, A.B. (1989). User participation—A design methodology for school and grounds design and environmental learning. *Children's Environmental Quarterly, 6*, 15–30.

Stoneman, D. (1988). *Leadership development: A handbook from the youth action program of East Harlem block schools.* New York: Youth Action Program.

Sutton, S.E. (1985). *Learning through the built environment: An ecological approach to child development.* New York: Irvington Publishers.

Sutton, S.E. (1992). Enabling children to map out a more equitable society. *Children's Environments, 9*, 30–33.

Wilson, T.C. (1974). *An alternative community-based secondary school education program and student political development.* Unpublished doctoral dissertation, University of Southern California, Los Angeles.

Winn, E., Morado, C., & West, H. (1992). *Resource manual for SEED.* Ann Arbor, MI: Students Educating Eachother about Discrimination.

Zimmerman, M. (1995). Empowerment theory: Psychological, organizational and community levels of analysis. In J. Rappaport & E. Seidman (Eds.), *Handbook of community psychology.* New York: Plenum Press. In press.

III

CHANGING PRACTICE TO INCLUDE FAMILIES AND COMMUNITIES

Part III of this book examines the changes in practice required to implement a community- and family-centered approach. These chapters discuss how service providers understand and create community, how they bring community to bear on work with individuals and families, and how they can work with families as full partners in the design and delivery of services.

To include community in practice, Eric W. Rothenbuhler argues in Chapter 11, professionals first need to lay the groundwork for intervention and change. Reconceptualizing community as a legitimate part of professional practice spreads responsibility for resolving issues of concern and expands available resources. However, the very diversity that provides new points of view and resources may also be a barrier to developing a common identity that promotes sharing. As an ideal, community evokes emotional ties and identifications that are expressed as hopes, promises, disappointments, appeals, and attempts at change. Identification with a community helps to transcend the narrow bounds of individualism: *our* successes and failures are also *my* successes and failures.

The problem is that such commitment to community is seldom present, at least to the degree required for effective problem solving. But commitment can be created in actions that symbolize *and* create the kind of community involvement that is desired. Expanding the professional role to legitimize community work would encourage and enable social workers to participate as community members and, in so doing, to begin to construct the kind of community in which sharing of responsibility is the rule rather than the exception.

Carol R. Swenson agrees in Chapter 12 that to move away from an individualistic focus on therapy and self-help, social workers need to develop a new vision of community. Two assumptions drive this quest: first, that the individual, family, and community exist as multiple, nested systems and that interventions need to address relationships within and across all these levels; and second, that clients and workers need together to create new meanings of community. While psychotherapy in general has tended to turn social problems into personal ones, reinforcing an ideal of self-contained individualism, social work has maintained a broader perspective, including a focus on the person-in-environment and community intervention. However, even in social work, most change efforts remain within the bounds of the self or the family.

In-depth interviews with clinical social workers reveal that they have rich conceptions of the role of community in their own lives and participate actively in creating and maintaining these personal communities, but have a much narrower view of community in the lives of their clients. Clinicians talk about community in utilitarian terms, as a resource and support for clients, and recognize community as an important aspect of identity, but they do not acknowledge or promote commitment or reciprocity between clients and their communities. Clients are seen only as "receivers," not as "givers," if community relationships are considered at all.

Although these social workers seemed unaware of this narrow and disempowering approach to community in their practice, their lack of attention relays to clients that community is unimportant, reinforcing the individualism dominant in society. Practice can only be reshaped by integrating into theory and practice a new concept of self-in-community that values attachment and commitment as well as autonomy.

Although working with individuals may appear to be "easier" than including complex family and community systems in professional practice, William H. Quinn shows in Chapter 13 that it is often less effective. Individuals cannot be understood apart from the relationships in which they are embedded—both past and current. If assessment omits information about key family members such as noncustodial parents or about wider social networks, family and community resources important to problem resolution may be overlooked. This broader view must include family and community strengths, especially those used in coping with stressful environments. It must also extend beyond narrow professional boundaries and bring in the perspectives and resources of other disciplines. Work with youths and their families who are experiencing problems with school failure or criminal behavior shows how more inclusive practice works.

The examples provided by Quinn demonstrate how practitioners can overcome the tendency to focus on individuals by employing principles derived from innovative practice in the diverse fields represented in this volume: first, by working with the family's environment to promote positive experiences and early intervention; second, by using family and community information and resources in interventions; and third, by adapting professional mandates to address family and community issues as well as individual needs and to promote environments supportive of personal well-being and productive living.

The final chapter by Robert Cohen and Christopher Lavach deals with some of the social policy and professional issues raised by this new approach to human services. Families have often been blamed for their children's problems by service providers, particularly in the mental health system. In addition, neither social policy nor service delivery systems have been responsive to families' needs for support, often offering placement of the child outside the home as the only alternative for overburdened caregivers.

In contrast, recent federal initiatives encourage parental participation "in all aspects of the planning and delivery of services" and the development of comprehensive systems of care that include home-based interventions, day treatment, and respite care to alleviate the financial and social burden on caregivers. However, professionals' perceptions of families, the reliance on institutional care, and a lack of intermediate level services place considerable barriers in the way of achieving these goals.

To involve parents fully as partners in interventions and service delivery, their contributions as experts in their situation, advocates, change agents, and supporters of other parents must be recognized and valued by professionals. In turn, professionals must make use of interventions that reduce blame, increase support, and recognize diversity. These include parent groups, clergy and natural helpers, and family therapy to help families cope with the stress of serious mental illness.

In addition to developing new skills in collaborative problem solving and involvement of formal and informal helpers, professionals need empowering administrative structures and incentives that reward engagement of families and mobilization of resources rather than the logging in of service hours. Finally, changes in policy are needed to support parent involvement and more inclusive professional practice. Specific examples include ending requirements that parents relinquish custody to receive inpatient treatment for their children and developing interagency coalitions to assure integrated systems of care.

These changes in the thinking and behavior of practitioners and agencies cannot be achieved without commitment, training, and resources. However, the examples of innovative community and family-centered practice in this volume can provide a starting point for the hard work involved in reinventing human services.

11

Understanding and Constructing Community: A Communication Approach

ERIC W. ROTHENBUHLER

The promise of community is that it is a kind of plural individuality, a corporate identity. This is recognized in the use of first person plural pronouns and verb tenses. *We* are members of a community; a community is something we claim as *ours*. We have hope for community-centered practice because we can imagine that it would take the form of "our solution to our problem." Similarly, we can imagine that although a community might need some outside help, a significant portion of whatever redistribution of resources was necessary could be advanced through pooling and sharing. We imagine a group accepting responsibility for a problem, choosing their own solution, and setting out to implement it.

The "we" of community-centered practice must transcend at least differences in practices and differences in resources. These resources could include ideas, information, time, energy, and experience. In addition, any kind of background, such as education, ethnicity, class, or political party connections, that might be relevant to the problem or solution, is an issue on which the community needs diversity.

DEFINING COMMUNITY

The definition of the term community and whatever logic derives from it should not be taken for granted. For some authors in this volume "community" is another word for neighborhood or locality. For community-centered practice this may often be adequate; for theoretical analysis it is not. A community may be in a place, but the concept is not exhausted by place. There are things we hope and expect of community above and beyond being a location. A community is an aggregate of individuals, in a group, in a place, engaged in patterns of activity, holding ideals they hope govern that activity, identifying themselves with this constellation, with feelings about the happiness of it all.

The individuals of a community are not a simple aggregate, but are a group. This implies some level of integration of their activities into a system that defines the group (e.g., Park & Burgess, 1921/1969). Another form of integration is some level of identification of the members with the group (Pitts, 1961). Both forms of integration imply acceptance of limits on choice (Parsons, 1937/1968; Parsons & Shils, 1951). But other than as a theoretical model, no system is fully integrated. We should expect variance in level of integration, and level of attention to integration, across time, places, activities, and people (Shils, 1975, pp. 48–90, 164–181).

Community as Place

To make place only part of the definition of community raises the question of whether it is necessary at all. Communities that are based in modes of communication and transportation rather more than place are interesting phenomena (e.g., Webber, 1963), but not our primary concern here. Besides, despite the tremendous changes in geographical mobility, transportation, and communication in the last 150 years, place continues to be a key base of personal and social identification, as well as a primary material reality (Calabrese, 1991; Howell & Frese, 1983; Hummon, 1986; Kirby, 1989; Rivlin, 1982; Sampson, 1988; Suttles, 1984; Wellman, 1979). The relevant place could be an institutional setting for a colleagial community or a geographical setting for a settlement community; but our concern here is with communities anchored in place.

Even if place is important, making it only one of the elements of community opens up some logical possibilities that have important empirical implications. People can be located in a place, but not, by other criteria, be members of the community. Analogously, there may be people who are members of the community, by most of the criteria, but who are not located in the primary place of the community. At the system level, a place could have problems that the community does not, while a community could have resources for a solution that the place alone could not provide. For example, everyone might agree that a particular neighborhood was poor; but it could be just one part of a larger community that is not poor, or at least not too poor to go to work on improving its conditions.

Some participation in community activities is expected of members and status or other sanctions are allocated partly on the basis of participation (e.g., Bell & Newby, 1971; Gans, 1962; Lynd & Lynd, 1937; Vidich

& Bensman, 1968; Whyte, 1955). But, of course, people vary in their levels of attention, interest, and participation and in their susceptibility to the sanctioning power of community relations (Fischer, 1975; Fischer et al., 1977; Greer, 1967; Janowitz, 1967; Jeffres & Dobos, 1984; Jeffres, Dobos, & Lee, 1988; Jeffres, Dobos, & Sweeny, 1987; Kasarda & Janowitz, 1974; Rothenbuhler, 1991; Stamm, 1985; Stamm & Guest, 1991; Tsai & Sigelman, 1982).

Community as Ideal

Just as there is a long and living tradition of identifying community with place, so there is a long and living tradition of identifying community with a set of ideals (Nisbet, 1982; Quandt, 1970; Strauss, 1968; Tinder, 1980). Communities are thought of as being based on primordial ties that create commonalities that are more important than other social differences; these ties produce consensus, a concern with the other as a whole and particular person, and an emphasis on concreteness and particularity rather than the abstract generalizations of modern professionalism (Tönnies, 1887/1988). Communities are thought to be nurturing and healthful; places where we accept and care about each other (e.g., Bellah, Madsen, Sullivan, Swidler, & Tipton, 1985; Stein, 1960). Of course these ideas are not very useful for describing actual communities, but they are ever-present in attempts to create and maintain them. These ideals are a part of the reality of communities in the form of hopes, promises, disappointments, appeals, and attempts.

Identification of the individual with the group is a key element of community that has two important implications for this chapter. First, through identification, the community becomes a part of who individuals think they are, and thus the mechanism by which the first person plural is a correct grammatical form. Second, it is through identification that individuals accept community contingencies as their own. When we identify with a social group or institution—a family, place of work, neighborhood, school, political party, sports team, city, nation, ethnicity, whatever—then even though outside of us, to some degree it is experienced as an internal check on our thoughts, emotions, choices, and speaking ultimately, our will. Growth, development, success, failure, plans, goals, setbacks, and other phenomena of group life become analogous phenomena for the individual; *our* successes and failures are also *my* successes and failures.

Alongside this elemental phenomenon, in most human affairs there is some semiconscious ceremonial of participation; humans need to be and enjoy being in groups. So while the average sports team loses 50% of its games, the average sports fan is loyal, even though disappointed, throughout the season. Analogously, at work and at home, we accept the groups we find ourselves members of, and to one degree or another, we strive to be good members. Hence ideals, expectations, sanctions, and so on become relevant inducements aiding the integration of the individuals' activities. In turn, this reinforces the social presence of community—in the form of integrated activities, expectations, etc.—thus its attractiveness for identification and its power for sanctioning.[1]

Finally, an important part of any community is the range of feelings of its members about their membership. Community is an important thing; it generates a broad array of strong emotions. Disappointments and frustrations and how they are dealt with are no less prevalent or important to how communities work than are happiness and satisfaction.

So a community-centered practice would be something done by a group of individuals who identify themselves with the group and the place, whose activities exhibit some degree of integration, with some distribution of community ideals in mind, some distribution of knowledge and ideas about community actualities, ideas about discrepancies between the preferences and the actualities of the place they all live in, and ideas about what to do about it.

COMMITMENT TO COMMUNITY

But we need to compare our definitions, and the hopes for community-centered practice that derive from them, to the record of empirical community studies. That record is clear; membership varies. As pointed out above, so long as membership is defined as something more than just living in a place, the people that live in a place may well vary in their membership on any other dimension. (See the literature cited in the previous section.)

One interpretation of this record of empirical variance in community membership is that people's devotion of time, energy, and resources to community is a rational response to their circumstances.[2] People who need more from the community will devote more to the community. So will people whose other activities put them in more frequent contact with community activities. People who need less from the community will offer it less and expect it to demand less of them. Property owners are more likely to pay attention to local affairs and participate in local politics. Parents of school-aged children will tend to be more involved in a variety of community affairs, from car pooling and babysitting to PTA meetings, school board elections, and bond issues. Young adults with good incomes and no children are notoriously uninvolved in the places they live and quick to move for improvements in lifestyle or property values. Janowitz (1967) called this whole complex "the community of limited liability:" like limited liability participation in a corporation, people's willingness to devote time, energy, and resources to a community is proportional to what they expect of the community; they will quickly withdraw if the community needs more of them than they are willing to commit.

The community of limited liability is a serious threat to community-centered practice. The balance of presumption is tipped toward the benefits of community membership and away from responsibilities. A community of limited liability is conceived as something from which the individual receives rather more than it is something to which the individual gives or in which the individual participates. The value of community is cast in terms of the satisfaction of individuals. A place to live is conceived as a means to an end; that end could be as general as happiness or satisfaction with life, or as specific as status, leisure opportunities, good schools, access to shopping, or easy transportation. Decisions about participation, staying, or moving are presumed to be based on a quasieconomic form of reasoning about the costs of desired ends (e.g., Fischer, 1982; Fischer et al., 1977, esp. pp. 139–186; Rossi, 1956).

Inefficiencies and Disutilities

Quasieconomic thinking can motivate people to action only when they can calculate a reasonable chance of a reasonably sized reward, depending on the size of the investment. But community-centered practice depends on a conception of community that can hold diverse individuals together in relations of mutual obligation, even in the face of gross inefficiencies and disutilities. To the extent community is thought of only as a place where one lives as a means to other ends, or due to a lack of means to make other choices, then the rational response to community problems is withdrawal. Withdrawal, of course, can range from small reductions in attention, caring, or simple presence on the street (withdrawing inside the home) through reductions in community activities and devotion of time, energy, and other resources to, at the extreme, leaving the neighborhood. (See Fischer et al., 1977; and Fischer, 1982, for a constraints model in which the happiness of a community and the people in it is dependent on the voluntariness of its residents, which in turn is dependent on their own means and choices.)

For community-centered practice to work as I have sketched it here, people's conception of a community must be such that a redistribution of resources that perhaps hurts them as economic individuals could be experienced as a gain because it helps the community. Imagine people volunteering time to help a school bond issue pass. They are giving a resource to the community that they could keep or invest for personal gain. In a community of limited liability, the only people who would do that are those for whom the investment had an individual payoff of corresponding size—those whose children would be in the local schools for a given number of additional years, for example. But in a community of committed group members, there would be many who could imagine an improvement of the community being an improvement of themselves and, thus, not experience the donation of time as either a sacrifice or an investment.

Normative and Instrumental Action

Our proposal for community-centered practice depends on people equating the communal good with their own well-being. But at the same time, research indicates that people often do not think that way, inviting explanations such as Janowitz's (1967) community of limited liability and Fischer's (1982) constraints model. In addition, quasieconomic thinking of the sort that threatens the viability of community-centered practice has a long and vital intellectual history and is presumed in policy debates (see, e.g., Fisher this volume).

However, quasieconomic thinking is not the only possibility. One theme in sociological theory has worked to overcome the intellectual dominance of quasieconomic thinking, to refute the empirical claims of quasieconomic models, and to synthesize an alternative perspective that can account for when people do calculate utilities as well as for when they do not. The two schools of thought can be conveniently, if not entirely accurately, captured by the labels instrumental and normative (Alexander, 1982–83; Parsons, 1937/1968; Weber, 1922/1978).[3]

Instrumental action is calculated by a rule of efficiency. Actions are presumed to be means to ends, ends are arbitrary matters of individual choice, but means are chosen for their efficiency. Such a theory does not presume to explain how or why people value what they do, but takes their chosen ends as data and uses these to predict and explain the action choices that they make. This is the standard model for economic decision making and is presumably the kind of thinking that lies behind the community of limited liability. People can choose to pursue whatever ends they want, but having made the choices, their actions are rational only if they pursue those ends efficiently. Instrumentally, a community that obligated the individual without immediate return would be an inefficient choice of a place to live.

By contrast, normative action is calculated by a rule of rightness. Actions are presumed to be, at least sometimes, ends in themselves; other times, when actions are means to ends, instead of being chosen on the basis of efficiency, they may be chosen because some other idea is valued more than efficiency. For example, Weber (1922/1978) coined the term value-rational to refer to those cases in which some action that might be irrational from the point of view of economics or empirical science nevertheless follows rationally from a belief or value that is taken as itself requiring no justification. Nearly any theory that identifies the ends of action as predominating over the means will be classified under the normative model, for it would expect people to do what is right, important, preferable, or meaningful, rather than what is efficient. While the community of limited liability would bargain with its members, a normative community would inspire them to do what is right, provide them the foundation of a meaningful life, or be an end in itself.

This classic debate between normative and instrumental theory has contributed importantly to the new communitarian movement (see the journal *The Responsive Community*), which argues that the economic models are wrong (e.g., Etzioni, 1988, 1991). Human being is a thoroughly socialized state and instrumental calculation for individual gain is not natural to it. In fact, it is not even empirically prevalent. Some form of community participation is necessary to individual health and happiness just as it is necessary to community health. The proposed alternative is a normative community from which individuals would accept responsibilities, in return for meaningfully integrated lives. (The *locus classicus* for these ideas is Durkheim, 1893/1964, 1897/1966, 1912/1965; they continue to be thick throughout the sociological literature.)

For those responsive to the appeal of normative reasoning, the new communitarians present a powerfully compelling set of ideas. But, of course, going any further than this simple proposal requires that we be specific about what norms the community should be based on, what responsibilities will be whose, and what kind of meanings will integrate whose lives in what ways. This cannot be done without fundamental political debate. To avoid this difficulty many theorists and lay thinkers base their ideas of community on an assumed preexisting normative consensus and a vision of some basic homogeneity of the people involved. In real life that turns out to be an ideological move and one that usually splits communities or only holds them together by dominance.

Problems with the Normative Model

The normative model has some problems. Normative systems are conventionally conceived as orderly things that guide action, as elements of the world of ideas that exist before we make our individual choices of action. They function for the social theorist, then, as explanations for why we take our actions and why our actions are orderly, at both the individual and social levels. In short, vis-à-vis the actor, normative systems are conceived as independent, a priori entities. This gives rise to three major problems.

First there is a logical problem. The presumption of a priori normative systems often leads to a confusion of evidence and claim that results in circular reasoning. We appeal to the existence of a normative system to explain the observable regularities in people's behaviors, but the primary evidence of the normative system *is* the observable regularity in people's behavior. If norms are to guide action, they must exist independently; and yet, their only social presence, their only reality for actors, and their only observability for scholars is *in* action. I will argue that this circularity is apparent rather than vicious, but seeing so depends on a shift in perspective, from theories of social action and order to theories of performance and communication.

Second there is an ideological problem. The model of an a priori normative system that guides social action is a model of a stable entity. This immediately shifts attention to the issues of consensus and integration. Order, apparently, will result only if the actors are members of the same normative system or if their individual normative commitments are largely overlapping or corresponding. When such thinking is brought into the world of practical affairs it results in hiding normative variety and dissensus, inhibiting normative debate, or, at the extreme, splitting communities into ever smaller groups of homogeneity, fundamentalist commitment, essentialist politics, and orthodox interpretation. Such communities strive to ignore or expel problems rather than work on them.

Third is a disabling problem. Where do social workers, service providers, and, in the larger sense, anyone interested in social change, begin to work to fix things, when success depends on a priori normative systems? If a community has the kind of norms that produce an ability to recognize, accept responsibility for, and go to work on problems, then what do they need social workers for?[4] On the other hand, if they do not, what can social workers do about it?

SOME HELP FROM COMMUNICATION THEORY

We need to deemphasize the idea of an a priori normative system that guides action and reemphasize the idea of normative references *in* action. It is tremendously useful to see that normative action is a symbolic performance, that it has communicative value. The action of talking, for example, can be defined in terms of its physical work as, for example, a speech therapist would. But the *value* of talking is extrinsic to that physical work; it is not produced directly by it and is defined in wholly other systems—certainly a semiotic system, for starters, but also systems of connotative meanings, aesthetics, morality, tradition, and histories of relationship. That is a gross example, but it establishes the principles of analysis. Normative action is, at one level, simply what it does as behavior; simultaneously it is what it symbolizes as normative. The growling of dogs and the swearing in of presidents accomplish little material work, but they signify much (see Rothenbuhler, 1993).

The communicative value of a symbolic performance, such as a normative action, is realized only in social circumstances, when there is more than one actor, at least one of which is oriented to the other. So when the communicative value of a normative action actually pays off, the action will always be part of the environment of some other actor—an observable externality.

But observable externalities can have communicative value only when they are interpreted. The recognition, not just that something was done, but of the significance of the action and the communicative value its performance in a given context has, depends on an act of interpretation that must be *willful*. Nothing can be interpreted without the participation of an interpreter. So the communicative value is, in this phase, also internal to the observer as well as the original actor.

But for communication, interpretations must be socially coordinated and that depends on systems that transcend individuals. Languages and other sign systems are not the personal property of individuals but collective properties of societies. Yet, simultaneously, communication depends on signs being interpreted, as given by someone with some intention. So communicative value always depends on bringing together the individual and the collective (see Shepherd & Rothenbuhler, 1991).

To the extent the communicative value of an action hinges on its normativeness, that property must be established in a collective system of interpretation, even as it is recognizably the action of an individual.

So norms exist simultaneously both independently of individual actors and only in the aggregate of individual actions. But that is not because of anything magical about norms (or illogical about the theory). It is because normative actions operate as communication. To engage in a normative action is not only to do something, it is to say something; and to say something is to articulate together the individual and collective, internal and external.

Communicative Constitution

That normative actions can, via their communicative value, be simultaneously individual and collective, internal and external, is theoretically important. But for any sort of interesting application, we have to push the reasoning further.

The mode of the communication in normative action is performance. Hence it is a form of being, as well as saying and doing. This is the basis of two important capacities (see Rothenbuhler, 1993). One is that such action brings the normative into being, it works, then, toward the creation of a normative world. The other is that it commits the actor to the norm. The performance identifies the actor with the action; any social results of the action, then, are undeniably the responsibility of the actor. These capacities seem obvious when it is action that we are talking about. If I buy dinner for a friend, then I have made a small contribution to the on-going creation of a world in which such things are done and I have identified myself with a relationship and a mode of conducting it. I have been, and presumably will continue to be, that kind of person.

But consider the case in which the normative action is talking or some other sort of messaging behavior. Here the communicative value of normative action is carried by the communication. This is a system in which normatively guided communication contributes to the construction of a normative world and identifies the actor with the norm, the world, and the promise implied by the communication. If I say what is nice, then I am being nice, constructing a nice world, and since my performance means that I cannot deny that I have in fact been nice, I am also promising that I actually am nice and so will continue to be nice in the future. If I make a promise, I commit myself to a world in which promises hold sway. If I say something thoughtful, I create and commit myself to a thoughtful world.

When we begin to see these ontological powers in every little bit of talk by every person on every day, we see how social worlds are communicatively constructed (see Shepherd, 1993).

IMPLICATIONS FOR COMMUNITY-CENTERED PRACTICE

How can these considerations help us develop a basis for community-centered practice? Successful community-centered practice will be based in social circumstances in which communication forms routinely wed actors' destinies together, mutually obligating them, and providing a variety of symbolic means for routinely transcending social differences. When we find ourselves in a community in which a diversity of individuals controlling a diversity of resources already think of themselves as a group with mutual obligations, we will also find that they are already engaged in a variety of communicative and ceremonial expressions of their community, including working together on problems. When we find ourselves in a place without a diversity of individuals or resources, where people do not think of themselves as a group with mutual obligations, we will also find that they lack a variety of communicative and ceremonial expressions of community and that they are not working together on problems. What can we do about it?

The conventional models of rhetoric and persuasion would call for us to use communication to construct community. Speeches, editorials, and the work of educators could be devoted to entreating people to act as a community and to work together on their problems. Events could be planned to celebrate what communal feelings exist and to promote their growth. Newspaper, radio, and television stories could be designed to increase knowledge about the history and current resources of the community as well as its problems. Such communicative strategies can result in increasing feelings of commitment and responsibility to a community. These are important resources for community-centered practice.

But my proposal here is a supplement to this traditional model and one that I expect would work better. It is based on the communicative value of normative action being such that, when we engage in normative actions, we communicatively construct a normative community. When we do what is right to help a community and its members, then we perform our membership in, as we construct, a community in which such things are done. So the first condition of a professional social worker's being able to promote community-centered practice is that that social worker engage in normative actions that perform his or her own commitment to normative community. This will often require the setting aside of standardized, professional practices, and replacing them with the simple human act of being a good neighbor.

NOTES

1. These are specifications of the original Durkheimian idea of the integration of the individual and society; see especially Durkheim (1912/1965; 1924/1953).

2. Note that this problem and the explanation of it that follows in the main text derive directly from methodological individualism. Once community membership is conceived as an observable individual characteristic, or a correlate of observable individual characteristics, such as the behavior of attending local meetings, knowing the names of one's neighbors, or paying attention to local news, then it is inevitable that there will be individual variance. Hence we will "discover" that there are individual differences in community membership; this will require explanation, and unless we work hard at being consistently sociological in our thinking, we will generate an individualistically biased theory of community.

3. Those with a clinical or consulting background will be familiar with another use of the term normative. In those contexts a normative model is one that prescribes and it is distinguished from an empirical model, which purports to describe. The prescriptive model is a model for action; the descriptive model is a model of action. My discussion is of descriptive models. So the distinguishing issue is not whether the model tells us what we ought to do or not, but whether the model claims that people's choices of things to do are or are not normatively ordered.

4. Note that just this kind of suspicion of social work, at least as it has been conventionally practiced, lies behind some of the proposals of Smale (1984; this volume; and Smale, Tuson, Cooper, Wardle, & Crosbie, 1988) and Adams and Krauth (this volume).

REFERENCES

Alexander, J.C. (1982–83). *Theoretical logic in sociology* (4 vols.). Berkeley, CA: University of California Press.

Bell, C., & Newby, H. (1971). *Community studies: An introduction to the sociology of the local community*. London: George Allen & Unwin.

Bellah, R.N., Madsen, R., Sullivan, W.M., Swidler, A., & Tipton, S.M. (1985). *Habits of the heart: Individualism and commitment in American life*. New York: Harper & Row.

Calabrese, A. (1991). The periphery in the center: The information age and the 'good life' in rural America. *Gazette, 48,* 105–128.

Durkheim, E. (1953). *Sociology and philosophy* (D. F. Pocock, trans.). Glencoe, IL: Free Press. (Original work published 1924.)

Durkheim, E. (1964). *The division of labor in society* (G. Simpson, trans.). New York: Free Press. (Original work published 1893.)

Durkheim, E. (1965). *The elementary forms of the religious life.* (J. W. Swain, trans.) New York: Free Press. (Original work published 1912.)

Durkheim, E. (1966). *Suicide* (J. A. Spaulding & G. Simpson, trans.). New York: Free Press. (Original work published 1897.)

Etzioni, A. (1988). *The moral dimension: Toward a new economics.* New York: Free Press.

Etzioni, A. (1991). *A responsive society: Collected essays on guiding deliberate social change.* San Francisco: Jossey-Bass.

Fischer, C.S. (1975). Toward a subcultural theory of urbanism. *American Journal of Sociology, 80,* 1319–1341.

Fischer, C.S. (1982). *To dwell among friends: Personal networks in town and city.* Chicago: University of Chicago Press.

Fischer, C.S., Jackson, R.M., Stueve, C.A., Gerson, K., Jones, L.M., with Baldassare, M. (1977). *Networks and places: Social relations in the urban setting.* New York: Free Press.

Gans, H.J. (1962). *The urban villagers: Group and class in the life of Italian-Americans.* New York: Free Press.

Greer, S. (1967). Postscript: Communication and community. In M. Janowitz, *The community press in an urban setting: The social elements of urbanism* (2nd ed.) (pp. 245–270). Chicago: University of Chicago Press.

Howell, F.M., & Frese, W. (1983). Size of place, residential preferences and the life cycle: How people come to like where they live. *American Sociological Review, 48,* 569–580.

Hummon, D.M. (1986). City mouse, country mouse: The persistence of community identity. *Qualitative Sociology, 9,* 3–25.

Janowitz, M. (1967). *The community press in an urban setting: The social elements of urbanism* (2nd. ed.). Chicago: University of Chicago Press.

Jeffres, L.W., & Dobos, J. (1984). Communication and neighborhood mobilization. *Urban Affairs Quarterly, 20,* 97–112.

Jeffres, L.W., Dobos, J., & Lee, J. (1988). Media use and community ties. *Journalism Quarterly, 65,* 575–581, 677.

Jeffres, L.W., Dobos, J., & Sweeney, M. (1987). Communication and commitment to community. *Communication Research, 14,* 619–643.

Kasarda, J.D., & Janowitz, M. (1974). Community attachment in mass society. *American Sociological Review, 39,* 328–339.

Kirby, A. (1989). A sense of place. *Critical Studies in Mass Communication, 6,* 322–326.

Lynd, R.S., & Lynd, H.M. (1937). *Middletown in transition.* New York: Harcourt Brace.

Nisbet, R. (1982). *The social philosophers: Community and conflict in western thought* (concise edition, updated). New York: Washington Square Press.

Park, R.E., & Burgess, E.W. (1969). *Introduction to the science of sociology* (3rd rev. ed., M. Janowitz, Ed.). Chicago: University of Chicago Press. (Original work published 1921.)

Parsons, T. (1968). *The structure of social action* (2 vols.). New York: Free Press. (Original work published 1937.)

Parsons, T., & Shils, E.A. (1951). Values, motives, and systems of action. In T. Parsons & E. A. Shils (Eds.), *Toward a general theory of action* (pp. 45–275). Cambridge, MA: Harvard University Press.

Pitts, J.R. (1961). *Introduction* (Part three: Personality and the social system). In T. Parsons, E. Shils, K. D. Naegele, & J. R. Pitts (Eds.), *Theories of society: Foundations of modern sociological thought* (pp. 685–716). New York: Free Press.

Quandt, J.B. (1970). *From the small town to the great community: The social thought of progressive intellectuals*. New Brunswick, NJ: Rutgers University Press.

Rivlin, L.G. (1982). Group membership and place meanings in an urban neighborhood. *Journal of Social Issues, 38*, 75–93.

Rossi, P. (1956). *Why families move*. Glencoe, IL: Free Press.

Rothenbuhler, E.W. (1991). The process of community involvement. *Communication Monographs, 58*, 63–78.

Rothenbuhler, E.W. (1993). *Ritual*. Unpublished manuscript.

Sampson, R.J. (1988). Local friendship ties and community attachment in mass society: A multilevel systemic model. *American Sociological Review, 53*, 766–779.

Shepherd, G.J. (1993). Building a discipline of communication. *Journal of Communication, 43* (3), 83–91.

Shepherd, G.J., & Rothenbuhler, E.W. (1991). A synthetic perspective on goals and discourse. In K. Tracy (Ed.), *Understanding face to face interaction: Issues linking goals and discourse* (pp. 189–203). Hillsdale, NJ: Lawrence Erlbaum Associates.

Shils, E. (1975). *Center and periphery: Essays in macrosociology*. Chicago: University of Chicago Press.

Smale, G.G. (1984). Self-fulfilling prophesies, self-defeating strategies and change. *British Journal of Social Work, 14*, 419–433.

Smale, G., Tuson, G., Cooper, M., Wardle, M., & Crosbie, D. (1988). *Community social work: A paradigm for change*. London: National Institute for Social Work.

Stamm, K.R. (1985). *Newspaper use and community ties: Toward a dynamic theory*. Norwood, NJ: Ablex.

Stamm, K.R., & Guest, A.M. (1991). Communication and community integration: An analysis of the communication behavior of newcomers. *Journalism Quarterly, 68*, 644–656.

Stein, M.R. (1960). *The eclipse of community: An interpretation of American studies*. New York: Harper & Row.

Strauss, A.L. (1968). *The American city: A sourcebook of urban imagery*. Chicago: Aldine.

Suttles, G.D. (1984). The cumulative texture of local urban culture. *American Journal of Sociology, 90*, 283–304.

Tinder, G. (1980). *Community: Reflections on a tragic ideal*. Baton Rouge, LA: Louisiana State University Press.

Tönnies, F. (1988). *Community and society (Gemeinschaft und Gesellschaft)* (C. P. Loomis, trans; new introduction by J. Samples). New Brunswick, NJ: Rutgers University Press. (Original work published 1887.)

Tsai, Y., & Sigelman, L. (1982). The community question: A perspective from national survey data—the case of the USA. *British Journal of Sociology, 33*, 579–588.

Vidich, A.J., & Bensman, J. (1968). *Small town in mass society: Class, power and religion in a rural community* (rev. ed.). Princeton, NJ: Princeton University Press.

Webber, M.W. (1963). Order in diversity: Community without propinquity. In L. Wingo (Ed.), *Cities and space: The future use of urban land* (pp. 23–54). Baltimore: Johns Hopkins University Press.

Weber, M. (1978). *Economy and society* (G. Roth & C. Wittich, Eds.). Berkeley: University of California Press. (Original work published 1922.)

Wellman, B. (1979). The community question: The intimate networks of East Yorkers. *American Journal of Sociology, 84,* 1201–1231.

Whyte, W.F. (1955). *Street corner society* (2nd. ed.). Chicago: University of Chicago Press.

12

Professional Understandings of Community: At a Loss for Words?

CAROL R. SWENSON

If strengths-focused, community- and family-centered approaches to services are to be developed successfully, service providers, planners, and policymakers need to have a rich and elaborated vision of families and communities. However, there are strong cultural and professional forces supporting an ideology of individualism and diminishing commitment to families and communities. Numerous social commentators (Bellah, Madsen, Sullivan, Swidler, & Tipton, 1985; Bellah, 1987; Cushman, 1990; Lasch, 1978; Rieff, 1963/1987; Sampson, 1977, 1988) have implicated therapies and self-help movements, as well as broad cultural forces, in contributing to the ideology of individualism. Effective community- and family-centered approaches are not easily implemented in such a context.

To learn more about helping professionals' understandings of community, the Community Research Group[1] undertook a small qualitative research project. Our questions were: How do helping professionals think about and experience community in their own lives? How do they think about and address community in their professional work? We selected respondents who would be likely to provide an informative perspective on our questions: clinical social workers who were known to be interested in community. They were interviewed with an open-ended format, and a conceptualization was developed from their responses. This approach is known as grounded theory (Glaser & Strauss, 1967). Grounded theory is particularly useful to conceptualize behavior in complex situations, to explore unresolved or emerging social problems, and to understand the impact of ideologies (Chenitz & Swanson, 1986).

This chapter will report selected findings from the study that have particular relevance for community- and family-centered approaches to services. Key concepts of these approaches are discussed at length elsewhere in this volume. Particularly relevant to this study are the ways in which client problems and solutions are conceptualized. All problems have community dimensions as well as individual and family dimensions. At the same time, clients and communities have unique strengths and resources and are partners with helping professionals in creating solutions.[2] There are two key assumptions that guide this study. The first is that helping professionals need to conceptualize individuals, families, and communities as multiple, nested systems, rather than as autonomous entities. An individual cannot be understood adequately without understanding his or her contexts—especially family and community. Likewise, interventions need to be addressed to all systems levels and the relationships between them. Even when working with one individual, interventions need to be conceptualized in terms of relationships, both the intimate relationships of the family and relationships within the community. At all times, an appreciation of strengths needs to be preserved.

A second assumption is that, among other things, helping professionals engage in the co-creation of new meanings with clients and communities (Bruner, 1986; Kegan, 1982; Saari, 1991). In this meaning-making process, anything that occurs verbally, nonverbally, or contextually will convey meanings. Practice cannot be value free (Rhodes, 1986; Dean & Rhodes, 1992). When professionals talk in certain ways, or do not talk, about community relatedness, they convey meaning and values. Practice will embody some stance on the individual and community, if not explicitly, then implicitly.

This chapter continues with a more extensive critique of individualism. Then various practice approaches are evaluated in relation to the concepts of individualism and community. Next, our method of inquiry and selected findings are presented. The following discussion will emphasize clinicians' languages of community. I relate these findings to alternative conceptions of the individual and community. Finally, implications for strengths-focused, community- and family-centered services are discussed.

CAUSE FOR CONCERN?

Individualism and the Empty Self

Numerous voices have been raised about the dominance of individualism and the decline of commitment to community in America. Lasch (1978) identified a "therapeutic sensibility" in contemporary U.S. culture that reflects a hunger "for the feeling, the momentary illusion, of personal well-being, health and psychic security" (p. 7). Above all, according to Lasch, the therapeutic sensibility is dominated by a notion of the Self as a fully-bounded and autonomous individual who shapes his or her own destiny through sheer strength of will. Lasch (1978) and the other critics find the tendency to turn "collective grievances" into "personal problems amenable to therapeutic interventions" deeply disturbing. After redefinition through a therapeutic interpretive paradigm, social discontent comes to be seen as a reflection of personal inadequacy. Under this regime, participation in public life becomes merely another avenue for individual, personal fulfillment (Rieff, 1963/1987).

The problem as viewed by these writers, however, is not only that personal ills are substituted for social ills. Lasch takes pains to point out that the therapeutic sensibility is not the balm for "inner emptiness" and "inauthenticity" that it imagines itself to be. He argues that by proscribing "excessive dependence on others" and extolling the virtues of independent self-management, the therapeutic perspective turns us away from an alternative view of personal life as socially significant. It can minimize the value of the interconnectedness of human beings and of the social embeddedness of human life.

Sampson (1977, 1988) examined the historical and cultural context that gave rise to the current hegemony in (American) psychological discourse of "self-contained individualism." He notes that this concept of the self is not the dominant view in other cultures or other historic eras. While consistent with the goals of modernism, this view is less suitable for an emerging global society. Sampson points to the Encounter, Sensitivity and Growth Group movements as therapies by which "persons are helped to separate themselves even further from others" (1977, p. 777). His criticism stems from these movements' emphasis on people focusing their attention inwardly rather than toward others.

Bellah, Madsen, Sullivan, Swidler, and Tipton (1985) and Bellah (1987) have studied the languages of white, middle-class Americans, including therapists, and found them dominated by individualism. Their respondents overwhelmingly explained their commitments and values by references to what they felt or wanted and the costs and benefits of those preferences. The authors call these languages expressive and utilitarian individualism, respectively, and identify them with the languages of therapy and economics. The participants were largely devoid of other language to articulate their commitments and values.

The critique is continued by Cushman (1990), who describes the current self as an "empty self," and analyzes the role psychologists have played in creating this self. He examines the current cultural situation and evaluates the concept of the self embedded in a variety of current theoretical frameworks (he chooses primarily psychodynamic theories). He points to the increasing preoccupation in psychological discourse with personality disorders, especially those defined as narcissistic and borderline disorders. Cushman concludes, "psychology has continued to decontextualize the individual. . . . While psychologists have been treating the empty self, they have, of necessity, also been constructing it, profiting from it, and not challenging the social arrangements that created it" (p. 609).

The critics offer several ideas about what an alternative language of community might include. Lasch (1978) suggests the personal life as socially significant, the social embeddedness of human life, the value of the interconnectedness of human life, and definitions of problems as social ills, collective grievances, and/or social discontent. Rieff (1963/1987) talks of participation in public life. Sampson (1977) suggests that people can focus their attention toward others, rather than inward. He develops (1988) the concept of "ensembled individualism," in contrast to "self-contained individualism." Bellah et al. (1985) and Bellah (1987) identify commitment to the common good; shared history and traditions; evocative rituals and symbols; common goals, values, and obligations. This group identifies republican democracy and Biblical religion as powerful alternative languages that have been historically present in America and are now eclipsed by the languages of expressive and utilitarian individualism. Cushman (1990) concurs, mentioning family, community, tradition, and a sense of the meaningfulness of life as what an "empty self" has lost. Throughout we find mention of working for the common good, compassion, commitment to something larger than the self, service to others, taking responsibility, shared fate, common future, cooperating, and collective power.

Social Work and Community

It is important to note that there are some differences between clinical social work and other helping professions. Social work values have historically incorporated a sense of community. Social work has been concerned with the client's social context and the social causes of problems. People have been seen as interdependent in casework; mutual aid has been a tenet of the group work and community organization traditions; and social activism has embodied the visions of a caring community and of social justice. In addition, the "person-in-situation" framework common to social work conceptualizations has provided a context for a broader perspective. However, even within social work, there has been recurrent concern that clinical social workers are too strongly identified with other therapeutic professions at the expense of social work values and perspectives (recently, Specht, 1990). Thus, it seems worthwhile to look at contemporary clinical social work to see whether it embodies a positive valuation of community in its theory and practice or if it appears more supportive of expressive or utilitarian individualism.

An examination of various practice theories utilized in clinical social work showed a pattern both similar to and different from the critiques of psychotherapy (see Swenson et al., 1993 for more detail). A large number of clinical social workers draw from psychodynamic theories. Other social workers utilize problem-solving, task-centered, cognitive, behavioral, and other interventive approaches that maintain, at least in part, an "autonomous, bounded self." Still other clinical social workers have adopted family systems perspectives, most of which, however, seem to focus on an autonomous, bounded *family*.

On the other hand, there are a variety of approaches developed in social work that frame a different relationship of the individual and the community. Some of these are the ecological approaches including the life model (Germain & Gitterman, 1980), the membership and interactionist approaches in social group work (Falck, 1984; Schwartz 1971, 1974), varieties of radical and empowerment practice (Breton, 1989; Lee, 1994; Solomon, 1976), and, of course, the family- and community-centered approaches at the heart of this volume.

There are also a variety of perspectives shared by mental health professions suggesting a different relationship of individual and community than that deplored by the "therapeutic critics." These include social psychiatry, community psychology (Speer et al., 1992), some aspects of cognitive psychology (Kegan, 1982), and ecological family perspectives (Imber-Black, 1986). Interesting developments in psychodynamic theory include the work of Roland and at the Stone Center (Miller, 1984; Surrey, 1984). From his experiences with Indian and Japanese cultures, Roland (1988, 1990) developed concepts of familial, spiritual, and expanding selves to extend the Western concept of an individual self. The Stone Center has proposed a theory of development from a feminist perspective, emphasizing a self-in-relation in contrast to the more traditional theories of separation-individuation (Blanck & Blanck, 1979). In addition, there are emerging narrative and constructionist perspectives in both psychodynamic and family systems approaches (Dean, 1993; Hoffman, 1991; McNamee & Gergen, 1992; White, 1992). These approaches understand individuals as participants in a community of socially created meanings. However, even in these various approaches, the idea of the self in relation to community may be implicit, a cultural analysis missing, or potential implications for practice overlooked.

Examining these various approaches suggests that perhaps the critique of individualism in the therapeutic professions is somewhat overstated. However, it is also clear that an important consideration in a practice theory, which has been given insufficient attention to date, is the concept of the individual in relation to community. The critics have taught us that such ideas are political, as well as professional. The perspective of the dominant culture will prevail, if an alternative is not consciously developed as part of a practice theory. It is particularly important for the development of community- and family-centered services that a vigorous professional conversation be generated about ideas of self and community. An alternative conception of self and community must be nurtured.

OUR MODE OF INQUIRY

Our study was carried out by a research team, consisting of a faculty member, a doctoral candidate, and nine Master of Social Work students concentrating in clinical practice. It was part of the Master of Social Work (MSW) students' second-year curriculum as described by Reinherz, Regan, and Anastas (1983). To become a "team" and to understand the terrain of study more fully, we immersed ourselves in the critiques of individualism and in various therapies, mainstream clinical practice theories, and definitions of community in sociology and social work. We refined the mode of inquiry as a group. The grounded theory approach emphasizes the creative, thematically associative role of the researchers, while demanding that they stay close, and therefore faithful, to the data (Rennie, Phillips, & Quartaro, 1988). Since grounded theory emphasizes the interpretive process (Jones, 1990; Sherman, 1987), we needed to develop a core of common understandings and a shared language. Extensive discussion and a team log, where individuals wrote thoughts, questions, and reflections on the process, were used to create a convergence of thinking. The multiple points of view of the research group ultimately added richness to the interpretation.

The Sample

The sample was selected to include both similarities and differences. It consisted of 17 clinical social workers with MSWs and at least 5 years of experience. We sought experienced practitioners, so that their thinking and practice would be well developed. An effort was made to be inclusive in regard to age, gender, sexual orientation, race, years of experience, theoretical orientation, and fields of practice, because we thought that these differences might influence ideas about community. The sample generally achieved that inclusiveness, with ages distributed relatively evenly from the 30s to the 60s, about 25% being male, two identifying themselves as gay, four being people of color, and various ethnicities represented among the white respondents. About half of the sample were practicing in mental health settings with the other half in various other settings such as health and criminal justice. The experience level was relatively evenly distributed from 5 to over 30 years. Less diverse, but understandable in view of the era of their training, was theoretical orientation. The great majority of the participants (13) described their training as psychodynamic, at least originally, although many said that they had incorporated cognitive, behavioral, and family/systemic approaches over time. Consistent with the majority of mental health professionals, the participants worked most frequently with individuals, but also included couples, families, and groups in their practice. Some had program development and administrative responsibilities as well.

All of the clinicians practiced in the Boston metropolitan area, a part of the country with a strong individualistic psychodynamic tradition, as well as flourishing family systems approaches. Massachusetts was a leader in some aspects of the community mental health movement in the 1960s and early 1970s. However, the state recently has been experiencing numerous economic and political pressures, leading to reductions in services, more conservative definitions of problems and solutions, staff layoffs, and, consequently, a turn to private practice by experienced clinicians. With these multiple pressures, Boston was an informative location for the study.

Study Method

The research team developed an interview guide to provide topics, about which the interviewers were free to explore, probe, and question (Patton, 1987). Thus the interviews were co-created by the interviewer and interviewee (Mishler, 1986). The interview guide was structured to allow the respondents to embed themselves first in personal experiences and meanings of community. During this process, respondents were also developing a common understanding and shared language with the interviewers. Once the respondents were immersed in their subjective, personal understandings of community, the interviewers moved on to respondents' constructions of community within the professional context. Potential respondents were contacted, and informed about the study and their rights as human subjects. They were then interviewed and the interviews audiotaped. The first 10 interviews were transcribed by the interviewers and intensively analyzed. A second round of seven interviews was conducted to allow for a more thorough examination of some of the categories that emerged from the first 10 interviews. This was a modest effort at theoretical sampling, the practice of collecting additional data to refine emerging categories and their relationships (Chenitz & Swanson, 1986). Summary notes were written of these interviews. Ideally, data gathering should continue until saturation of categories occurs. In this study, it appears that we achieved saturation in relation to constructions of personal community; however, understandings of community in professional practice may benefit from further exploration. The transcribed interviews were analyzed line by line in search of themes and categories. We transferred each identifiable idea from the interviews to separate white cards (for personal community) and yellow cards (for community in practice). Each card, representing one data unit, was assigned to as many categories as applicable. When none of the categories fit, a new category was developed.

The research group members also recorded their own ideas about emerging themes and categories and possible relationships among categories in "memos." Memos are the researchers' written records of the analytical process. It is in memos that categories are created, recorded, compared, verified, modified, or eliminated as new data are gathered (Strauss & Corbin, 1990). Memos assist the researchers to move from single examples to the identification of themes and patterns in the data. We used the memoing process and comparison with the literature to develop a higher-level conceptualization about clinical constructions of community. We also used memoing to puzzle over the many interpretive decisions that are involved in constructing a meaningful account (Riessman, 1993). Discussion of our data follows. Pseudonyms are used throughout.

THE LANGUAGES OF COMMUNITY

Our first level of analysis was descriptive and classificatory. The interviews indicated that most clinicians had a concept of community in their own lives that they could, with varying degrees of fluency, articulate. Generally communities were identified first in terms of geography: neighborhood, town, city, and so forth. Then participants began to think about communities in terms of affiliation, identification, and participation. These nongeographic communities can be shared statuses: age, sex, race, sexual orientation, or medical condition. They can be religious, professional, and political affiliations. They can be support and self-help groups. They can be shared interests. For a few respondents, "the community" was the human race, and, indeed, the whole planet.

The qualities of communities that participants identified most often as important were those that emphasized commonality: mutual trust, belonging, support, safety, shared feelings. Also important were validation, affirmation of identity, and enhancing personal growth. Reciprocity of giving and receiving was mentioned, as well as shared interests. Mentioned less frequently were shared goals and values. Mentioned even less often were shared tradition and history, ritual and other symbols, and common purposes and achievements. Some participants mentioned belonging to something that transcends the self, a spiritual sense of the interconnectedness of all people and living things. Also mentioned were inclusiveness, diversity, and collective power.

The Community in Clinical Work

The participants were noticeably less detailed and eloquent regarding the importance of community in their work with clients than in their personal lives. However, several different areas of focus did emerge: ways of thinking about work with clients, community and clients' presenting concerns, assessing community connections, and community-related interventions.

Most of the social workers did think about community in their work. Pam spoke for many when she said that the notion of community was important to her and that she believed that "clients do better in life if they are connected." A number of the social workers tended to equate "community" with belonging to some group and to see group membership as a universal human element. It is something inherent. The therapist's task is to help clients recognize and acknowledge it. While community connections may offer the individual a meaningful identity, and may provide practical resources, there is also another level of community. According to Deb, "Everybody has a right to live in a community" and has something valuable and unique to offer to it. "Communities benefit from this fuller membership, this sort of inclusion."

The clinicians' interventions around community were analyzed and broken down into specific activities. There were eight types of interventions identified: encouraging existing community connections, mediating community friction, developing new community connections, referring to community self-help groups, networking with other professionals, discussing self-in-community with clients, creating an experience of community in the clinical work, and responding to community needs on an agency level. All of these descriptive findings are discussed at length elsewhere (Swenson et al., 1993).

Community connections can be supported through encouragement or through addressing conflicted or ruptured ties to existing communities. Sometimes new connections can be developed. For example, Juan described setting up a parent support group around concerns over street violence involving children. He also described bringing the teen members of the community directly to the home of a young client who was phobic about going out after being victimized in his community. The community intervention most frequently mentioned was referring clients to self-help groups, especially Twelve-Step Programs. Other groups mentioned were for battered women, single parents, incest survivors, the widowed, the divorced, and the agoraphobic, as well as day treatment programs for the mentally ill. Networking with other professionals on behalf of clients is a way to mobilize a segment of the community: professional caregivers.

Most of the clinicians intervene by discussing self-in-community. They make a concerted effort to discuss the rationale and benefits of being part of a community. One respondent observed that therapy is an effort to balance being an individual with being part of something bigger than the self. Clinicians point out to their clients how their AA group is positively influencing them, or how their lack of connection limits their reflected sense of self and, therefore, their self-esteem.

Juan sees most presenting problems as appeals for community. "I try to reframe it in terms of how they might feel disconnected or how they might feel isolated," and then he helps the client to use his/her own capacity for connection to begin helping him/herself.

Some clinicians intervene to create an experience of community in the therapeutic relationship. Juan says, "It's only [in a crisis that] most people really release their defenses and allow others to see them for who they really are, so [they experience] community. . . . What clients want is to experience sharing and communicating with someone who is actively listening to them." Juan's technique for creating this safe environment is to reveal some of his "own broken parts" to help the client "feel a little bit more attached or a part of a massive sense of brokenness among human beings." He referred to clients' "inherent capacity. . .to experience community for themselves. . . . I try to see how they can take that experience and generalize it to other important areas in their lives. . .[how they, themselves can be] helping others build communities in their own lives."

One interviewee, Jan, also stressed that her agency is reaching out to specific community groups. Speaking of the agency's community, she noted that it "has a growing gay and lesbian-identified population," and "We are in the process of trying to make ourselves more sensitive [about diversity] and are also trying to target services to a more diverse group." She later described the process of building a neighborhood clinic: "We perceived the need. . . . We had some meetings in the neighborhood to talk about the needs and about placing a clinic there. They thought it was a good idea. . . . We spent a lot of time working out the details and developing relationships with the local school and health clinic and the church. It ran successfully for ten years until funding was cut, eliminating it."

These, then, are some key considerations that our sample of clinicians discussed when they thought about community in their professional role. While several of our participants had much to say about the different issues involved, there were others who had very little to say. For some, attention to community varied depending on the client's situation. For others, it was unavoidable, a central focus of their work.

Alternative Conceptions of Community

In addition to the descriptive findings just summarized, we were able to move to a higher order of conceptualization. This work derived from the memoing process and extensive discussion within the research team. As we examined the interviews and the categories, we began to discriminate some different languages of community. These are briefly illustrated with excerpts from the interviews.

The instrumental community. We found a strong tendency on the part of our participants to use rather limited languages of community. One of these was a concrete description of community as a locality, or a group of people who share a characteristic, such as age or race. This language seems largely instrumental. It provides a convenient way of categorizing people or organizing services. It overlooks the possibility that the "community" so identified might be meaningful for the person or for the collectivity. This language reduces community to something akin to "being a Chevrolet owner"—useful if a recall of defective cars is needed, but not likely to be a significant grouping to anyone except General Motors. Community, here, is located "outside" of individuals or families. This is community at its most utilitarian. The corresponding "Self" or family is indeed bounded, masterful, and self-contained. Curtis exemplifies this limited idea of community:

> Community, to Curtis, is synonymous with his city. Alternatively, it means outreach. He lives in the city where he works (though he would have other geographically convenient alternatives) and he finds it "difficult." Still maintaining the definition of community as that city, he discounts its importance in his own life. He tries to get away on evenings and weekends...he has family and friends and plays golf.

> At one point, Curtis gave quite an articulate and broad definition of community. But he declined repeated invitations by the interviewer to utilize that view in describing his work. Most definitively, Curtis said, "We use the concept of community and agency and networking and have strong relationships with different town departments and agencies and people that help us to get to clients that we might not ordinarily get to, but I think once you're involved with the client, I don't know how much I think about community at that point. . . . I don't think I'm thinking about community when we're actually involved with someone on a regular basis. . . . It's a guaranteed path to getting referrals for people who need help and just don't pick up the phone and call the clinic. That's my literal view of community."

Community as social support. A somewhat less limited language of community involves social support. This language is seen pervasively throughout the discussion of presenting problems, assessment, and intervention skills. While the support provided may be instrumental, informational, or emotional, this way of languaging is still largely utilitarian in that the primary question is, "What uses can the community serve for the individual or family?" Clients, in particular, are viewed as recipients of social support; they are unimagined as providers:

> David described work with a client who had no income and was breaking up with his girlfriend, with whom he had been living. "He doesn't know where he is going to go. . . . We even talked about a homeless person that he knows who has made it on the street and that is also a community. . . . So we talked about how he could tap into the homeless community, friendship community, and his family of origin. Those are communities that are supportive of him. . . . That is what communities can do; they can support us when we are in need."

> Ofelia described a prisoner with AIDS. He was refusing AZT. "You have to respect the rights of the individual. [And also,] you have to make some intervention in the medical community so that they don't feel insulted, so they can see he should keep getting other services even though he refuses AZT."

Community-self. Another language of community describes the community's significance for the individual's sense of self. It could be called community-in-self (Fleck-Henderson, 1993). The language is one of identification, embeddedness, belonging, relatedness, and affiliation. All these are significant ways of making meaning and living life. This language expresses a self-in-relation, or ensembled individualism, not self-contained individualism. Respondents applied this language both to themselves and to clients, though the greatest richness appeared as they talked about their own lives:

> Rachel defines community largely in terms of ethnic, racial, and religious groups and their significance in developing a sense of personal identity. A person might be variously embedded, in conflict with, or in creative relation to such communities. She helps clients explore these issues: "I think about identity in an intrapsychic way and an interpersonal way, and in a sociological way. . . . Usually a client comes in with a, a particular relational issue. And it may take us some time to get to the other levels."
>
> Rachel recognizes the significance and complexity in her own life of these identifications and sees herself as needing to learn the specific meanings of these identifications in her clients' lives. She remarked that in her training these "other levels," especially religious and spiritual connections, were de-emphasized, and, indeed, somewhat suspect.
>
> David is beginning to understand himself as elderly, about which he laments, "guidelines of how to be an elderly gay person are not very clear." Perhaps related to his life stage, he said, the commitment that most powerfully moves him presently is Native American spirituality. This is a very solitary and somewhat marginal connection, however. "I like going up into the mountains and into the desert by myself. . .but it still feels to me as if I am a member of a community that is 2000 years old, though I am an outsider. I walk around the perimeter of that community because I feel that as a white person, non-Native American, I. . .cannot puncture that circle but I can be on the edge of it, learning from it. . . . That's a community that is very different from what I have lived, it's not industry. . .automobiles and wealth. . . . It is much more eco-centered. . . . I feel that spiritually I can be the brother of other people out there by persuasion and by spirituality rather than by skin color or training."
>
> He gave an example of talking about attending Mass with a Roman Catholic client who was having trouble coming to terms with the death of her mother. The client went to Mass, and, as David imagined, the client felt a sense of connection with her mother ". . .and other people from her past and had a feeling of tranquillity."

The community of identification and belonging is still a one-directional concept: what the community contributes to the individual's well-being. There was little mention of reciprocity or mutuality, even though these are key concepts of self-in-relation theory. The respondents, even those familiar with self-in-relation theory, seem not to have noticed the omission. There was little discussion of obligation or responsibility to attend to the well-being of the community. In their own lives, these clinicians were often intensely involved in maintaining and enhancing communities; however, they were not apt to articulate their activities in these terms. Respondents virtually never considered that it might be important to address a client's contribution to or obligations to their communities. This language maintains a strong thread of individualism. It suggests that if individuals have a strong sense of self, community will "happen." Or if it does not, that is not a particular concern of clinicians.

Community as interconnectedness. Some participants expanded the community that provides affiliation and identification into a spiritual or existential sense of the interconnectedness of people:

> Sharon described herself as becoming a "citizen of the world" through her involvement with peace and justice work. She moved from "survival of the world" and "are we gonna blow ourselves up?" into "spiritual thinking. And then the spiritual, very much, got fed back into the social work, my way of talking with people." She tries to bring about understanding and dialogue between people whose relationships may have been ruptured, for example, a parent of a deformed child and a doctor who "brings all the medical students around to look at this freak."
>
> Juan has a concept of community that transcends ethnic, racial, and class divisions. While himself a person of color and deeply concerned about culturally sensitive practice, he moved to a different level in discussing community. Community is "communication, or communicating...that ability to share one's vulnerability, with one another. Part of experiencing community for me is being able to tolerate differences, diversities."
>
> Juan discussed working with a client who had become agoraphobic after being shot in a drive-by shooting. He visited the client at home and encouraged peers to visit, but also walked with the client in the neighborhood, sharing his fears and experiences, "helping the client to feel safe about sharing his own fears and anxieties."

Those clinicians who articulated a spiritual sense of community spoke easily and fluently and clearly described their responsibility to act toward other people in ways consistent with their values. However, these thoughts were not likely to be articulated to clients. It seems that clients were not expected to have a similar experience of community or to have a similar responsibility.

The spiritual/existential sense of community was invested with substantial moral worth by the few respondents who described it. Sometimes, this language included a specific religious tradition with shared ritual, symbols, and history. If so, it occurred only in relation to the participant's personal life. However, these respondents were apt to suggest to their clients that they consider participating in *some* religious activity. Sharon described the one instance where the spiritual entered the room: "[A client] and I start every session with a silent meditation, which is wonderful." This client had participated with Sharon in another context in which meditation had occurred, so for them it was a shared tradition.

Community as commitment. Finally, there was a language of community that was a language of commitment and social participation. It is important to understand oneself as part of something larger than the self; in addition, the goals and values of the community become significant. They serve as an imperative for one's own action. In this language of community, there is responsibility and obligation, reciprocity and mutuality, and the power of collective action. Participants used this language when talking about taking part in socially significant activities, pursuing goals such as social justice, creating community contexts for other people, developing needed community resources, and so on. This language was used almost exclusively in relation to clinicians' own lives:

> Deb sees her colleagues as a professional community with shared values "that have to do with working with people in need of assistance, and that have to do with empowering people, and that have to do with helping people build communities of their own. And I think primarily that have to do with making the community a more inclusive and, in my mind, a better place. . . . The interviewer asked, "Are you saying that your belief is that communities should change themselves to be able to incorporate a variety of people without those people having to change themselves?" Deb replied, "Right. . . . [What] we as providers did for a long time was create communities for people with disabilities that were separate and outside of the community. . . . There was a very clear and very rigid boundary between the community-within-the-house and the larger community. . .and that's what we are changing now. . . . It isn't the community providing assistance to the disabled person. It's a community in which everyone [including the disabled] has membership and everyone has a role and everyone can contribute."

Only two of the respondents, Deb and Sharon, even hinted at talking with clients in these terms. The following excerpts give the quality of their unusual approach:

> Sharon talked about a client who had organized a small protest against the absence of any women in a panel discussion. "I said to her, `Do you think that your willingness to stick your neck out and do this in front of your colleagues is in any way related to what you know I did [engage in civil disobedience]?' She said, `Oh, of course.'"

> Deb described a poignant case of a single professional man who "believes very strongly in his obligation to be a contributing member of the community [he volunteers as a Red Cross emergency response worker and flies rescue missions] "but it hasn't brought with it connections which are sustaining, which help him to get through difficult times or have satisfaction or happiness in his life. . . . Any focus that we've had on community, and we've been talking about it more, leaves him with the sense of what he doesn't have. . . . He's overwhelmed with not having it. . . . And so it's been

> very hard work. . . . [He feels] this emptiness, this just gray, dead emptiness. But I think that's where he lives, and so I think that's where we need to be together in order [for him] to leave it. And that is the work."

We found it curious that these clinicians often seemed reluctant to discuss the idea of community with their clients. Instead there was a resort to the ostensibly value-neutral canons of technique such as "waiting for the client to bring it up" or "listening for it." Most respondents conveyed a sense that doing differently was inappropriate. Even Deb, whose speech was otherwise so fluid and articulate, floundered:

> The interviewer asked: "Can we shift gears here and talk about people you see in private practice where you're looking more at what actually happens in your conversation with [clients]?" Deb stopped and searched for words. "Yeah. . . . It's really, I don't, I'm trying to think about how differently I think about it. In practice, it's quite different. You know, it's easy for me to think about community in every way that I just described, when I think about our organizational work. It's more complicated when I think about it in individual therapy work. So, I think I would say that, I would say that, I am much less directive around this issue. I mean, part of it is just training and style, but I would be more likely with individual clients to be listening for things than to be talking about what I think." She eventually identifies community as "what is it in their environment. . .that might help or hinder their ability to get through this [difficult] time?"

It seemed that participants felt that they had a choice about "community," but that all clients had a "self" that was at the heart of the work. The idea that "community" is as central as "self" to human identity and social existence seems not to have been put into practice by these clinicians. And yet, if asked, most would probably say that they were committed to the concept.

We were also interested that our respondents seemed not to notice that they had constructed quite a bifurcated view of community. The "community" for themselves was quite rich and alive, a central part of the ways they made meaning, and they were active in their commitment. The "community" for their clients was much more restricted and limited; community as a source of meaning-making was overlooked and clients were viewed primarily as passive recipients of support or services. Gail defines community as "a spiritual connection between people who have similar beliefs concerning the meaning of life." However, in relation to her work with clients, she talks about community primarily as support for a troubled individual. In Ofelia's personal life, community means friends, family, and "crowds." In discussing her professional work, the communities she refers to are helping professionals and formal organizations: DSS, medical professionals, and the church. Another respondent consciously created communities in her personal life, but this was not the case in her work:

> Pam actively recruited friends to her neighborhood, she helped start a day care center, she encouraged her church to develop community action projects; she even started a group for her *puppy*. And yet, when asked where issues or values about community appeared in the therapy, she replied, " I'm not sure it really does, usually."

These clinicians do not seem to have questioned, either for themselves or with their clients, what kind of world is being constructed by using therapy in such highly individualistic ways. They likewise generally did not seem to have a sense *that* a way of life was being enacted. The ideology of the "bounded, masterful Self" seems to be so pervasive that it becomes unseeable. In this pervasiveness, its political dimensions are concealed. Whether clinicians "choose" to focus or not on community, some type of community is being enacted.

NOT AT A LOSS FOR WORDS—NONETHELESS, CAUSE FOR CONCERN

Do, then, the data support the claim that the dominant languages of the therapeutic professions are individualistic? Are community and commitment subordinated? Do strengths-focused, community- and family-centered approaches to services face an uphill struggle against not only the dominant American culture, but also professional ideologies? The answer would have to be both a "yes" and a "no." The data support the assertion that there are strong social and professional interests maintaining an individualistic perspective. On the other hand, there are audible alternative languages and a vigorous scholarly effort to reexamine the ideas of self and community.

The most profound implication of this work is the need to explicate a concept of self-in-community and to integrate it consistently into our theories and practices. We need an expanded view of a "mature" or "whole" self. This Self would be differentiated, but would also have relationships and a sense of overlapping boundaries with a complex array of "Others." The Others would include the family, local communities defined by geography, affiliation, and participation, and the "global" community of the human race and the biosphere. This Self would have attachments and commitments as well as autonomy; would be able to give as well as to receive; would value the traditions, rituals, and symbols of a community of memory; and would commit actively to community purposes and goals.

If such a view of the person is developed and gains professional acceptance, it will substantively support strengths-focused, community- and family-centered services. These services are already pointing the way to practice consistent with the concept of self-in-community. A next step will be elaborating the language of community and commitment in practice at all levels with individuals, families, and communities.

There *are* beginnings, described in this study, upon which a more elaborated professional language of community can be built. Most important, professionals tend to have a rich and meaningful experience of community in their own lives from which they can draw as they think about clients. They can be encouraged further to articulate and apply this experience. Many professionals recognize that absence of community is a significant part of some clients' distress, even when the clients themselves may not. Professionals can expand the universe of clients for whom they think about "community" from "some" to "all."

Community interventions are already actively discussed and facilitated, especially referrals to self-help and support groups. Such groups can be emphasized even more. Discussing community involvement and commitment to others as a fulfilling and morally sound way to live can be amplified, buttressed by postmodern awareness that we are always conveying values and that professionals need not support the culturally dominant ideology of individualism. Smale, and others in this volume, describe powerful alternative experiences and visions. Finding ways to talk about these experiences with clients comes easily to some professionals, whereas others need help sorting out possible objections or finding the words. And, finally, the language of mutual aid and empowerment, of benefit both to *self and others* remains a potent and underutilized resource for individual, family, and community change. Let us work on learning this language and discovering its implications.

ACKNOWLEDGMENTS

I want to thank the members of the Community Research Group for their substantive contribution to this chapter and the clinicians who shared so generously of their time and expertise. I also appreciate the editorial suggestions of Ann Fleck-Henderson, MSW, Barry Kahn, MSW, and Kathleen Hannigan Millstein, DSW, and those of the Obermann Faculty Research Seminar.

NOTES

1. The members of the Community Research Group were Dina Carbonell, MSW, project co-director and Terry Bowes Bayer, Elizabeth J. Carleton, Nancy Costikyan, Richard P. Curtiss, Mark Gallagher, Gregory Lippolis, Mary Nada, Ian Shapiro, and Laura Weingast.

2. I use the words "client" and "problems" with some reservations, since they seem to locate difficulties *within* individuals and families, precisely what I am trying to avoid. However, they are the only terms with widespread use at the current time.

REFERENCES

Bellah, R. (1987). America's cultural conversation. In R. Bellah, R. Madsen, W. Sullivan, A. Swidler, & S. Tipton (Eds.), *Individualism and commitment in American life* (pp. 3–10). New York: Harper & Row.

Bellah, R., Madsen, R., Sullivan, W., Swidler, A., & Tipton, S. (1985). *Habits of the heart: Individualism and commitment in American life.* Berkeley: University of California Press.

Blanck, G., & Blanck, R. (1979). *Ego psychology: Vol. II.* New York: Columbia University Press.

Breton, M. (1989). Liberation theology, group work, and the right of the poor and oppressed to participate in the life of the community. *Social Work with Groups, 12* (3), 5–18.

Bruner, J. (1986). *Actual minds, possible worlds.* Cambridge, MA: Harvard University Press.

Chenitz, W.C., & Swanson, J. (1986). *From practice to grounded theory.* Reading, MA: Addison-Wesley.

Cushman, P. (1990). Why the self is empty. *American Psychologist, 45,* 599–611.

Dean, R. (1993). Constructivism: An approach to clinical practice. *Smith Studies in Social Work, 63,* 127–146.

Dean, R., & Rhodes, M. (1992). Ethical clinical tensions in social work practice. *Social Work, 37,* 128–132.

Falck, H. (1984). The membership model of social work. *Social Work, 29,* 155–160.

Germain, C., & Gitterman, A. (1980). *The life model of social work practice.* New York: Columbia University Press.

Glaser, B., & Strauss, A. (1967). *The discovery of grounded theory: Strategies for qualitative research.* Chicago: Aldine.

Hoffman, I. (1991). Toward a social-constructivist view of the psychoanalytic situation. *Psychoanalytic Dialogues, 1,* 74–105.

Imber-Black, E. (1986). Families, larger systems, and the wider social context. *Journal of Strategic and Systemic Therapies, 5* (4), 29–35.

Jones, M. (1990). Understanding social work: A matter of interpretation? *British Journal of Social Work, 20*, 181–196.
Kegan, R. (1982). *The evolving self*. Cambridge, MA: Harvard University Press.
Lasch, C. (1978). *The culture of narcissism*. New York: Norton.
Lee, J. (1994). *The empowerment approach to social work*. New York: Columbia University Press.
McNamee, S., & Gergen, K. (1992). *Therapy as social construction*. London: Sage.
Miller, J. (1984). *The development of women's sense of self*. (Work in Progress, No. 12). Wellesley, MA: Stone Center Working Paper Series.
Mishler, E. (1986). *The research interview: Context and narrative*. Cambridge: Harvard University Press.
Patton, M. (1987). *How to use qualitative methods in evaluation*. London: Sage.
Reinherz, H., Regan, J., & Anastas, J. (1983). A research curriculum for future clinicians: A multimodel strategy. *Journal of Education for Social Work*, 19 (2), 35–41.
Rennie, D., Phillips, J., & Quartaro, G. (1988). Grounded theory: A promising approach to conceptualization in psychology? *Canadian Psychology, 29*, 139–150.
Rhodes, M. (1986). *Ethical dilemmas in social work*. Boston: Routledge.
Rieff, R. (1987). Therapy and technique. In R. Bellah, R. Madsen, W. Sullivan, A. Swidler, & S. Tipton (Eds.), *Individualism and commitment in American life* (pp. 3–10). New York: Harper & Row. (Reprinted from *Therapy and Technique*, 1963, pp. 8–24.)
Riessman, C. (1993). *Narrative analysis*. Newbury Park, CA: Sage.
Roland, A. (1988). *In search of self in India and Japan*. Princeton, NJ: Princeton University Press.
Roland, A. (1990). The self in cross-civilizational perspective: An Indian-Japanese-American comparison. In R. Curtis (Ed.), *The relational self: Theoretical convergences in psychoanalysis and social psychology* (pp. 160–180). New York: Guilford Press.
Saari, C. (1991). *The creation of meaning in clinical social work*. New York: Guilford Press.
Saleeby, D. (Ed.). (1992). *The strengths perspective in social work practice*. New York: Longman.
Sampson, E. (1977). Psychology and the American ideal. *Journal of Personality and Social Psychology, 35*, 767–782.
Sampson, E. (1988). The debate on individualism: Indigenous psychologies of the individual and their role in personal and societal functioning. *American Psychologist, 43*, 15–22.
Schwartz, W. (1971). On the use of groups in social work practice. In W. Schwartz & S. Zalba (Eds.), *The practice of group work* (pp. 3–24). New York: Columbia University Press.
Schwartz, W. (1974). The social worker in the group. In R. Klenk & R. Ryan (Eds.), *The practice of social work* (2nd ed.) (pp. 208–228). Belmont, CA: Wadsworth.
Sherman, E. (1987). Hermeneutics, human science and social work. *Social Thought, 13*, 34–40.
Solomon, B. (1976). *Black empowerment: Social work in oppressed communities*. New York: Columbia University Press.

Specht, H. (1990). Social work and the popular psychotherapies. *Social Service Review*, *64*, 345–357.

Speer, R., Dey, A., Griggs, P., Gibson, C., Lubin, B., & Hughey, J. (1992). In search of community: An analysis of community psychology research from 1984–1988. *American Journal of Community Psychology*, *20* (2), 195–209.

Surrey, J. (1984). *The "self-in-relation": A theory of women's development* (Work in Progress, No. 13). Wellesley, MA: Stone Center Working Paper Series.

Strauss, A., & Corbin, J. (1990). *Basics of qualitative research: Grounded theory procedures and techniques*. Newbury Park, CA: Sage.

Swenson, C., Carbonell, D., Bayer, T.B., Carleton, E.J., Costikyan, N., Curtiss, R.P., Gallagher, M., Lippolis, G., Nada, M., Shapiro, I., & Weingast, L. (1993). *Clinical constructions of community*. Unpublished manuscript, Simmons College, Boston.

White, M. (1992). Deconstruction and therapy. In D. Epston & M. White (Eds.), *Experience, contradiction, narrative, and imagination* (pp. 109–149). Dulwich, S. Australia: Dulwich Centre Publications.

13

Expanding the Focus of Intervention: The Importance of Family/Community Relations

WILLIAM H. QUINN

Family and community have been obscured in human services by a focus on selfhood and the quest for self-actualization. Explaining social problems using an individual lens helps to simplify strategies for intervention. For example, it is sometimes thought to be "easier" to repeatedly try to correct, punish, or help a student in a school setting than to assess, or resolve, the family processes in which that unmotivated, troubled, or self-doubting student is embedded. It is "easier" to reprimand, adjudicate, or punish a juvenile delinquent than to engage a family to resolve their abusive tendencies, marital conflict, or personal parental stresses. It is "easier" to control the environment of one drug-abusing adolescent or adult than to vitalize a life wrought with disappointment and failure by reconstructing a social environment that includes affection and tolerance.

Reconstructing a social environment requires the inclusion of other human beings (a seemingly distant father, a demanding stepparent, a destructive and troubled set of peers, even professionals with other affiliations and agendas) in a helping process. This at first seems like a complicated social network with conflicting motives, life circumstances, and needs that cannot be practically joined (e.g., work schedules), or more threatening yet, understood. Like the inexperienced family therapy trainee who suffers the illusion that seeing one person is actually easier than seeing a family, because one life can be understood more clearly than several lives with interconnected linkages, helpers in human service agencies routinely assume that drawing a boundary around the individual allows for coherence and simplifies recordkeeping.

However, individuals are embedded in social systems, such as families and communities, that contain reciprocal influences, and these reciprocal influences must be acknowledged in human service delivery if positive and durable outcomes are to occur. For example, the value of family therapy in treating adolescent drug abuse is well known (Quinn, Kuehl, Thomas, & Joanning, 1988; Joanning, Quinn, Thomas, & Mullen,

1992; Todd & Selekman, 1991) and must for ethical and clinical reasons supersede the desire for simplicity through warehousing of youth.

THE DARKNESS IN THE INDIVIDUAL LENS

A quick gaze at assessment instruments that are used in case management shows that they routinely omit family and relational data. For example, in a recent case involving a juvenile delinquent, data were gathered on a youth and his current home situation including information about his custodial parent, the mother, and two siblings. The family had endured severe financial hardship and the mother was admittedly unable to provide sufficient supervision of the children. It was discovered by an intervention team, some time later, that the boy had a ritual of getting his hair cut every Friday. This seemed somewhat unusual and puzzling to the team until it was discovered that the barber was his father. Getting a haircut was a "legitimate" reason for seeing his father in the face of severe conflict between two ex-spouses. This discovery made it possible to include the father in decision making about the boy and his school situation and promote the father–son relationship. However, this was slow in developing because the data collection method did not include information regarding family members living outside the home. Strengths in families can be located, but often only if a wider social arc is drawn. This point is not meant to level criticism at the already overburdened social service, educational, and juvenile justice systems, but to document that understanding problems only at the individual level fails to utilize family and community resources that would in fact support the efforts of formal systems.

It is "easier" to employ a singular lens (within-the-skin focus) because it is perceived that, whatever the original source, the child's problem has become embedded in the child's biological system, and certainly, if this is the case, then the resolution of the problem is also embedded in that same system. This perspective can sometimes be reinforced by family members unwilling to share responsibility for change. This reasoning limits the probability of successful outcomes as the following situation illustrates. An 84-year-old man made weekly visits to a physician for ailments that could not be substantiated through tests or examinations. After several visits, the frustrated physician requested the author, then serving as the behavioral scientist in a medical school, to interview and evaluate the patient:

Family Therapist (FT): "Where do you live?"
Elderly Man (EM): "In a nursing home."
FT: "Do you have any family members that you see?"

EM: "I have one son who lives in town."
FT: "How often do you see him?"
EM: "Rarely, I used to see him a lot but now that I am in a nursing home, only when he brings me to see the doctor."

Clearly, this man's psychosocial needs were more relevant than his medical condition. Trips to the physician were a justifiable way for him to seek contact with his son. As it became clear that the older man was yearning for more frequent contact with his son, the son was included in a family session (older father and adult son) that resulted in trips to a restaurant or around town instead of to the medical clinic. The son had erroneously assumed that his father's social needs were fully met when he moved to a nursing home.

This example illustrates another limitation in current approaches to intervention. For a positive outcome to occur in this case, two atypical actions were needed. First, the physician was obliged to seek help from someone else who could offer some insight or an alternative perspective outside the boundaries of the medical profession. Second, the therapist expanded his view to include the social system of the older man through a series of questions about the man's family and, as a consequence, included the son in the attempt to resolve the older man's problem.

NEW DIRECTIONS IN SOCIAL ANALYSIS

The interest in examining new paradigms has grown in part out of the failure of traditional approaches, which emphasize pathology and dysfunction. Hoffman (1991) offers the "art of lenses" as a way of conceptualizing the needed shift. Jessor (1991) delineates key developments that have contributed to a newer model of inquiry, grounded in a contextual framework. One change was a growing sense that a multidisciplinary perspective was needed "to encompass the socially organized environment of human action" (p.117). Jessor proposes a model that places the individual (e.g., adolescent) in the center of overlapping circles and that includes the family, school, and neighborhood, set in a backdrop of the larger social-structural, economic, political, and cultural environment.

A response to Bronfenbrenner's (1986) "call to context" to embed human behavior in the family and community is the multidisciplinary and ecosystemic studies supported by the MacArthur Foundation. One such study in Philadelphia is exploring the strategies that families use to protect adolescents from the risks, dangers, and illegitimate opportunities characteristic of disadvantaged neighborhoods. Located in an inner-city neighborhood, the study focuses on how families manage problematic environments, negotiate with local institutions such as school or police, seek out necessary resources for their children, buffer against drug use and peer pressures that lead to problem behaviors, and even locate a safer environment. These are proactive strategies that promote family change by utilizing skillful transactions in the extrafamilial environment.

An additional contribution is the stage–environment fit paradigm. Eccles et al. (1993) describe school and family experiences that are chronically disturbed because of the traditionalism, rigidity, and inattention to student needs of educational institutions. One vivid example is the clash between the developmental needs of early-adolescent youth and the impenetrable structure of junior high school, which often ends in youth maladjustment.

Context with a Capital "C"

The pitfall of mental health service as it currently exists is that human misery is viewed as an isolated expression of personal failure rather than a consequential expression of failed relationships. These failed relationships emanate from a benign neglect, a self-centered compulsion, or a disquieting anger that contagiously infects young children and youth who desperately need, instead, a nurturing experience to solidify their competencies and sense of worth and social commitment.

Adler identified an important cornerstone of this idea in his concept of "Gemeinschaftsgefühl," or social interest. Other English translations include social feeling, community feeling, fellow feeling, sense of solidarity, communal intuition, community interest, and social sense (Ansbacher & Ansbacher, 1956).

The notion of self-other in contemporary society seems almost forgotten in moment-to-moment human interactions and, more specifically, in the mental health system and other institutions, which emphasize the perceived well-being of the individual rather than the common good. Of course, at one level this is impossible, since individuals are embedded in social environments from which they cannot escape and from which flow particular social consequences.

As Adler stated, "before the individual life of man [sic] there was the community. In the history of human culture, there is not a single form of life which was not conducted as social. Never has man [sic] appeared otherwise than in society" (p.128). Adler proposed that the individual could be understood by the observation of behavior in context. He suggested that "we have to close our ears. We have only to look. In this way we can see as in pantomime" (Ansbacher & Ansbacher, 1956, p. 18).

To understand any individual requires an exploration of that person's past experiences in relation to other significant social relationships, such as family. An example from my own experience will illustrate this: Quite a few years ago (1979), I interviewed men and women (mostly women) in old age to assess needs of the frail elderly. Early one evening I came upon an older woman rocking on her front porch in a very rural area of southwest Virginia. I approached her cautiously, introduced myself and explained my presence, and asked if she would be willing to answer some questions. She obliged and invited me to sit next to her. She told me initially that she was 76 years old. In the standardized interview itself I had to ask her for her birthdate. She told me it was July 5, 1898. Doing a little math, I discovered an incongruity between her report of her age and the actual years between her birth and the present. I asked her if she was sure of this and she said, "oh yes, my older sister was born in 1896 and my kid sister was born in 1899. I'm sure." Reluctantly, I told her that if she really was born in 1898, then she was now 81 years old and not 76 as she had told me earlier. The woman leaned toward me in her rocker, looked me in the eye and quietly remarked, "you don't say." She seemed confused but accepting of this "news of a difference."

To explain how this could happen the woman told me a story. She said that she never married and lived alone most of her life, but in her later years her sister's husband had died and the two sisters decided to move in together. Each year they festively celebrated each other's birthday when it came along. When I asked the woman about her sister, she remarked that her sister had died 5 years previously, and so she stopped celebrating birthdays! Thus, she remained 76 for 5 years because her birthdays were never acknowledged when they came along.

Group life (or culture), in other words, defines the individual life. If the group contains pathology, then the individual cannot be healthy. In contemporary terms this might be applied to unsafe school, neighborhood, and family environments that impair human cooperation and civility. Although the goal in these environments is often to promote individual growth and development, the social climate required for growth is ignored. This can be the case in any institution that focuses on the individual.

As the story illustrates, each of our truths is socially constructed. To understand and empathize with the condition of another person requires that relational partner (spouse, parent, social service worker, educator) explore the social experience of that person, their history, relational circumstances, and environmental conditions. This is not to say that socially constructed truth is not helpful in life. While in this case the woman did not appear to experience any dire consequences of "not knowing" her chronological age, too often statistics (bits of information) disguise the complexity of a problem.

Statistics serve a purpose; however, they do not generate solutions because they do not reflect the individual-in-context. Statistics too often are used to justify a "pick yourself up by the bootstraps" mentality that protects persons who are not "statistics" and creates an "us–them" dichotomy. Instead, statistics should be seen not as aggregates of individual problems, but as reflections of social and structural problems. Otherwise, institutions fall prey to the same self-defeating patterns of behavior in their efforts to address human problems.

TWO DOMAINS OF PROBLEMATIC SITUATIONS

There are a number of social structures that have a limited approach to human problems and their solutions. Two domains of youth problems, criminal behavior and school failure, are illustrative of these social structures.

In dealing with these issues only one reference point is usually established, that of the child and the behavior that society categorizes as a problem. A youth's juvenile delinquency can be unequivocally identified, categorized, and summarized. The same is true for school failure. The life experiences of youth that might explain delinquency and school failure are, however, more complex.

The School Arena

Research over the years has documented that parent involvement in their children's education results in better attendance, more positive attitudes about education (Henderson, 1989), and, more crucially, higher student achievement (Smith, 1968; Epstein, 1983). An example of the strength of family influence is found in a study of academic achievement of children in over 200 Indo-Chinese refugee families in the United States (Caplan, Choy, & Whitmore, 1992). Parents set standards and goals for weeknight evenings that facilitated academic progress, even when the parents lacked education and proficiency in English. After the table was cleared and chores were completed, homework began; older children helped younger siblings and read stories. Instead of personal efficacy, a family efficacy was present. Parents who attributed greater importance to fun and excitement in their lives had children with lower grades, while children whose parents emphasized the values of their past family history received higher grades.

Parental involvement in the school is strengthened when school personnel enlist parental participation in decision making and problem resolution. When this occurs, the impact of the family on a child's school performance can be documented (Bronfenbrenner, 1986). Family therapists are working in several programs with school-related problems to incorporate school–family collaboration (Wetchler, 1986; Amatea & Sherrard, 1991; O'Callaghan, 1991; Vob, 1993; Weiss, Edwards, Zelen, & Schwartz, 1991). An example of a recent family/community collaborative approach to pervasive school problems is the Ackerman Institute's project in New York City, which includes families in school planning and goal setting to diminish adversarial relations when problems emerge during the school year (Weiss & Edwards, 1992).

Another illustration comes from my own practice. Colleagues and I have used a family–school intervention team in a multisystemic effort to resolve chronic school problems (Quinn, Michaels, Sutphen, & Gale, 1994). In this model, the interventionist is outside the communication problem-solving process and serves as a facilitator of conversation to foster reconciliation and collaboration among the participants (see Table 13.1).

A school–family collaboration, like any collaboration between people, requires meaningful conversation that allows good outcomes to emerge.

Table 13.1. The Professional Role in Fostering Family–School Collaboration

1. Emphasize that changes in parent and family behavior can affect a child's school behavior and, consequently, academic and social performance.
2. Make the problem-solving collaboration more convenient. Ask parents to choose a time and day for a meeting, have meetings at the school or home, and consider transportation needs and work schedules. Even more importantly, the nature of collaboration influences results. Asking, "Can you meet on Tuesday at four, that's when the school psychologist will be here," isn't nearly as helpful as, "What time could you (and your husband) meet with us?"
3. Open the floor to any participant who expresses concerns. The goal is to steer conversation toward a pragmatic consensual plan. Essential ingredients include questions, paraphrasing, and clarification.
4. Change conversation from a "gripe-gripe-gripe" style that is unwittingly negative and inhibiting to one that focuses on "what can we do to change it?" Explanations are also not helpful since analysis and causation are not directly linked to solutions.
5. Expel destructive dichotomies from the model of collaboration. Examples are being a good child or a bad child (or a good parent or a bad parent), having a good or bad childhood, and being a capable or incapable student. The school and family, or members within one of these systems, can utilize the dichotomy to argue with each other and reduce their own personal responsibility, evident in adversarial relationships that develop around who is at fault: the family, the child, or the school.

The purpose of collaboration must be identified, so that competing cross-agendas do not hamper the constructive interaction needed to achieve a goal. Each participant in the collaboration must be involved. Everyone needs to feel a sense of belonging to the group, and thoughts and feelings that express needs and desired goals must be invited. A dominating individual will shut down shared ownership of the concern.

A description of the problem must be negotiated that does not depend on the perception of personal inferiority or inadequacy of any individual. Information needs to be woven together to provide a picture of the circumstances and context in which the problem is embedded. Patience and acknowledgment of expertise and constraints are required. Finally, inviting questions or final thoughts and reviewing, even recording, the plan before terminating any collaboration provide motivation and clear direction for action.

Juvenile Delinquency and Family/Community Intervention

Romig, Cleland, and Romig (1989) suggest that social characteristics such as having delinquent friends, lack of attachment to prosocial institutions (schools, church, community organizations), absence of a law-abiding parent, lack of empathy toward others, boredom, impulsive behavior, and drug and alcohol abuse are among the strongest indicators of potential to offend. These factors have not been established as unicausal. For instance, association with delinquent peers does not by itself predict criminal behavior, nor does income alone predict delinquency (Institute of Medicine, 1989; Rutter, 1980; Sameroff & McDonough, 1984; Schorr, 1988), and several of these risk factors are environmental (Zigler, Taussig, & Black, 1992).

The importance of taking into account these wider issues has been proposed in studies by Nelson (1990) and Henggeler, Melton, and Smith (1992), which demonstrate the value of family-based intervention for juvenile offenders. A recent attempt in my own work to reduce the rate of repeat offenses and to interrupt the cycle of criminal behavior offers an example of a multisystemic approach (Quinn, Michaels, Sutphen, & Gale, 1994). To resolve the offending tendencies of their children, multiple family groups are formed. These groups utilize each other's help, counsel, and resources to develop more effective ways of thinking about family life and child development, to problem solve together, to share responsibility for change, to reorganize their neighborhoods to rid them of crime, and to offer each other help in monitoring the behavior of children in the neighborhood.

This has led us to develop an entirely family–community-based model and to create a program that is flexible and adaptable to the immediate needs of the participants. The goal was not to have a preset agenda, but to develop a program that was both (1) sensitive to feedback from the families and facilitators participating in the program and (2) sufficiently fluid to self-correct its operations. In this approach, families are viewed as doing better when they can voice their ideas together in a collaborative fashion. Each person in each family is invited to tell the story of his or her situation. Peers respond collaboratively to help normalize the problems, offer other perspectives on the issues, and suggest possible solutions.

The program allows all parts of the system to provide feedback. Each night, the families evaluate the program and state what they want and need that night. While certain themes (i.e., family communication, school problems, neighborhood issues) are structured into the program, these are seen as "working drafts" that can be modified at any time. For instance, one night when the focus was to be on problem-solving communication, the issue of the cost of athletic shoes came up. This led to a group discussion on finances and budgets and to the development of a worksheet that families could utilize in their financial planning.

The program is designed to lead to discussion on topics that are relevant to the particular neighborhood and community. Community leaders (e.g., school counselor, youth services worker) facilitate discussion in such areas as working with the schools and surviving street crime. Eliciting participation and support from the community is a gradual and continual process. Various churches are used as locations for programs that help inform the clergy of the community effort for juvenile delinquents and families. Role plays on conflict resolution with facilitators enacting initially angry or resentful youths or parents and a graduation night talent show produce a down–up motion as well as an up–down motion in which action or change can be initiated or occur within any part of the family–facilitator network.

Finally, family advocates, helping professionals on the project who also serve as group facilitators, are connected to each family in the program to be available for collaboration if further problems are encountered. These advocates are helpful in resolving feelings of injustice families sometimes experience with regard to the judicial system. In fact, a juvenile court judge attends one meeting to discuss the history and role of the juvenile court, reminding families that juvenile courts came into being over 100 years ago to protect the interests of children. Advocates provide encouragement and a proven relationship that resolves families' fear that they will simply be caught up within another system that does not understand their needs.

Requests from the Consumer/Client

Using ethnographic methods and lengthy interviews with families selected at random, we have learned what families appreciated about the program as well as their suggestions for improvement. For instance, the youth volunteered that they benefited most from role plays; parents expressed appreciation for the manner in which the group became a validating body and support in the face of family adversity.

The consumer/client does not often have the opportunity to describe the experience of engaging with a helper in the human service network. Some accounts do exist in addition to the few brief examples given above. In this section a more elaborate set of findings will be reported. Inquiries allowed clients in family therapy to tell the stories of their experiences.

Three domains of meaning emerged (Quinn, 1995). The first was labeled *affirmation*, and comprised phrases such as "we count," "being able to stay with me" (on my level of thinking or feeling), "extending herself," "drawing me into her life," being brought into my spouse's feelings without being a dummy," and "not hiding" (showing courage to face adversity).

A second domain was labeled *discovery*, and was composed of client phrases such as "the light going on," "not clamming up," "throwing questions right back at us," "asking a question I never considered," "putting a new wrinkle to something," "experiencing great organization of the brain," "not knowing it's working" (change is occurring), and "giving me permission to take on a new role."

The third domain was labeled *congruence*, and included phrases such as "connecting what was happening," "keeping me in balance," "pinpointing the problem," "knowing where I need to go," "putting myself through this little session in my mind" (during the week between sessions), "building up the talk," and "someone who can help in that area."

These categories, affirmation, discovery, and congruence, reflect the importance of social interaction and group properties in the production of better outcomes for individuals and families. Some of these better outcomes include resolution of personal problems, new and more helpful ways of thinking about self and/or world, and the experience of human comfort.

An extrapolation of these consumer voices to human service delivery systems might foster some different thinking about collaboration or partnership by service providers. First, the consumer is requesting from the service provider some communication that offers a sincere acknowledgment of his or her perspective. This acknowledgment includes a respect for one's needs and situation, and a sincere attempt to remain connected ("not hide") and not retreat from the problem.

Second, the consumer is asking for a new idea from the helper that might contribute to the resolution of the problem ("discovery"). Innovative and co-created ideas are privileged over standard, predictable, and bureaucratic responses. Examples of the latter might be overutilized ideas or strategies for problem resolution expressed by a caseworker or a family member who is rigidly adamant about another person's need to take responsibility for change.

And third, the helper should engage in focused interaction that sets in motion actions that are meaningful to the consumer and the helper. This is possible if the helper solicits input from the consumer about whether a plan, its components, and its implementation are sensible and relevant.

EXPANDING FAMILY AND COMMUNITY RELATIONS

A relational lens viewing both human development and social problems leads to the following three practice principles:

1. The condition and development of human beings are embedded in an ecology of human interaction, physical conditions, and cultural beliefs. As such, to consider the needs of individuals requires the broadest understanding of their ecologies. Where needs are unfulfilled in such social contexts, impediments to development and personal productivity and relational satisfaction must be addressed. Specifically, more emphasis is needed on organizing ecologies at the familial, social, and political levels to promote productive and meaningful life experiences. This should include prenatal and infant care, parental skill development, early learning environments, and community support resources for parents. Also, intervention programs should begin early in life for at-risk children. Many programs provide "too little too late" to help in any meaningful way and substitute for the support needed to prevent or ameliorate human despair and hardship. One example is the importance of early childhood intervention in preventing juvenile delinquency (Zigler, Taussig, & Black, 1992).
2. Intervention must account for the ecological variables that influence problems in living. Family data are essential in constructing service delivery plans, whether within the educational system, the human service system, or the family system. It is essential to assess the level of motivation

for change, to determine the location of resources, and to understand influences on current behavior. Family members themselves, including noncustodial but actively involved parents, and both parents in a two-parent household, should be part of every decision-making process in educational, juvenile delinquency, and mental health interventions. For example, one of the challenges in our multiple family intervention program for first offender youth is to engage both parents if they live together or in the same community rather than accept the presence of just one parent.

3. Total environmental quality is essential for personal well-being and productive living. Tagiuri (1968) includes four dimensions: culture (belief systems, values, and cognitive structures), milieu (characteristics of persons and groups such as race and ethnicity, morale), social system (patterned relationships of persons and groups such as leadership, emotionally focused utility, and communication), and ecology (the physical and material aspects of the environment). The goal is a social system that includes emotion and communication in ways that allow for good outcomes.

Environmental quality is what this chapter has attempted to emphasize as essential for personal well-being and productive living. Social systems too often fail to acknowledge the significance of environmental conditions. Lack of availability during evening hours, service that is not accessible due to location, and employment pressures and restrictions on familial behavior are illustrations of unresponsiveness. An organizational climate conducive to building or enhancing total environmental quality is required.

CONCLUSION

The process of service delivery can fail due to a lack of understanding of the change process and the definitions helpers construct of their roles. This chapter addresses the question of what can be done to facilitate human development for vulnerable youth and families. New thinking is needed to engage families and communities in striving for an adequate environment to promote the well-being of youth by rejecting the deprivation/pathology model in favor of a resource model that assists youth and families without extreme dependence on public services, agency support, and helping professionals. Two institutional domains, school–family difficulties and juvenile delinquency, provide examples of problematic thinking and new program models. Finally, practice principles for future human service activity are delineated: (1)

expanding the social ecology for individual development and problem resolution, (2) increasing the use of family data (intra- and extrafamilial) in interventions, and (3) examining the professional structure and climate in which interventions occur to adapt to individual, family, and community needs.

ACKNOWLEDGMENTS

Acknowledgment must be given to the U.S. Office of Juvenile Justice and Delinquency Prevention and the Georgia Children and Youth Coordinating Council for their support (93J-16-9304-0016).

REFERENCES

Amatea, E.S., & Sherrard, P.A.D. (1991). Systemic practice in schools provides a new frontier. *Family Therapy News, 22,* 5–6.

Ansbacher, H.L., & Ansbacher, R. (1956). *The individual psychology of Alfred Adler.* New York: Harper & Row.

Bronfenbrenner, U. (1986). Ecology of the family as a context for human development. *Developmental Psychology, 22,* 723–742.

Caplan, N., Choy, M.H.., & Whitmore, J.H. (1992). Indochinese refugee families and academic achievement. *Scientific American, 266,* 36–42.

Eccles, J.S., Midgley, C., Wigfield, A., Buchanan, C.M., Reuman, D., Flanagan, C., & MacIver, D. (1993). Development during adolescence: The impact of stage-environment fit on young adolescents' experiences in schools and in families. *American Psychologist, 48,* 90–101.

Epstein, J.L. (1983). Longitudinal effects of family-school-person interactions on student outcomes. *Research in Sociology of Education and Socialization, 4,* 101–127.

Henderson, A. (1989). *The evidence continues to grow: Parent involvement improves school achievement.* Columbia, MD: National Committee for Citizens in Education.

Henggeler, S.W., Melton, G.B., & Smith, L.A. (1992). Family preservation using multisystemic therapy: An effective alternative to incarcerating serious juvenile offenders. *Journal of Consulting & Clinical Psychology, 60,* 953–961.

Hoffman, L. (1990). Constructing realities: An art of lenses. *Family Process, 29,* 1–12.

Institute of Medicine. (1989). *Research on children and adolescents with mental, behavioral, and developmental disorders: Mobilizing a national initiative (Contract N. 278-88-0025).* Washington, DC: Department of Health and Human Services, National Institute of Mental Health.

Jessor, R. (1991). Behavioral science: An emerging paradigm for social inquiry? In R. Jessor (Ed.), *Perspectives on behavioral science: The Colorado lectures* (pp. 309–316). Boulder, CO: Westview Press.

Joanning, H., Quinn, W., Thomas, F., & Mullen, R. (1992). Treating adolescent drug abuse: A comparison of family systems therapy, group therapy, and family drug education. *Journal of Marital and Family Therapy, 18,* 345–356.

Nelson, K.E. (1990). Family-based services for juvenile offenders. *Children and Youth Services Review, 12,* 193–212.

O'Callaghan, J.B. (1991). Therapists and schools can construct workable partnerships and collaboration. *Family Therapy News, 22,* 7–8.

Quinn, W.H., Hill, J., Wiley, G., & Dotson, D. (1994). The family-school intervention team (FSIT) model: A meta-level and multi-systemic approach. Transitioning from individual to family counseling. In C. Huber (Ed.), *The family psychotherapy and counseling series* (pp. 87–106). Alexandria, VA: American Counseling Association Press.

Quinn, W. H. (1995). The client speaks out: Three domains of meaning. *Journal of Family Psychotherapy*. In press.

Quinn, W.H., Kuehl, B.P., Thomas, F.N., & Joanning, H. (1988). Families of adolescent drug abusers: Systemic interventions to attain drug-free behavior. *American Journal of Alcohol and Drug Abuse, 14,* 65–87.

Quinn, W.H., Michaels, M., Sutphen, R., & Gale, J. (1994). Juvenile offenders: Characteristics of at-risk families and strategies for intervention. *Journal of Addiction and Offender Counseling, 15,* 2–23.

Romig, D.A., Cleland, C., & Romig, J. (1989). *Juvenile delinquency: Visionary approaches*. Columbus, OH: Merrill.

Rutter, M. (1980). *Changing youth in a changing society: Patterns of adolescent development and disorder.* Cambridge, MA: Harvard University Press.

Sameroff, A., & McDonough, S. (1984). The role of motor activity in human cognitive and social development. In E. Pollitt & P. Amante (Eds.), *Energy intake and activity* (pp. 331–353). New York: Alan R. Liss.

Smith, M.B. (1968). School and home: Focus on achievement. In A. H. Passow (Ed.), *Developing programs for the educationally disadvantaged* (pp. 87–108). New York: Teachers College Press.

Schorr, L.B. (1988). *Within our reach: Breaking the cycle of disadvantage.* New York: Anchor Press.

Tagiuri, R. (1968). The concept of organizational climate. In R. Tagiuri & G.H. Litwin (Eds.), *Organizational climate: Exploration of a concept* (pp. 10–32). Cambridge, MA: Harvard University Press.

Todd, T.C., & Selekman, M.D. (1991). *Family therapy approaches with adolescent substance abusers.* Boston, MA: Allyn and Bacon.

Vob, R. (1993). Systemic consultation and interdisciplinary cooperation: Appeal for an ecosystemic model of action in the human sciences. *International Journal of Prenatal and Perinatal Psychology & Medicine, 5,* 1–16.

Weiss, H.M., & Edwards, M.E. (1992). The family-school collaboration project: Systemic interventions for school improvement. In S.L. Christensen & J.C. Conoley (Eds.), *Home-school collaboration: Enhancing children's academic and social competence* (pp. 215–243). Silver Spring, MD: The National Association of School Psychologists.

Weiss, H.M., Edwards, M.W., Zelen, M., & Schwartz, F. (1991). Systemic interventions produce innovative school change. *Family Therapy News, 22,* 9–10.

Wetchler, J.L. (1986). Family therapy of school-focused problems: A macrosystemic perspective. *Contemporary Family Therapy, 8,* 224–240.

Zigler, E., Taussig, C., & Black, K. (1992). Early childhood prevention: A promising preventative for juvenile delinquency. *American Psychologist, 47,* 997–1006.

14

Strengthening Partnerships between Families and Service Providers

ROBERT COHEN and CHRISTOPHER LAVACH

Historically, families of children with serious emotional or behavioral disturbances (EBD) have borne multiple burdens. First, as primary caregivers they have had to cope with the unpredictable and sometimes explosive behavior of their offspring without the benefit of adequate or appropriate services. Available services are either too restrictive (e.g., long-term, out-of-community placements) or not intensive enough to meet the children's needs (Knitzer, 1982; National Mental Health Association, 1988; Saxe, Dougherty, Cross, & Silverman, 1987). Necessary related services have generally been delivered in a fragmented, discontinuous manner with the major child-serving agencies rarely working together (Tuma, 1989). In addition, families entering the service delivery system have often been confronted with hostile, judgmental, and rejecting attitudes on the part of service providers (Cohen, Singh, Hosick, & Tremaine, 1992; Friesen & Koroloff, 1990).

Given the long-standing schism between parents of children with EBD and child-serving professionals, reorienting the child service system toward family inclusion will not be an easy task. The purpose of this chapter is to review the obstacles to family responsiveness and to identify constructive efforts to strengthen the partnership between parents and professionals. We will also offer recommendations about providing opportunities for families to have input into the treatment process while enhancing the service system's capacity to provide support and assistance.

Service providers' insensitivity and antipathy toward families may be attributed to several factors. First, unlike many other western nations, the United States has not generally included families as a major element in social policy. From the absence of any mention of families in the Constitution to the emphasis on addressing social problems through crisis-oriented categorical service programs, there has been a strong tendency to assure individual rights without considering the larger environmental context (Langley, 1991). The lack of explicit recognition of family needs in mental health policy and program structure has certainly contributed to many families' sense of exclusion.

Etiological and treatment theories and beliefs have also contributed to the disenfranchisement of parents within the child serving system. Many of the theoretical constructs that form the basis for clinical treatment explicitly refer to parents as causing child behavioral and emotional disorders (Collins & Collins, 1990). The phenomenon of "mother blaming," which attributes psychopathology to inappropriate interaction between mothers and their children, has contributed to the rift between professionals and parents. A survey of major clinical journals between 1970 and 1982 revealed that 42% of articles that dealt with the etiology of psychopathology cited earlier literature that linked a child's pathology and the mother's behavior without, in most instances, questioning the validity of this literature (Caplan & Hall-McCorquodale, 1985).

While family functioning may have an impact on child behavior, research does not support the theory that parental behavior causes childhood psychosis and other serious disorders (Forehand, 1993; Hingtgen, Bryson & Gair, 1972). In spite of this absence of support and a growing body of evidence indicating a strong genetic component in these disorders, parent blaming still exists (Peschel, Peschel, Howe, & Howe, 1992). Outdated professional training and clinical practice continue to imbue service providers with negative perceptions of parents. In light of the stigma that has been attached to emotional disorders, it is not surprising that parents have been reluctant to challenge these perceptions and to insist on greater participation in the service delivery process.

In recent years, the orientation of services for children with serious EBD has shifted considerably (Duchnowski & Friedman, 1990). The federally sponsored Child and Adolescent Service System Program (CASSP) provided an impetus for states to develop systems of care that share a common set of core values and principles. One of the basic principles of CASSP is that "the families and surrogate families of emotionally disturbed children should be full participants in all aspects of the planning and delivery of services" (Stroul & Friedman, 1988, p. III). The importance of family inclusion is also emphasized in the Individuals with Disabilities Education Act of 1990 (IDEA), which mandates and provides guidelines for parent participation in the Individual Education Plan (IEP) process.

In contrast to traditional approaches that force children to fit into one of a limited number of standard programs, CASSP emphasizes planning and delivery of comprehensive services that are shaped by the needs of each child and family. In addition, CASSP promotes service delivery in the child's natural environment, in home and community settings rather than institutions, whenever possible (Stroul & Friedman, 1986). As indicated in other chapters of this volume, home and community-centered services involve more than simply a change of location. They signify an approach in which professionals consider parents not as "objects of concern," but as genuine partners who are responsible and resourceful participants in the endeavor to help their child. Services are provided by and for the community and children and families remain the responsibility of the community. Finally, CASSP underscores the importance of being sensitive and responsive to cultural differences.

BARRIERS TO PARENTAL INVOLVEMENT

Barriers to effective parental involvement exist at multiple levels. First, there are the impediments at the level of professional practice cited above. As Friesen and Koroloff (1990) have observed, the absence of effort to support families "is related at least in part to deep-seated beliefs about the nature and cause of emotional disorders in children" (p. 15).

Second, the design and structure of program services are not typically family-friendly. The inappropriate reliance on restrictive institutional services (Knitzer, 1982; National Mental Health Association, 1988) disrupts the child's connection with the family. The lack of "intermediate" level services between traditional outpatient and highly restrictive inpatient services (Knitzer, 1982), such as home-based services, day treatment, and respite care that provide the intensity and support to enable youth to remain in home and community settings encourages overreliance on institutional placement. The absence of these services places families caring for children with EBD in a difficult and precarious position. They are forced either to place their children in institutional settings, often at some distance from home, or to settle for services that are not intensive enough to meet the needs of the child and family.

A host of system-level problems also impede parental involvement. Children with EBD and their families have multiple needs that bring them into contact with a variety of non-mental health systems of care, such as education, health, child welfare, and juvenile justice (Tuma, 1989). The lack of clarity of roles and responsibilities among child serving agencies has resulted in a fragmented service system characterized by poor interagency relationships, nonproductive expenditure of energy, and territorial squabbles (Cohen et al., 1992). In addition to being uncoordinated, the child serving system also lacks adequate financial resources (National Advisory Mental Health Council, 1990) and suffers a host of bureaucratic regulations that make it even less responsive.

Families' Views of the Service System

Earlier survey research conducted with families who had adult offspring with mental illness indicated that families generally experience high levels of objective burden (e.g., financial costs, disruption of everyday routines) and subjective burden (e.g., emotional costs, feelings of overload, entrapment/exclusion) (Thompson & Doll, 1982). Families perceived significant differences between the type of assistance they sought from professionals and the kinds of help they received. Families wanted practical information about what to expect of their offspring and how to help them, but instead received therapy (Hatfield, 1983). Families were also dissatisfied with staff behavior toward them (Bernheim & Switalski, 1988) and with the nature and level of involvement in their child's treatment (Holden & Lewine, 1982).

Recently families who have children and adolescents with EBD have received more attention. Consistent with earlier studies, researchers find that families with younger offspring also perceive services to be suboptimal and do not view professionals as being supportive of families (Collins & Collins, 1990; Fine & Friesen, 1988; Tarico, Low, Trupin, & Forsyth-Stevens, 1989). One of the most frequently voiced complaints is that professionals seem to minimize, overlook, or deny a child's problem, often conveying the message to parents that they were overreacting or not responding appropriately to their child's behavior (Tarico et al., 1989). Parents experienced difficulties not only with mental health professionals, but also with pediatricians, teachers, and other gatekeepers to the mental health system.

Professionals' Views of Family Involvement

Only a few attempts have been made to systematically assess mental health professionals' perceptions of families of the individuals that they treat. In their survey concerning patients in a state-operated psychiatric hospital, Bernheim and Switalski (1988) collected data on staff attitudes toward families. Inpatient and outpatient staff responses to families were generally favorable. Less than one-fifth thought that mental illness was attributable to the way patients were treated as children or that families ceased to care about children once they were hospitalized. In spite of the relatively favorable attitude of staff toward families, their beliefs did not translate into action. The majority of staff reported that they spent less than 1 hour per week in contact with families, with most of those contacts being initiated by the patient or relative.

Significant discrepancies also exist between professionals' perceptions of current and ideal practices in relation to family involvement (Bailey, Buysse, Edmondson, & Smith, 1992). Although many professionals believe that parents should be given high levels of choice and responsibility within the child service system, they perceive the current approach to service delivery as being professionally dominated, offering parents only a minor role in the planning and delivery of services.

ESTABLISHING A FRAMEWORK FOR FAMILY–PROFESSIONAL PARTNERSHIPS

To effectively restructure the relationship between families and the child service delivery system, we must define the desired outcome (i.e., how parents should be involved), identify what needs to be changed, and develop effective strategies for strengthening the partnership between parents and service providers. Traditionally, when parents were allowed to be a part of a system of care, they were assigned the role of "patient" based on the belief that the family caused the child's problem and needed to change for the child to improve (Friesen & Koroloff, 1990). While parents and other family members certainly may have personal needs that require therapeutic intervention, including those associated with the stresses of raising a child with EBD, it is inappropriate and demeaning to label family members as patients. A more constructive approach is to recognize both the strengths and needs parents bring as equal collaborators with professionals and to identify their unique roles and contributions, which include

- parents as experts and teachers, offering first-hand knowledge about their children to mental health professionals;
- parents as advocates on behalf of their children, working to ensure that their needs are met;
- parents as advocates for improved services for all children and families;
- parents as change agents in the family environment, learning more about helping their children while also becoming better able to cope with having a child who has EBD;
- parents as participants in mutual support activities assisting other parents, as well as professionals, to cope with and overcome the

> many barriers and frustrations in providing comprehensive services to children with EBD (Cohen, Singh, Hosick, & Tremaine, 1992; Duchnowski & Friedman, 1990; Friesen & Koroloff, 1990; Moroney, 1986; Slentz, Walker, & Bricker, 1989).

One promising vehicle for parent involvement is the self-help or mutual support group, which can fulfill multiple objectives including enhancing parent–professional collaboration; increasing family members' ability to negotiate with the child-serving system; reducing feelings of isolation, guilt, frustration, and anger; and increasing participation in developing programs and policies pertaining to children with EBD (Corp & Kosinski, 1990).

Within the treatment and service planning process, family members who are, in fact, primary caregivers must be fully involved in the decision-making process, functioning as bona fide members of a multidisciplinary team rather than simply reacting to decisions and plans that have been formulated by professionals prior to meeting with the parents (Collins & Collins, 1990).

Consider the difference between the traditional and emerging relationship of families, persons with disabilities, and professionals. In the traditional relationship, the professional defines the client's and family's needs, prescribes how to satisfy these needs, and designs formal service programs and policies to meet them. In an emerging, more responsive approach, the person with the disability and the family are collaborative partners in the service development process. Each identifies their own needs, chooses the extent to which they will work with professionals as well as with informal networks, and forms partnerships to design both formal and informal service programs. Family members of persons with disabilities also choose the degree to which they participate in modifying programs, policies, and systems to make them more responsive (Turnbull & Turnbull, 1986).

Constructive family involvement in the child service system can be assessed and enhanced by using the following health care system indicators: availability of the most appropriate services to all citizens; accessibility of services to those needing them in terms of geography, time, and cost; and continuity of care, including ease of movement from one level of care to another (Penchansky & Thomas, 1981; Stefl & Prosperi, 1985). Patients and families should have a minimum of clerical personnel to whom they convey information. Services must be of good quality, delivered by staff who have appropriate training and a high level of competence for their specific duties and must be acceptable to the population in need.

In emphasizing involvement of caregivers it is important not to lose sight of the perspective of the child as well as other family members. Provision should be made to include the child in planning and decision-making activities and to recognize the strengths and needs of each member of the family, even though this adds complexity to the process.

STRENGTHENING THE FAMILY–SERVICE PROVIDER PARTNERSHIP

In recent years, there have been exciting developments in the field of child mental health. Not only has family involvement with service providers increased, but their participation has resulted in the creation of innovative service programs, responsive to child and family needs, and structures for providing comprehensive, coordinated systems of care at the local and state levels. In the following section we will describe some of these exemplary initiatives as well as strategies for improving practices, programs, and policies to involve families. While not exhaustive, this summary offers examples for providers, administrators, and policymakers who wish to improve services for children with EBD and their families.

Developing Constructive Staff Practices

As noted above, one of the major barriers to family involvement is the often deep-seated belief among staff that the child's problem is, in large part, due to parental influence and that contact with parents may have a toxic effect on the child's progress during treatment (Collins & Collins, 1990). One promising treatment approach is family therapy, which incorporates the entire family into the treatment process to alter family interaction (Nichols, 1984). Simply working with the family unit is not enough, however. Therapists must be sensitive to the many stresses experienced by families so as not to unwittingly reinforce feelings of guilt and inadequacy among parents. If therapists acknowledge the significant impact that factors associated with having a child with EBD may have on families (e.g., economic and social stresses) and bring a nonjudgmental attitude to their interaction with parents, positive parental participation will be more likely. Even in situations in which there may have been abuse or neglect, it is important to focus on what can be done to help the child and how the parents can participate constructively to achieve this goal. If parents view therapists as nonblaming and supportive of the family's desire to participate as full partners in the treatment of their children, they may be more willing to examine how family structure and dynamics can exacerbate or reduce their child's troubling behavior.

Service providers cannot be converted to a family-centered approach simply by offering them pertinent information and a new repertoire of skills. One of the underlying sources of staff resistance to parents is the "adoption process" that occurs in institutional settings (Palmer, Harper, & Rivinus, 1983). Staff in these settings may assume the role of surrogate parent, thus placing themselves in an adversarial relationship with the child's biological or adoptive family. This attitude is understandable within the historical context of institutions as the only viable option for long-term care for children with EBD, but it is counterproductive in maintaining the child's connection to the family and encouraging parents to participate as equal collaborators with service providers.

Service providers will need to alter these traditional attitudes to work in partnership with parents (Friesen & Koroloff, 1990). Inservice training, as well as administrative direction and support and modified patterns of service delivery (e.g., structure and location) will be needed to enable providers to shift from blaming families to facilitating family empowerment, recognizing and enhancing family strengths (Collins & Collins, 1990; Dunst, Trivette, Starnes, Hamby, & Gordon, 1993). In their process of self-examination and relearning, professionals should honestly assess what factors contribute to maintaining a distant, judgmental relationship with families. Parents may be used as teachers to help professionals understand more fully how their behavior impacts family members' attitudes and willingness to work collaboratively.

Providers must also develop sensitivity to the diversity of individuals and families they serve, in order to take into account ethnic and cultural factors, as well as gender and class differences (Cross, Bazron, Dennis, & Isaacs, 1989). The first step is to acknowledge diversity as a strength rather than a problem. If service providers adopt a positive attitude toward differences among families, recognition of and accommodation to cultural differences are more likely to occur. This will, in turn, increase the probability of effective involvement of family members. Factors such as language (Gomez, 1979) and cultural attitudes toward seeking help (Acosta, 1979; Takeuchi, Leaf, & Kuo, 1988) may serve as impediments to parental involvement unless service providers and administrators consider cultural diversity as an important parameter in service delivery. If practitioners who are linguistically and culturally proficient are not available, it may be necessary to enlist the assistance of individuals from the family's culture. African-Americans have been reluctant to seek help from mental health professionals, preferring instead to use other sources, including ministers (Neighbors, 1985). Therefore, providers should seek creative ways to involve the clergy and other informal help givers.

It is sometimes assumed that white, middle- and upper-class parents who have greater access to individual treatment meetings and educational workshops with professionals speak for all parents. Minority and low socioeconomic families should also be encouraged to represent themselves and professionals should accommodate their preferences and needs (Turnbull & Turnbull, 1989). Given the degree of discomfort many parents experience in service planning meetings and related functions, it would be helpful to offer training for parents on how to participate effectively in these activities. This training will be most beneficial if conducted by both service providers and other parents who have successfully mastered the service delivery maze.[1]

Merely shifting conceptual paradigms will not be sufficient. Service providers also will have to develop new skills in the area of collaborative problem solving and individualized service planning based on creative utilization of formal and informal resources. Administrators will have to find ways to develop alternative incentives for service providers who are being asked to replace traditional service delivery approaches with family-focused practices. For example, productivity is traditionally measured by indicators such as number of therapeutic contacts with identified patients and the length of time required to move patients off the agency's caseload. With a family-centered approach, it might be more appropriate to assess the extent to which a practitioner provides assistance to families in mobilizing needed resources and the degree to which families are engaged with service providers to help meet their needs. If service providers' job expectations encompass family inclusion objectives and performance evaluation and salary increases are based, in part, on their performance in this domain, there is a high probability that staff will become more family responsive (Friesen & Koroloff, 1990).

Altering Service Delivery Patterns

Training alone will be of limited value if the structure of the workplace is not modified. Genuine reform of the service delivery system will require the incorporation of organizational strategies, including democratic management principles, that empower staff to work collaboratively with families. While workplace changes are necessary to achieve significant reform, they are not sufficient. Providing comprehensive services in a manner that involves and strengthens families will require additional resources and services difficult to obtain in the current climate of scarcity. Nonetheless, there are some promising approaches that can enhance service delivery.

Even when the child is being served outside the home, it is possible to alter staff–parent relationships by adjusting structure and roles. Family involvement can be improved by expanding hours and changing the format of service planning. In some hospitals parents spend as much time as possible on the unit, working together with direct care staff (Danziger, Carcl, Varsano, Tyano, & Mimouni, 1988; Doherty, Manderson, & Carter-Ake, 1987). In one hospital, staff actually call family members in to help deal with a crisis (Goren, personal communication, October 11, 1990). Kahan (1993) has suggested that "parental rooming in" may be an effective way to strengthen the working partnership between parents and staff, while maintaining the integrity of the family and providing additional information for assessment and treatment.

One of the primary shifts that has occurred in the field of child mental health has been to move the site of contact from an office or an institutional setting to the natural environment of the family, with services most frequently being provided in the home (Kinney, Madsen, Fleming, & Haapala, 1977; Nelson, Landsman, & Deutelbaum, 1990). Bringing staff into the home environment, when accompanied by a positive, collaborative attitude toward family involvement, increases understanding of family experiences and empathic responses to parental frustration. These changes in location and attitude also help to create a more egalitarian relationship in which a group of adults work together in a problem-solving mode.

The expansion of "intermediate level" services such as case management, home-based intervention, and day treatment has enabled children to remain with their families while receiving intensive services (Duchnowski & Friedman, 1990; Edna McConnell Clark Foundation, 1993; Jordan & Hernandez, 1990; Nelson, Landsman, & Deutelbaum, 1990). Services such as respite care (Gartner, Lipsky, & Turnbull, 1991) and parent support and education programs (Halpern, 1990) have been instituted to provide relief and assistance to families who maintain a child with EBD at home. Multisystemic family treatment has significantly reduced rates of criminal activity and incarceration of adolescents with serious emotional and behavioral problems through a range of interventions provided in the natural context of the home and community (Henggeler, Melton, Smith, Schoenwald, & Hanley, 1993).

While each of the service components used in treating the child and enhancing the well-being of the family is important, the case management function merits special recognition in strengthening the partnership between parents and professionals. Parents experience several benefits by having a single individual responsible for coordinating multiple aspects of the service program. First, they are relieved of some of the burden of procuring, tracking, and coordinating the multiple service components required to meet the needs of their child. Second, the case manager may serve as a single focal point for the family, not only providing assistance in navigating the complex system of services, but also serving as an advocate and ally for the family. Finally, the case manager can serve as a communication bridge within the family, facilitating interaction between child and parents.

Empowering Family Members

While service providers cannot "give" empowerment to family members, there is a legitimate role for providers and administrators in facilitating this process. Knowledge is a key element of empowerment and professionals can provide family members with current information about the origins, treatment, and management of childhood psychopathology (Collins & Collins, 1990; Hegar & Hunzeker, 1988). Agency administrators may also assist family self-help groups by providing financial and in-kind resources, by making available information related to children's programs, and by including family members in policy and program planning (Corp & Kosinski, 1990).

For a long time, strong parent support groups have been established in other disability areas (Dunst et al., 1993). In the past several years, with the support of the Families as Allies conferences and the encouragement of the National Alliance for the Mentally Ill, local support groups for families of children with EBD have been formed in many states (McManus & Friesen, 1986; Virginia Treatment Center for Children, 1987). These groups offer emotional support and information about the service delivery system and influence legislators and other policymakers to improve services for children with EBD and their families (Research and Training Center on Family Support and Children's Mental Health, 1991). In 1988, the Federation of Families for Children's Mental Health was formed with the purpose of bringing together parent-run organizations, professionals, and other interested persons to make services more family centered.

All families are not comfortable with the verbally oriented format of many support, advocacy, and administrative processes. Parents with limited higher education, who often have a great need for empowerment-oriented services, may be more responsive to individualized approaches that help them gain access to tangible resources needed to enhance child and family functioning. Other families may prefer to participate in multifamily peer groups, where they can benefit from the experience and feedback of other members. Providers should also not lose sight of the large number of children in the public sector who do not have easily identifiable families (Cohen, Singh, Hosick, & Tremaine, 1992). Although extra effort may be required to establish family connections, it is vital that every child have some family representation within the service delivery system. If it is not feasible to include a parent, an older sibling, grandparent, or another member of the child's extended family may be willing to participate in service planning and provision.

DEVELOPING COMPREHENSIVE FAMILY-RESPONSIVE SYSTEMS OF CARE

The manner in which services are coordinated, the extent to which resources are effectively utilized, and the policies and structures that govern service delivery have a powerful impact on service availability, accessibility, appropriateness, and quality (Duchnowski & Friedman, 1990). These factors also have a strong influence on family functioning and family relationships with the child in need of services and may serve as enabling or impeding forces in achieving full participation of parents within the child serving system. The policy of requiring parents to relinquish custody of their children in order to obtain intensive (usually residential) services is a good example of how system dynamics may operate. Even though severing this fundamental family bond may have a devastating impact on both child and parent, this is the practice of a variety of child serving agencies, ostensibly to be in compliance with state and federal policies. In fact, the primary reason behind the requirement that parents relinquish custody is a scarcity of public resources that forces agencies to rely on funding sources that were not originally intended for children with EBD (e.g., child welfare funds for children who have been abused or neglected) and to give priority to youth who are wards of the state (Cohen, Gottlieb, Harris, & Baker, 1991).

Several states have taken steps to make services available without breaking the bond between the child and family. For example, Minnesota enacted legislation that explicitly prohibits custody transfer for the purpose of obtaining services, while California has developed a system of coordinated services for children with EBD, including out-of-home care, that does not require custody transfer (Cohen, Preiser, Gottlieb, Harris, Baker, & Sonenklar, 1993). Iowa has established a system of 6-month renewable voluntary placement agreements that allows children with disabilities to obtain required services using public funds (Research and Training Center to Improve Services for Seriously Emotionally Handicapped Children and Their Families, 1989).

In recent years, a number of initiatives have attempted to develop comprehensive systems of care that provide individually tailored, family-centered, community-based services. One of the first, the Ventura Children's Demonstration Project, created interagency coalitions responsible for designing and developing holistic, community-based services for children with EBD. Interagency teams were given the authority to combine funds, staff, and services from the respective agencies to achieve this goal (Jordan & Hernandez, 1990). The program achieved dramatic outcomes including reducing out-of-county court-ordered placements, reducing the rate of state hospitalization for minors, and maintaining children at risk of imminent placement within their homes. These achievements, plus an avoidance of costs associated with residential care equivalent to 66% of the annual direct expenditures of the project, spurred the California legislature to expand support for "The Ventura Planning Model," enabling localities to design responsive systems of care compatible with local conditions.

Following the success of the Ventura Project, others initiated efforts to deliver comprehensive systems of care (e.g., Burchard & Clarke, 1990) with the most ambitious being the Robert Wood Johnson Mental Health Services Program for Youth, which established eight local demonstration projects to improve the organization, financing, and delivery of services to youth who are seriously mentally ill (Beachler, 1990).

These initiatives have demonstrated that effective implementation of family-centered services depends on having a receptive and supportive climate within the executive and legislative branches of government. The parent–provider partnership can play an important role in educating policymakers and administrators about the needs of children with EBD and their families and the programmatic and fiscal benefits of providing services that are tailored to meet the unique needs of each child and family. The development of broad-based family coalitions can provide a strong constituency to encourage public officials to provide effective programs for children with EBD and their families.

SUMMARY

Increased awareness of the inadequacy and inappropriateness of services for children with EBD, greater willingness of administrators and service providers to coordinate service delivery and funding, a growing technology of alternative service modalities, and a beginning effort to reconceptualize the role of parents offer considerable promise for improving services to children with EBD and their families. Substantial obstacles in the form of entrenched professional attitudes, bureaucratic rigidity, and limited resources pose serious challenges to those who are interested in service reform. Collaborative partnerships between family members and service providers have significant potential for long overdue reform at the individual child, agency, community, state, and national levels. These partnerships can best be achieved by altering attitudes and practices at the practitioner, program, and policy levels, recognizing the importance of serving the child within the context of the family, acknowledging both the strengths and needs of the family, and encouraging and supporting the inclusion of families as equal collaborators in all service planning and delivery activities.

NOTE

1. A number of curricula have been developed to assist staff to focus on empowering rather than blaming families. One such program is the family empowerment training program in Virginia, which is being offered to a wide range of direct service workers from child mental health, social service, juvenile justice, education, and health agencies (Musick-Hutchens, 1993).

The Parents and Children Coping Together (PACT) project in William County, Michigan provides a 1-year internship on family counseling and human services for upper level, undergraduate, and graduate students (Cabral & Callard, 1982). This program utilizes an ecological developmental framework that does not view family members and their problems in isolation, but considers them as "as a whole, dynamic, interacting unit with personal, cultural, environmental, and social influences operating together" (p. 17).

REFERENCES

Acosta, F.X. (1979). Barriers between mental health services and Mexican Americans: An examination of a paradox. *American Journal of Community Psychology*, *7*, 503–520.

Bailey, D.B., Buysse, V., Edmondson, R., & Smith, T.M. (1992). Creating family-centered services in early intervention: Perceptions of professionals in four states. *Exceptional Children*, *58*, 298–309.

Beachler, M.P.H. (1990). The mental health services program for youth. *The Journal of Mental Health Administration*, *17*, 115–121.

Bernheim, K.F., & Switalski, T. (1988). Mental health staff and patient's relatives: How they view each other. *Hospital and Community Psychiatry, 39*, 63–68.

Burchard, J.D., & Clarke, R.T. (1990). The role of individualized care in a service delivery system for children and adolescents with severely maladjusted behavior. *The Journal of Mental Health Administration, 17*, 48–60.

Cabral, R.J., & Callard, E.D. (1982). A home-based program to serve high-risk families. *Journal of Home Economics, 74*, 14–19.

Caplan, P.J., & Hall-McCorquodale, I. (1985). Mother-blaming in major clinical journals. *American Journal of Orthopsychiatry, 55*, 345–353.

Cohen, R., Harris, R., Gottlieb, S., & Best, A. (1991). States' use of transfer of custody as a requirement for providing services. *Hospital and Community Psychiatry, 42*, 526–530.

Cohen, R., Singh, N.N., Hosick, J., & Tremaine, L. (1992). Implementing a responsive system of mental health services for children. *Clinical Psychology Review, 12*, 819–828.

Cohen, R., Preiser, L., Gottlieb, S., Harris, R., Baker, J., & Sonenklar, N. (1993). Relinquishing custody as a requisite for receiving services for children with serious emotional disorders. *Law and Human Behavior, 17*, 121–134.

Collins, B., & Collins, T. (1990). Parent-professional relationships in the treatment of seriously emotionally disturbed children and adolescents. *Social Work, 35*, 524–527.

Corp, C., & Kosinski, P. (1990, February). Parents Involved Network: A self-help, advocacy, information and training resource for parents of children with serious emotional problems. *A System of Care for Children's Mental Health: Building a Research Base, 3rd Annual Research Conference Proceedings* (pp. 239–256). Tampa, FL: University of South Florida, Florida Mental Health Institute, Research and Training Center for Children's Mental Health.

Cross, T.L., Bazron, B.J., Dennis, K.W., & Isaacs, M.R. (1989). *Toward a culturally competent system of care*. Washington, DC: Georgetown University, Child Development Center, CASSP Technical Assistance Center.

Danziger, Y., Carcl, C.A., Varsano, I., Tyano, S., & Mimouni, M. (1988). Parental involvement in treatment of patients with anorexia nervosa in a pediatric day-care unit. *Pediatrics, 81*, 159–162.

Doherty, M.B., Manderson, M., & Carter-Ake, L. (1987). Time-limited psychiatric hospitalization of children: A model and three-year outcome. *Hospital and Community Psychiatry, 38*, 643–647.

Duchnowski, A.J., & Friedman, R.M. (1990). Children's mental health: Challenges for the nineties. *The Journal of Mental Health Administration, 17*, 3–12.

Dunst, C.J., Trivette, C.M., Starnes, A.L., Hamby, D.W., & Gordon, N.J. (1993). *Building and evaluating family support initiatives: A national study of programs for persons with developmental disabilities*. Baltimore, MD: Paul H. Brookes.

Edna McConnell Clark Foundation. (1993). *Keeping families together: Facts on family preservation services*. New York: Author.

Fine, G., & Friesen, B.J. (1988, December). *Relinquishing custody as a means of obtaining services*. Paper presented at the Next Steps Conference, Arlington, VA.

Forehand, R. (1993). Family psychopathology and child functioning. *Journal of Child and Family Studies, 2*, 81–87.

Friesen, B.J., & Koroloff, N.M. (1990). Family centered services: Implications for mental health administration and research. *Journal of Mental Health Administration, 17*, 13–25.

Gartner, A., Lipsky, D.K., & Turnbull, A. (1991). *Supporting families with a child with a disability: An international outlook*. Baltimore, MD: Paul H. Brookes.

Gomez, A.G. (1976). Some considerations in structuring human services for the Spanish-speaking population of the United States. *International Journal of Mental Health, 5*, 60–68.

Halpern, R. (1990). Parent support and education programs. *Children and Youth Services Review, 12*, 285–308.

Hatfield, A. (1983). What families want of therapists. In W.R. McFarlane (Ed.), *Family therapy and schizophrenia* (pp. 41–65). New York: Guilford Press.

Hegar, R.L., & Hunzeker, J.M. (1988). Moving toward empowerment-based practice in public child welfare. *Social Work, 33*, 499–502.

Henggeler, S.W., Melton, G.B., Smith, L.A., Schoenwald, S.K., & Hanley, J. (1993). Family preservation using multisystemic treatment: Long-term follow-up to a clinical trial. *Journal of Child and Family Studies, 2*, 283–293.

Hingtgen, J., Bryson, C., & Gair, D. (1972). Recent developments in the study of early childhood psychoses: Infantile autism, childhood schizophrenia and related disorders. *Annual Progress in Child Psychiatry and Child Development, 5*, 8–63.

Holden, D.F., & Lewine, R.J. (1982). How families evaluate mental health professionals, resources, and effects of illness. *Schizophrenia Bulletin, 8*, 626–633.

Jordan, D.D., & Hernandez, M. (1990). The Ventura planning model: A proposal for mental health reform. *The Journal of Mental Health Administration, 17*, 26–47.

Kahan, B.B. (1993). Parental rooming-in on psychiatric inpatient units. *Journal of Child and Family Studies, 1*, 323–327.

Kinney, J.M., Madsen, B., Fleming, T., & Haapala, D.A. (1977). Homebuilders: Keeping families together. *Journal of Consulting and Clinical Psychology, 45*, 667–673.

Knitzer, J. (1982). *Unclaimed children: A failure of public responsibility to children and adolescents in need of mental health services*. Washington, DC: Children's Defense Fund.

Langley, P.A. (1991). The coming of age of family policy. *Families in Society: The Journal of Contemporary Human Services, 72*, 116–120.

McManus, M., & Friesen, B. (Eds.). (1986). *Families as allies: Conference proceedings*. Portland, OR: Portland State University, Research and Training Center to Improve Services for Seriously Emotionally Disturbed Children and Their Families.

Moroney, R. (1986). *Shared responsibility: Families and social policy*. Hawthorne, NY: Aldine de Gruyter.

Musick-Hutchens, D. (1993). *VISSTA Course 105: Family empowerment*. Richmond, VA: Virginia Commonwealth University School of Social Work, Virginia Institute for Social Services Training Activities.

National Advisory Mental Health Council. (1990). *National plan for research on child and adolescent and mental disorders*. Washington, DC: National Institute of Mental Health, Alcohol, Drug Abuse and Mental Health Administration.

National Mental Health Association. (1988). *Final report and recommendations of the invisible child project*. Alexandria, VA: Author.

Neighbors, H.W. (1985). Seeking professional help for personal problems: Black Americans' use of health and mental health services. *Community Mental Health Journal, 21,* 156–166.

Nelson, K.E., Landsman, M.J., & Deutelbaum, W. (1990). Three models of family-centered placement prevention services. *Child Welfare, 69,* 3–21.

Nichols, M. (1984). *Family therapy: Concepts and methods.* New York: Gardner Press.

Palmer, A.J., Harper, G., & Rivinus, T.M. (1983). The "adoption process" in the inpatient treatment of children and adolescents. *Journal of the American Academy of Child and Adolescent Psychiatry, 22,* 286–293.

Penchansky, R., & Thomas, J.W. (1981). The concept of access: Definition and relationship to consumer satisfaction. *Medical Care, 19,* 127–140.

Peschel, E., Peschel, R., Howe, C.W., & Howe, J. (1992). *Neurobiological disorders in children and adolescents.* San Francisco, CA: Jossey-Bass.

Research and Training Center on Family Support and Children's Mental Health. (1991, Fall). Parents as policy makers: Challenges for collaboration. *Focal Point, 6,* pp. 1–10.

Research and Training Center to Improve Services for Seriously Emotionally Handicapped Children and Their Families. (1989). *Focal Point, 3*(1), 3–16.

Saxe, L., Dougherty, D., Cross, T., & Silverman, N. (1987). *Children's mental health problems and services: A report by the Office of Technology Assessment.* Durham, NC: Duke University Press.

Slentz, K.L., Walker, B., & Bricker, D. (1989). Supporting parent involvement in early intervention: A role-taking model. In G.H.S. Singer & L.K. Irvin (Eds.), *Support for caregiving families: Enabling positive adaptation to disability* (pp. 3–25). Baltimore, MD: Paul H. Brookes.

Stefl, M.E., & Prosperi, D.C. (1985). Barriers to mental health service utilization. *Community Mental Health Journal, 21,* 167–177.

Stroul, B.A., & Friedman, R.M. (1986). *A system of care for severely emotionally disturbed children and youth.* Washington, DC: Georgetown University, CASSP Technical Assistance Center.

Stroul, B.A., & Friedman, R.M. (1988). Principles for a system of care. *Children Today, 17,* 11–22.

Takeuchi, D.T., Leaf, P.J., & Kuo, H. (1988). Ethnic differences in the perception of barriers to help-seeking. *Social Psychiatry and Psychiatric Epidemiology, 23,* 273–280.

Tarico, V.S., Low, B.P., Trupin, E., & Forsythe-Stevens, A. (1989). Children's mental health services: A parent perspective. *Community Mental Health Journal, 25,* 313–426.

Thompson, E.H., & Doll, W. (1982). The burden of families coping with the mentally ill: An invisible crisis. *Family Relations, 31,* 379–388.

Tuma, J.M. (1989). Mental health services for children: The state of the art. *American Psychologist, 44,* 188–199.

Turnbull, A.T., & Turnbull, H.R. (1989). Families and community integration. In *Proceedings: Leadership Institute on Community Integration.* Syracuse, NY: Center on Human Policy.

Virginia Treatment Center for Children. (1987). *Collaborative advocacy for mentally ill and emotionally disturbed children and adolescents.* Richmond, VA: Author.

Biographical Sketches of the Contributors

Most of the authors participated in the Obermann Faculty Research Seminar at the University of Iowa Center for the Advanced Studies during July 1993. The editors of this manuscript, Adams and Nelson, were the seminar directors. Obermann Fellowships are awarded competitively to scholars nationwide and at the University. In 1993 the theme was Family- and Community-Based Approaches to Social Problems.

Paul Adams is Professor of Social Work at Portland State University. He has published widely on international social policy and service delivery issues. He was principal investigator of the federally-funded Patch Project which transferred to the United States a British model of community-centered practice and service integration.

Marcia Allen, Executive Director, National Resource Center for Family Centered Practice, is a nationally recognized expert on family-based, family preservation, and family support services. She has provided technical assistance and family systems training in more than 30 states and has been a key speaker at more than 60 national and state conferences and institutes.

Barry Checkoway, Professor of Social Work and Urban Planning, University of Michigan, has published widely on social planning, community organization, and neighborhood development.

Robert Cohen, Professor of Psychiatry, Virginia Commonwealth University and Director of the Commonwealth Institute for Child and Family Studies, has used his years of experience in clinical, administrative, and policy-making positions to establish a community-based psychiatric hospital that is a model for comprehensive service systems for children and adolescents.

Janet Finn, Assistant Professor of Social Work, University of Montana, has extensive professional practice experience in child welfare.

Peter S. Fisher, Associate Professor of Urban and Regional Planning at the University of Iowa, has conducted studies and published extensively on the interrelationship of welfare reform, state and local economic development programs, and policies to reduce the disparities in resources available to local governments.

Robert Halpern, a Professor at the Erikson Institute in Chicago, has published widely in the areas of child and family development and family support. His most recent work explores the need for community-based support for at-risk families.

Jo M. Hendrickson is an Associate Professor in the University of Iowa College of Education specializing in Curriculum and Instruction in Special Education. Her research interests include the development and effectiveness of community-based schools.

Karin Krauth, while an MSW student at the University of Iowa, was involved in every aspect of the Iowa Patch Project, as research assistant, intern, and employed team member. She is currently adapting patch principles to a school-based setting in rural Iowa.

Christopher Lavach is a graduate student in rehabilitation counseling at the Medical College of Virginia/Virginia Commonwealth University, and a research specialist at the Commonwealth Institute for Child and Family Studies, evaluating community-based foster care prevention and respite care programs.

Mary R. Lewis, Professor of Social Work at the University of Houston, has studied models of school-linked, community-based services in Europe, the United States, Canada, and Australia, under the auspices of the Organization for Economic Cooperation and Development's Center for Education Research and Innovation.

Salvador Minuchin, a founder of family therapy, internationally-known expert, and author of many books and articles, revives his early interest in the destructive impact of larger social institutions that create, maintain, and expand dysfunctional behavior patterns in poor families. He is Director of Family Studies, Inc. in New York City.

Kristine Nelson, Professor of Social Work at Portland State University, has conducted several major federally-funded studies and published widely on family-based services to prevent the out-of-home placement of children and on child neglect. She is co-author of *Evaluating Family-Based*

Services (Aldine, 1995) and *Alternative Models of Family Preservation: Family-Based Services in Context* (Charles C Thomas, 1992).

Donna Omer is the Supervisor of Special Projects for the School Board of Alachua County (SBAC) in Gainesville, Florida. She is responsible for desinging and/or providing oversight to all of the school district's grants and has been highly instrumental in marshalling resources to develop interagency school-based programs such as the SBAC Family Service Center.

Kameshwari Pothukuchi is a doctoral student in Urban, Technological, and Environmental Planning at the University of Michigan.

Salome Raheim, Assistant Professor of Social Work at the University of Iowa, whose work focuses on the empowerment of disadvantaged and oppressed groups, is studying the effectiveness of empowerment strategies to help welfare recipients become self-sufficient through the development of small businesses.

Eric Rothenbuhler, Associate Professor of Communication Studies at the University of Iowa, has written on communication rituals, popular culture, and the media. His recent work focuses on the importance of communication in establishing a sense of community.

Gerald G. Smale, Development Director, National Institute for Social Work, London, and Visiting Professor, University of Southampton, England, has been a leading figure in the development and theorizing of community social work in the United Kingdom. The National Institute offers a broad range of development work and consultancy both nationally and internationally.

Carol R. Swenson, Professor of Social Work and chair of the Clinical Practice Sequence at Simmons College and former chair of the Council on Social Work Education's Clinical Practice Symposium, has conducted several studies on mutual aid and natural helping networks. Her current interest is how clinicians conceptualize and use community in their practice with families and individuals.

Quint Thurman, Associate Professor of Criminal Justice at Washington State University and Co-Director of the Washington State Institute for Community Oriented Policing, has researched and written extensively about community policing innovations in the state of Washington.

William H. Quinn, Associate Professor and Director of the Marriage and Family Therapy Program at the University of Georgia, has many years of experience as a researcher, educator, trainer, and practitioner in the fields of family development and family therapy and has published extensively in these fields. His most recent work focuses on substance abuse and juvenile offenders.

Index